Colonial Justice in British India

Colonial Justice in British India describes and examines the lesser-known history of white violence in colonial India. By foregrounding crimes committed by a mostly forgotten cast of European characters – planters, paupers, soldiers, and sailors – Elizabeth Kolsky argues that violence was not an exceptional but an ordinary part of British rule in the subcontinent. Despite the pledge of equality, colonial legislation, and the practices of white judges, juries and police placed most Europeans above the law, literally allowing them to get away with murder. The failure to control these unruly whites revealed how the weight of race and the imperatives of command imbalanced the scales of colonial justice. In a powerful account of this period, Kolsky reveals a new perspective on the British empire in India, highlighting the disquieting violence that invariably accompanied imperial forms of power.

Elizabeth Kolsky is an assistant professor of History at Villanova University. She is co-editor of *Fringes of Empire: People, Power and Places on the Margins of Colonial India* (2009), author of many articles, and contributor to numerous books.

Cambridge Studies in Indian History and Society 17

Editorial board

Cambridge Studies in Indian History and Society publishes monographs
on the history and anthropology of modern India. In addition to its primary
scholarly focus, the series also includes work of an interdisciplinary nature which
contributes to contemporary social and cultural debates about Indian history and
society. In this way, the series furthers the general development of historical and
anthropological knowledge to attract a wider readership than that concerned with
India alone.

A list of titles which have been published in the series is featured at the end of the book.

Colonial Justice in British India

Elizabeth Kolsky

Villanova University

CAMBRIDGE
UNIVERSITY PRESS

CAMBRIDGE UNIVERSITY PRESS
Cambridge, New York, Melbourne, Madrid, Cape Town,
Singapore, São Paulo, Delhi, Tokyo, Mexico City

Cambridge University Press
The Edinburgh Building, Cambridge CB2 8RU, UK

Published in the United States of America by Cambridge University Press, New York

www.cambridge.org
Information on this title: www.cambridge.org/9781107404137

First published 2010
First paperback edition 2011

A catalogue record for this publication is available from the British Library

ISBN 978-0-521-11686-2 Hardback
ISBN 978-1-107-40413-7 Paperback

Contents

Figures

Maps

Tables

Acknowledgements

This book is the culmination of ten years of research and writing. It could not have been completed without the help of so many people, places, and institutions.

First and foremost, I acknowledge the love and support of my family: my parents Carol and Martin, my sisters Gretchen and Rebecca, and my brother-in-law Tim. My aunt Wicked pored over every page of this manuscript (as only a former book editor and practicing lawyer could) in a devoted effort to cure me of a comma affliction that I did not even know I had.

Friends and fellow scholars along the way provided critical insights, intellectual support, and many a good laugh. I would especially like to thank Sameetah Agha, Isolde Brielmaier, Nonica Datta, Harald Fischer-Tiné, Durba Ghosh, Sunila Kale, Katrina Karkazis, Jim Mills, Prabhu Mohapatra, Dard Neuman, Christian Novetzke, Sujani Reddy, Satadru Sen, Sudipta Sen, Radhika Singha, Mitra Sharafi, and Shana Sippy. Catherine Hall offered invaluable feedback in the final days of writing. Bethanne Moskov went over and above the call of duty to make life livable during many a hot summer in Delhi. And Janaki Bakhle was by my side from the first days of graduate school right through to the final revisions of this manuscript. She read every page and encouraged me to take the kinds of intellectual risks that I would never have on my own.

Much of what I know I learned at Columbia University first as an undergraduate and later as a graduate student. I thank all of those who taught me, especially Partha Chatterjee, Ayesha Jalal, Frances Pritchett, Gauri Viswanathan, and Patricia Williams. My mentor, Nicholas B. Dirks, provided constant guidance, gentle wisdom, and unflagging support as this book made its way to completion.

To my colleagues in the History Department at Villanova University I owe an especially large debt for demonstrating to me the very meaning of collegiality and for always being at the ready to help in so many different ways. Particular thanks are due to Hibba Abugideiri, Seth Koven, and Paul Steege who read and provided excellent comments and criticism of my work.

Thanks are due to all of the editorial and production staff at Cambridge University Press who assisted in the publication of this book. A particular debt of gratitude is owed to Marigold Acland, Jo Breeze, and Sarah Green. Thanks to the extremely careful copy-editing of Chris Jackson, this book is a whole lot easier on the eyes. Any and all remaining errors and inaccuracies are, of course, my own.

Research funding for this project was provided by Villanova University, the National Science Foundation, the British Academy, the Council of American Overseas Research Centers, the Fulbright–Hays Program, and the Pratt Institute. The staff at a range of research sites, including the British Library, the Indian Law Institute, the Lahore High Court Library, the Columbia Law Library, and the National Archives of India provided invaluable assistance in the location of materials.

This book is joyfully dedicated to the love of my life, my husband, my partner, my friend, Joseph Prunty, to my son Isaiah, and to my daughter Vivienne.

Glossary

adalat	court of law
chowkidar	watchman
diwani	right to collect revenues and administer justice on behalf of the Mughal Emperor
diwani adalat	civil court
mofussil	interior of the country
Nizamut Adalat	superior criminal court of Bengal
palanquin	hand-carried covered carriage on poles
punkhawallah	fan-puller
rattan	whip
ryot	peasant
Sadr Diwani Adalat	superior civil court of Bengal
sepoy	soldier
syce	horse groom
thana	police post
zamindar	landholder
zulm	oppression

Introduction

> The foundation of our empire in India rests on the principle of justice, and England retains its supremacy in India mainly by justice. Without justice we could not hold India for a moment.
>
> Sir Robert Fulton[1]

On January 15, 1784, Sir William Jones established the Asiatic Society of Bengal, a Calcutta-based center for the study of Indian laws, languages, and traditions. Jones' vision of India, which was shaped by a sense of racial tolerance and cultural connection between East and West, is generally taken as representative of a kinder and gentler brand of early British colonial rule. Just a decade after the founding of Jones' renowned research institute, indigo planter William Orby Hunter was tried in the Calcutta Supreme Court in connection with the torture of three of his female servants, who were discovered with their noses, ears, and hair cut off, their genitals mutilated, and their feet fettered in iron chains. Hunter was sentenced to pay a nominal fine and immediately set free.[2]

The appalling brutality uncovered at Hunter's trial provides a sobering counterpoint to current trends in the historiography of eighteenth-century India.[3] Rather than revealing an environment of assimilation and accommodation, Hunter's extraordinary case bears witness to the racial violence that was a constant and constituent element of British dominance in India. Bringing us right into the heart of darkness, this book examines how quotidian acts of violence simultaneously menaced and maintained British power in India from the late eighteenth to the early twentieth centuries. Physical violence was an intrinsic feature of imperial rule.

daily

---

[1] J. T. Sunderland, *India in Bondage: Her Right to Freedom* (New York: L. Copeland, 1929), p. 105.

[2] BL, IOR, O/5/4.

[3] W. Dalrymple, *White Mughals: Love and Betrayal in Eighteenth-Century India* (London: Viking, 2002); and M. Jasanoff, *Edge of Empire: Lives, Culture and Conquest in the East* (New York: Vintage, 2006). Dalrymple's amazing narrative offers a portrait of love, intimacy, and interaction even as it exposes the East India Company's aggressive and rapacious expansion.

This fact is widely acknowledged but narrowly explored, particularly in the Indian historiography. Although the archive is replete with incidents of Britons murdering, maiming, and assaulting Indians – *and getting away with it* – white violence remains one of the empire's most closely guarded secrets.

Even as major episodes of violence mark our understanding of the consolidation of British power in India, everyday acts of violence remain largely absent from the historical literature. This book argues that the history of violence in British India cannot be understood by traversing from one cataclysmic event to the next, from the Battle of Plassey to the Uprising of 1857 to the Jallianwallah Bagh massacre, as the micro-moments betwixt and between these macro-events are where the violence central to the workings of empire can be found. By focusing on crimes committed by a mostly forgotten cast of European characters – planters, paupers, soldiers, and seamen – this study demonstrates that violence was an endemic rather than ephemeral part of British colonial rule in India.

The growth of the British empire expanded the reach of British law, grounding and legitimizing colonialism in the power of legal practices and ideologies. In India, colonial administrators claimed that the promise of British justice was a cornerstone of its government, a guarantor of its liberty, and a key agent in its civilizing mission.[4] British officials not only used law to create the colonial state (the Permanent Settlement Act of 1793, for example, provided the early colonial state with a legal mechanism to collect land revenues), they also used the language of law to legitimize their rule.[5] The view that India had long been enslaved by the tyranny of Oriental despotism made law a critical instrument by which Britons simultaneously established their authority and differentiated colonial law and order from the anarchy of previous regimes.[6] In contrast to the personal and arbitrary rule of the Oriental despot, Britons saw their empire as an empire of law and liberty – not an empire of men, and certainly not an empire of violent men. By offering Indians an impartial judicial system and the equal protection of law, Britons assumed that the loyalty of their colonial subjects and the stability of

---

[4] For an African perspective, see M. Chanock, *Law, Custom and Social Order: The Colonial Experience in Malawi* (Cambridge: Cambridge University Press, 1985).

[5] B. Cohn, *Colonialism and Its Forms of Knowledge: The British in India* (Princeton: Princeton University Press, 1996), pp. 57–75.

[6] R. Travers, *Ideology and Empire in Eighteenth-Century India* (Cambridge: Cambridge University Press, 2007).

the empire would be secured. The assumption that British justice would
be beneficial and appealing to colonial subjects elided the fact that the
establishment of the colonial state and its laws required the displacement of a pre-existing order, a displacement achieved without the consent of the governed.

The relationship between law and violence in the empire was always a
tricky one. As Anthony Pagden has shown, imperial Britons in the early
modern period strove to distinguish their empire from the empires of their
European rivals, particularly Spain.[7] In contrast to what they saw as the
cruelty and bigotry of Spanish conquest, Britain's imperial authority
rested on ideas about reform, improvement, and the expansion of commerce. To widen its empire of trade, Britain required access to the land,
labor, and resources available in overseas colonies. As Britons viewed
conquest by force as illegitimate, other means were required to legitimately establish a global imperial polity.

In his *Second Treatise of Government* (1690), John Locke offered a theory
of property rights that justified the non-consensual nature of British
colonialism and the dispossession of indigenous peoples in the New
World.[8] Locke argued that he who mixed his labor with the land to
cultivate and improve it lawfully gained property rights and that once
settlement was established, natives who attempted to regain their lands
could "be destroyed as a lion or tiger, one of those savage wild beasts."[9]
This effectively conjoined the empire's rule of law to its theory of just war,
bridging the gap between colonial justice and colonial violence. According to Locke, rather than constituting an act of forceful expropriation,
British colonial expansion spread civilization and the bounds of law. And,
once established, British sovereignty could be legitimately enforced with
violence, when necessary.

Two centuries later in India, James Fitzjames Stephen restated and
reinforced Locke's theory on law, violence, and colonialism when he
evocatively observed that Britain had created a bridge by which "India
has passed from being a land of cruel wars, ghastly superstition, and
wasting plague and famine to be at least a land of peace, order, and vast
possibilities."[10] The two supports holding up Britain's imperial bridge,
Stephen claimed, were force and justice. But how could this be so? How
could Britain forcibly cement its power in India while simultaneously
ensuring justice? Unlike Britain's settler societies in the Americas which

[7] A. Pagden, *Lords of All the World: Imperial Ideologies in Spain, Britain and France, c. 1500–1800* (New Haven, CT: Yale University Press, 1998).
[8] J. Locke, *Second Treatise of Government* (1690).   [9] Pagden, *Lords of All the World*, p. 77.
[10] L. Stephen, *The Life of Sir James Fitzjames Stephen* (London, 1895), p. 895.

removed rather than ruled native peoples, the empire in India governed a vast population of colonial subjects purportedly according to an equal and impartial rule of law. Was it possible to administer equal justice to those who were legally and politically unequal?

India's colonial rulers promised to treat all subjects equally, but at the end of the day law's paramount purpose was to maintain Britain's hold.[11] Despite a rhetorical stance of legal equality, legal practice and conventions placed most Europeans in India above the law and, in effect, tolerated and condoned widespread physical assault and abuse. This violated the theory of equal protection that undergirded the rule of law and made law complicit in acts of racial violence rather than a guard against them. As the radical Indian nationalist Bal Gangadhar Tilak vividly noted in 1907, "The goddess of British Justice, though blind, is able to distinguish unmistakably black from white."[12]

This book demonstrates that the tension between the discourse of a rule of law and the practice of something different snapped around trials of violent Britons, exposing the fact that the scales of colonial justice were imbalanced by the weight of race and the imperatives of imperialism. By taking a classic colonial claim – of bringing law and order to pre-colonial chaos and mayhem – and turning it on its head, this study zeroes in on a rather unusual source of lawlessness and disorder: the Briton himself. The unsettling picture that emerges from our investigation of white violence and its handling in the colonial courts should not be brushed off as a list of exceptions, an epiphenomenal sideshow to the main stage of Pax Britannica. The exemplary cases selected for examination in this book represent a small fraction of those chronicled in the historical record. The innumerable other incidents of interracial violence that never made their way through official channels remain beyond the historian's reach. As James A. Sharpe argues, unrecorded crime is the "dark figure" impeding our understanding and statistical analysis of rates and patterns of crime and conviction over time.[13]

This study offers a history of colonial law and colonial violence that speaks strongly to current debates over the nature and impact of empire and to the persistent significance of race in British India. The problem of white violence exposed the messy work of empire and blurred the purportedly neat line dividing colonizers from colonized. Imperial ideology

[11] On the colonial rule of law and exceptional measures used to sustain British control, see N. Hussain, *The Jurisprudence of Emergency: Colonialism and the Rule of Law* (Ann Arbor: University of Michigan Press, 2003).
[12] *Kesari*, November 12, 1907, BL, IOR, L/PJ/6/848, File 453.
[13] J. A. Sharpe, *Crime in Early Modern England, 1550–1750* (London: Addison Wesley Longman, 1999), p. 61.

marweyer to dichotomy

rested on a series of dichotomies: white/black, colonizer/colonized, civilized/uncivilized, etc. These dichotomies manifested themselves in imperial architecture, city planning, sartorial prescriptions, and other means by which difference was made visible.[14] By the late nineteenth century, the frugal, disciplined, honorable, honest, vigorous, restrained, sporting, and superior Englishman was meant to stand in stark contrast to his inferior Indian other, cast as deceitful, extravagant, sensuous, effeminate, and weak.[15] This binary system was unwelcomingly upended by the white vagrants and planters and soldiers and sailors who drifted about India barefoot, drunk and disorderly, assaulting, burglarizing, and murdering those around them, muddying the lines of racial difference and threatening imperial stability from within. (See Figures 0.1 and 0.2.)

Despite concerted efforts to make colonial distinctions clear and clearly visible, the colonial world was not a world cut cleanly in two. Men like William Orby Hunter exemplified what might be called the third face of colonialism, comprised of whites in India who were neither official British rulers nor subjugated Indian subjects, but rather something in-between. Referred to as non-officials, Britons who did not work for the state in an official capacity functioned as both the bearers and the targets of colonial authority. As the bearers of British power, indigo planters like Hunter expanded the grip of the extractive colonial economy and provided crucial financial returns to the British Government. For this, they were granted advantageous market conditions and special legal privileges that essentially allowed them to police their own industries. At the same time, the unruly behavior of these shadowy figures on the social and physical fringes of the empire also made them the frequent targets of colonial control.

Concern about the tyranny of British colonial rule is practically coterminous with the East India Company's formal assumption of sovereignty in 1765. British efforts to manage the uses and abuses of official power culminated in the impeachment of Warren Hastings.[16] This book contends that non-official troubles and tyrannies are also an important, if lesser-known, chapter in the history of British India. The history of these others within reminds us that Britons in India did not constitute a monolithic ruling class. Furthermore, their mortal misconduct and steadfast

---

[14] D. Kennedy, *The Magic Mountains: Hill Stations and the British Raj* (Berkeley: University of California Press, 1996); P. J. Marshall, "The White Town of Calcutta under the Rule of the East India Company," *Modern Asian Studies*, 34 (2000), 307–331; and T. Metcalf, *Ideologies of the Raj* (Cambridge: Cambridge University Press, 1994).

[15] M. Sinha, *Colonial Masculinity: The "Manly Englishman" and the "Effeminate Bengali" in the Late Nineteenth Century* (Manchester: Manchester University Press, 1995).

[16] N. B. Dirks, *The Scandal of Empire: India and the Creation of Imperial Britain* (Cambridge, MA: Harvard University Press, 2006).

Figure 0.1 **Planters at drink, 1870s**

This group portrait of three "planters at drink" presents a rare image of the "wrong sorts" of Britons in India. Members of the non-official community who did not work for the state in an official capacity, such as the planters pictured here, made the task of running the empire both easier and more complicated at once. While British tea, indigo, and coffee planters in India provided critical financial returns to the colonial government, their drunk, disorderly, and murderous conduct both presented a serious law-and-order problem and also was an embarrassment to the "right sorts" of official Britons, such as those pictured in Figure 0.2.

refusal to submit to the restraints of law offer evidence of the fact that as the empire expanded, it was not just Indian peoples and territories that the colonial state sought to discipline and dominate. The literature on criminal law in colonial India chiefly emphasizes the ways in which British efforts to control Indian crime and criminality entrenched the power of the colonial state.[17] But the scourge of white crime was another "scandal of empire" that was endemic to the British presence in India and not necessarily an obstacle to its success. For even though the unlawful excesses of men like William Orby Hunter were a constant source of

---

[17] See, for example, R. Singha, *A Despotism of Law: Crime and Justice in Early Colonial India* (Delhi: Oxford University Press, 1998); and A. Yang (ed.), *Crime and Criminality in British India* (Tucson: University of Arizona Press, 1985).

Figure 0.2 **Viceroy's Council, c. 1864–1866**
This group portrait of the Viceroy Lord Lawrence and his Council presents a contrasting image of the "right sorts" of Englishman in India: moral, restrained, honorable, disciplined. In place of the planters' drinks and glasses are the legislators' pens and papers. The subjects pictured here are: (Secretaries standing behind from left to right) Edward Harbourd Lushington, Financial Secretary; Colonel Henry Norman, Military Secretary; Colonel Henry Durand, Foreign Secretary; Mr. Edward Bayley, Home Secretary; Colonel Richard Strachey, Public Works Secretary; (Members of Council seated in front from left to right) George Noble Taylor; Sir Charles Trevelyan; Sir Hugh Henry Rose (Lord Strathnairn); Sir John Lawrence (Lord Lawrence); Sir Robert Napier (Lord Napier of Magdala); Mr. Henry James Sumner Maine; Mr. William Grey.

consternation to the colonial government, their regulation also offered the state a pretext upon which to expand its power.

In his classic work, *The English Utilitarians and India*, Eric Stokes argued that law reform in colonial India was defined by the radical vision of Benthamites who sought "to redeem a people sunk in gross darkness and to raise them in the scale of civilization."[18] Stokes emphasized the intellectual and philosophical foundations of nineteenth-century colonial legal developments and described the codification of law in India as part of "the Utilitarian legacy."[19] Radhika Singha's meticulous history of crime

[18] E. Stokes, *The English Utilitarians and India* (Oxford: Clarendon Press, 1959), p. 302.
[19] Ibid., p. 234.

and justice in early colonial India offers a different perspective on the development of the colonial criminal law, which she argues should be read alongside the formation of the colonial state.[20] The argument advanced by this study is that the codification of the Indian law was neither born solely of an abstract English political philosophy nor designed to create a state to rule over only Indians in India. Instead, codification was the official response to the moral, legal, and political dilemmas posed by the unruly third face of colonialism.

Although non-official violence was discursively represented as a menace external to the official organs of governance, its constant presence was an unseemly reminder of the disquieting violence that inevitably accompanied imperial forms of power. Contradicting the imperial promise of law and order, the enduring problem of white violence vividly revealed the disorder and terror brought through colonial contact. The murderous violence and lawlessness of the many white vagabonds, imposters, burglars, beggars, planters, escaped convicts, and renegade soldiers who wandered about India's port towns and into the interior made them a menace to each other, to local Indians, and to the colonial government, which was either unable or unwilling to control them. Their behavior also challenged the ideologies of moral and racial superiority that were so central to the imperial mission, embarrassing the better class of official Britons who believed both in the right to rule and in the obligation to rule righteously.

By bringing the painful bodily experience of the Raj back into view, this study departs from the cultural concerns that have dominated the literature in recent years. Colonialism, we now know, was never exclusively a project of political, economic, and military domination. Colonial interventions also bore down brutally in the domain of culture.[21] Yet, in contrast to the rich literature on the violence of colonial knowledge, we know comparatively little about the physical violence of the colonial encounter. While there may be nothing novel about the claim that colonialism was violent, it is odd that so little attention has been devoted to the bloody clash of bodies involved in running the empire. It is also worth noting how much more fully the question of violence is explored in the scholarship on anti-colonialism than it is in studies of colonialism itself.[22]

---

[20] Singha, *A Despotism of Law.*

[21] E. Said, *Culture and Imperialism* (New York: Vintage, 1994); Cohn, *Colonialism and Its Forms of Knowledge*; and N. B. Dirks, *Castes of Mind: Colonialism and the Making of Modern India* (Princeton: Princeton University Press, 2001).

[22] The quintessential text on anti-colonial violence is F. Fanon, *The Wretched of the Earth* (reprint Manchester: Grove, 2005). For a good overview, see R. E. Young, *Postcolonialism: An Historical Introduction* (Oxford: Blackwell, 2001), pp. 293–307.

Of late, historians of certain British colonies have illuminated the intrinsic violence of imperialism, fracturing the benign and bloodless myth of Pax Britannica by showing its sometimes brutal core.[23] At the same time, some revisionist historians have downplayed and dismissed the violence of the British colonial encounter.[24] Aside from a few works that consider merciless British reprisals for acts of native violence,[25] most historians of British India evade the topic altogether, fortifying – perhaps unintentionally – the assumption that racial violence was marginal to the workings of empire in India.[26] Even a recent account of the embodied experience of the Raj devotes a scant eight pages to the history of corporeal violence.[27]

An important review essay on empire and violence attributes the paucity of histories on colonial violence to a paucity of source material.[28] This argument does not hold in British India, as the archives plainly show. In 1860, *Times* correspondent William Howard Russell exposed the reading British public to the atrocities committed by Britons in response to the Indian Uprising of 1857. As Russell informed his readers: "that force is the basis of our rule I have no doubt; for I have seen nothing but force employed in our relations with the governed."[29] In the ensuing decades, polite notices posted on the walls of colonial hotels openly reminded white patrons that "Gentlemen are earnestly requested not to strike the servants."[30] By the close of the nineteenth century, newspapers across India

---

[23] Recent publications on non-military colonial violence include C. Elkins, *Imperial Reckoning: The Untold Story of Britain's Gulag in Kenya* (New York: Henry Holt, 2004); J. McCulloch, *Black Peril, White Virtue: Sexual Crime in Southern Rhodesia, 1902–1935* (Bloomington: Indiana University Press, 2000); S. Pierce and A. Rao (eds.), *Discipline and the Other Body: Correction, Corporeality, Colonialism* (Durham, NC: Duke University Press, 2006); and M. Wiener, *An Empire on Trial: Race, Murder, and Justice under British Rule, 1870–1935* (Cambridge: Cambridge University Press, 2009).

[24] K. Windschuttle, *The Fabrication of Aboriginal History* (Paddington: Macleay Press, 2002).

[25] C. Herbert, *War of No Pity: The Indian Mutiny and Victorian Trauma* (Princeton: Princeton University Press, 2008); and R. Mukherjee, *Awadh in Revolt 1857–1858: A Study of Popular Resistance* (Delhi: Oxford University Press, 1984).

[26] Exceptions include J. Bailkin, "The Boot and the Spleen: When Was Murder Possible in British India?," *Comparative Studies of Society and History*, 48 (2006), 462–493; and D. Ghosh, "Household Crimes and Domestic Order: Keeping the Peace in Colonial Calcutta, c. 1770–1840," *Modern Asian Studies*, 38, 3 (2004), 598–624.

[27] E. M. Collingham, *Imperial Bodies: The Physical Experience of the Raj, c. 1800–1947* (Cambridge: Cambridge Polity Press, 2001).

[28] J. McCulloch, "Empire and Violence, 1900–1930," in P. Levine (ed.), *Gender and Empire* (Oxford: Oxford University Press, 2004), pp. 220–239.

[29] W. H. Russell, *My Indian Mutiny Diary* [reprint of *My Diary in India, in the Year 1858–59*, 1860] (London: Cassell, 1957), p. 29.

[30] M. Edwardes, *Bound to Exile: The Victorians in India* (London: Sidgwick and Jackson, 1969), p. 195.

were reporting daily on the menace of white violence and the scandalous acquittals of Britons accused of brutalizing Indians. In July 1892, the editor of *Vrittanta Chintamony* wondered what was so distinctive or different about this vaunted gift of British justice, as "Englishmen now grind down the natives in the same way as the Brahmins did the other classes in former days. If Englishmen commit any crimes, their deeds are not regarded as criminal, while the same deeds performed by others become serious crimes."[31]

T/O   This study joins the lively debate about the impact of empire on Indian society by raising serious questions about the manner in which colonialism sustained itself. Although the book borrows from the insights and arguments offered by colonial and post-colonial theorists, discourse is not its main protagonist. Nor is this a book about how Britons viewed their empire or how the empire was viewed by Indians. Rather, this study highlights the everyday practices of racial violence committed by individuals in local settings while insisting that the brutality of a man like William Orby Hunter cannot be separated from a legal system and a colonial structure that made his actions possible. Hunter may not have conformed to the standards of the ideal English gentleman, but in his nonconformity, and in his brutality, he too enacted and enforced imperial power.

The consistent failure to punish European defendants in so-called "racial cases" gave the lie to the imperial promise of a fair and certain rule of law and highlighted the enduring presence of race in the colonial administration of justice.[32] What outraged Indian journalists and nationalists in the late nineteenth century was not simply the fact of white violence but its handling in the criminal courts. Race had a clear, obvious, and ongoing influence over legal decision-making as Britons accused of assaulting and murdering Indians were booked on lesser (if any) criminal charges, which resulted in little to no punishment. Contrary to David Cannadine's controversial claim that rank and status were more important in the empire than race, British police, judges, and juries in India routinely collaborated across the hierarchies of class to buttress the racial basis of colonial dominance.[33]

If white violence was a common rather than exceptional component of British rule in India, then law was its most reliable and consistent

[31] *Vrittanta Chintamony*, July 15, 1891, BL, IOR, L/R/5/106.
[32] On race and the limits of the rule of law in colonial Australia, see J. Evans, "Colonialism and the Rule of Law: The Case of South Australia," in B. Godfrey and G. Dunstall (eds.), *Crime and Empire 1840–1940: Criminal Justice in Local and Global Context* (Portland, OR: Willan Publishing, 2005), pp. 57–75.
[33] D. Cannadine, *Ornamentalism: How the British Saw Their Empire* (Oxford: Oxford University Press, 2002).

accomplice. This book analyzes over 150 years of cases of violent crime. Despite changes to the colonial legal system over time, what remained relatively constant was the law's collusion in protecting and normalizing certain kinds of violence. This makes the history of colonial law central to our investigation of the history of colonial violence.

What this also suggests is that while there undoubtedly were "tensions of empire"[34] that pulled at the fabric of British colonial society, in some ways whiteness was monolithic. Whiteness was certainly experienced as monolithic by colonial India's beaten and battered coolies and *punkhawallahs* – what difference did it make to them that the white planter and soldier and magistrate were not of the same class? Even though racial boundaries were blurred and unstable, colonial law created conditions that consistently allowed white people to behave violently towards Indians with utter impunity. In this sense, imperial whiteness sometimes worked in monolithic ways.

Under its first royal charter, the East India Company was authorized to make laws to govern only its official representatives in India. By the early eighteenth century, in an effort to govern natives by native law and Englishmen by English law, the Company established parallel sets of laws and law courts in the Presidencies (Crown Courts) and in the *mofussil* (Company Courts). The Crown Courts were tribunals of English law with jurisdiction over everyone within the limits of the Presidency and in all cases involving Britons. The Company Courts administered a plurality of laws and mostly had jurisdiction over Indians and non-British Europeans in the interior. This dual system gave non-official Britons practical impunity from local prosecution and punishment, and established a place of white lawlessness at the center of the Indian empire that would never be wholly controlled. With law far and London even further away, non-officials in the Indian interior posed a persistent threat to the lives of local people and to the stability of the government precisely because of the legal vacuum in which they operated.

In the early nineteenth century, the problem of European misconduct and the prospect of an expanded white settlement prompted the colonial authorities to reform the judicial system by establishing a uniform set of laws and law courts. A central theme of this book is that a codified rule of law was designed by colonial administrators to control both unruly British citizens and colonized Indian subjects on the subcontinent. Colonial justice, however, did not grow more just as a result of the codification and rationalization of the Indian law. In fact, violent whites were more

[34] F. Cooper and A. L. Stoler (eds.), *Tensions of Empire: Colonial Cultures in a Bourgeois World* (Berkeley: University of California Press, 1997).

likely to be punished, and to be punished more harshly, in the late eighteenth century than they were one hundred years later. There were far more executions of Europeans in India pre-1860 than there were after the promulgation of the Indian Penal Code (after 1860 there are only four recorded executions of non-military Europeans in India). And, in the eighteenth century, Britons in the *mofussil* could be rounded up and deported, "their Magna Charta [sic] and birth-rights included."[35]

Colonial officials were inconsistent and ineffective in their efforts to subject members of the ruling race to the jurisdiction of the ordinary criminal courts. The notion of a rule of law as a system of principles designed to govern and protect equal subjects – a notion introduced into India by Britons themselves – was blatantly contradicted by the institutionalization of racial distinctions in the statutory law and by the overt partiality of white police, judges, and juries. As an Indian journalist frankly observed: "our rulers may say what they like but there is one law for the Europeans and another for the Indians."[36]

Legal historian Lauren Benton argues that the possibility of a shared legal identity in the colonial world was disrupted by "the task of structuring difference."[37] In addition to documenting a history of white violence, this book also demonstrates how law constructed race in British India. Having provided special privileges to European British subjects in the law, the state was required to establish the boundaries of race. That is, race was not already there. It had to be delineated, and the work of defining race was partly done by law.[38] Whites in India were not only ill-behaved: they were also ill-defined, and a race-based legal system raised the pesky problem of determining who was entitled to the privileges of Britishness.[39] In India, the legal question of who counted as a European British subject was contested and reworked over time, offering evidence of how law participated in the determination and institutionalization of racial difference.[40]

[35] H. C. Mookherji, "The Anti-Penal Code Meeting," in *Selections from the Writings of Hurrish Chunder Mookherji* (Calcutta: Cherry Press, 1910), p. 273.

[36] *Muhammadan*, June 6, 1901, BL, IOR, L/R/5/110.

[37] L. Benton, *Law and Colonial Cultures: Legal Regimes in World History, 1400–1900* (Cambridge: Cambridge University Press, 2001), p. 12. Also see M. Chanock, *The Making of South African Legal Culture, 1902–1936: Fear, Favour and Prejudice* (Cambridge: Cambridge University Press, 2001).

[38] N. S. Bose fails to consider race as a historical construction in *Race, Indian Nationalism and the Struggle for Equality* (Calcutta: Firma KLM Limited, 1981).

[39] On how this question played out at home, see L. Tabili, "The Construction of Racial Difference in Twentieth-Century Britain: The Special Restriction (Coloured Alien Seamen) Order, 1925," *Journal of British Studies*, 33, 1 (1994), 54–98.

[40] For a comparative perspective, see I. H. López, *White by Law: The Legal Construction of Race* (New York: New York University Press, 2006).

Scholarship on law and colonialism tends to adopt one of two analytical perspectives. The first takes law as a core institution of colonial control and domination:[41] as Ranajit Guha puts it, "the state's emissary."[42] The second focuses on the use of law as a weapon of the weak, a discourse of right borrowed from an imposed legal order to resist and constrain the power of might.[43] This book combines both perspectives and concludes that colonial law and colonial justice, when viewed through the prism of white violence, were both unjust and ambiguous. On the one hand, the special rights and privileges provided by law to European British subjects normalized and enabled their brutality. On the other hand, the terror induced by individual Britons uncovered the violent basis of imperial power and created a terrain for claims-making and critique. Even though the gap between the promise of equal justice and the practice of something different produced startlingly biased legal decisions, it also exposed the government to the criticism of a variety of historical actors in India and abroad. The publicity devoted to white violence and the efforts to control it suggest that while the legal system may not have been equal or impartial, the promise of colonial justice did restrict the gross exercise of power by offering a language and a means to imprison India's rulers within their own rhetoric.[44] In this way, colonial justice sustained and destabilized the empire at once.

This book is primarily intended to offer an account of the history of white violence and its relationship to law in colonial India. But still we must ask why. Why was there such excessive violence in colonial India? Why did so many Britons rape, maim, mutilate, and murder Indians? Why were these unthinkable acts of brutality consistently condoned in court? And why has so little been said about this in the historical literature? The evidence suggests that there is no single or overarching answer to these vexing questions. Just as the conditions of colonialism in India changed over time, so too did the motives and mindsets of those Britons who committed the kinds of appalling violence against Indians documented here. And while the primary question driving this study is not why violent

[41] S. E. Merry, *Colonizing Hawai'i: The Cultural Power of Law* (Princeton: Princeton University Press, 2000).

[42] R. Guha, "Chandra's Death," in R. Guha (ed.), *A Subaltern Studies Reader, 1986–1995* (Minneapolis: University of Minnesota Press, 1997), p. 40.

[43] On the limits of these antithetical approaches, see J. L. Comaroff, "Symposium Introduction: Colonialism, Culture, and the Law: A Foreword," *Law and Social Inquiry*, 26, 2 (2001), 305–314.

[44] See S. E. Merry, "Law and Colonialism," *Law and Society Review*, 25, 4 (1991), 889–922; S. E. Merry, "Resistance and the Cultural Power of Law," *Law and Society Review*, 29, 1 (1995), 11–27; and E. P. Thompson, *Whigs and Hunters: The Origin of the Black Act* (New York: Pantheon, 1975).

Methodology

Britons did what they did, it is certainly important to provide some frameworks to explain and account for the violence.

The first concerns the matter of race. European ideas about race changed over time.[45] In eighteenth-century British parlance, the concept of race generally referred to a people or a nation. By the nineteenth century, cultural and territorial notions of race gave way to a scientific discourse that defined race in genetic, biological, and physically observable terms.[46] The growth of imperialism helps to explain why the abolition of slavery in the British empire in 1833 did little to diminish the persistence of race in British life. The empire, which practiced a politics of exclusion and subordination, required mechanisms of differentiation to describe and legitimize who the rulers were and who the ruled were. As the empire expanded, race became a primary register of difference that was used to establish and naturalize imperial inequality.

As important as it is to historicize and unpack the constructions and meanings of race, it is equally important to remember the enduring constancy of British imperial ideas about the inferiority of "others". Seymour Drescher suggests that the scientific racism of the nineteenth century did not signal a radical shift in British racial attitudes but a reworking of them within new frames of reference.[47] Similarly, in the context of post-colonial Britain, Stuart Hall describes cultural difference and biological difference as racism's "two logics."[48] And, as John Comaroff points out, the fact that there were tensions of empire did not necessarily make colonialism any less coercive or exploitative.[49] Nor, it would seem, did it make the embodied experience of colonial power any less painful. To put it bluntly, what difference would it have made to a dead Indian whether his British murderer saw him as culturally or biologically inferior?

Of course, the identity of the colonizer was not monolithic. Nor were the boundaries of race in the colonial world secure and self-evident.[50] As Ann Stoler and Frederick Cooper observe: "the otherness of colonized

---

[45] C. Bolt, _Victorian Attitudes to Race_ (London: Routledge and Kegan Paul, 1971); and P. D. Curtin, _The Image of Africa: British Ideas and Action, 1780–1850_ (Madison: University of Wisconsin Press, 1964).

[46] N. L. Stepan, _The Idea of Race in Science: Great Britain, 1800–1960_ (London: Macmillan, 1982).

[47] S. Drescher, "The Ending of the Slave Trade and the Evolution of European Scientific Racism," _Social Science History_, 14, 3 (1990), 415–450.

[48] S. Hall, "Conclusion: The Multi-Cultural Question," in B. Hesse (ed.), _Un/settled Multiculturalisms: Diasporas, Entanglements, Transruptions_ (London: Zed Books, 2000), p. 223.

[49] Comaroff, "Symposium Introduction," p. 306.

[50] A. L. Stoler, "Making Empire Respectable: The Politics of Race and Sexual Morality in 20th-Century Colonial Cultures," _American Ethnologist_, 16, 4 (1989), 634–660.

persons was neither inherent nor stable; his or her difference had to be defined and maintained."[51] The ideas that justified British dominance both changed over time and took on different forms within a particular historical context. As Catherine Hall demonstrates in her magisterial study of colonial Jamaica, while there was disagreement between abolitionists and slave-holders about the legitimacy of slavery, this did not simply mean that abolitionists were non-racists and slave-holders were racists. British missionaries in Jamaica who spent their lives critiquing the brutal treatment of slaves still saw themselves as the tutors of their "children" within the "universal family of man."[52] The missionaries' sense of racial superiority could combine with a sense of responsibility for those less fortunate and a belief that whites were their only hope.

In India, too, Britons were not of a mind in any given historical moment about how Indians should be treated. Some were horrified by the murderous conduct of their countrymen, and others saw no problem with it. On March 14, 1808, Peter Hay, James Reilly, and John Reid entered the home of an Indian woman named Buxee Begum and seized her by the throat. When her *chowkidar* tried to protect her, Hay grabbed his bludgeon and struck the *chowkidar* on the head three times, killing him. After the European jury in the Calcutta Supreme Court returned a manslaughter conviction, Judge Henry Russell was scandalized and exploded in outrage:

What justifies you in saying that this amounts to less than murder? The crime of Peter Hay was either murder or it was nothing…The Natives look up to our laws for protection. We owe to them that protection. We live here among them in ease and safety. They give to us their services, their obedience, their wealth – God forbid that they should ever have to tell that we set less value upon their lives than upon the vulgar of our own country who come among them.[53]

A century later, officials such as Henry Cotton and Viceroy Curzon voiced a similar disgust about the behavior of their countrymen, the tea planters of Assam who physically brutalized the tea workers there. The Reverend Charles Dowding worked tirelessly in Assam to protect the tea workers from physical violence and economic exploitation.[54] However, when Dowding wrote to Curzon's government to condemn the planters and their deadly system, he never suggested that the empire was itself immoral. Instead, "on behalf of my coolies," he pressed for a *stronger* colonial government to assert its power over the planters, "strong enough

[51] Cooper and Stoler, *Tensions of Empire*, p. 7.
[52] C. Hall, *Civilising Subjects: Metropole and Colony in the English Imagination, 1830–1867* (Chicago: University of Chicago Press, 2002), p. 338.
[53] BL, IOR, O/5/8.
[54] C. Dowding, *Coolie Notes* (Dibrugarh, 1895), BL, IOR, L/PJ/6/832, File 3639.

to keep them in their place, and make them understand that they must obey the law as instantly as their native neighbours."[55]

While the legitimacy of an excessive sort of white violence was periodically questioned and condemned, the legitimacy of imperialism rarely was. The fact that some Britons at some moments urged a more humane treatment of Indians is meaningful, as it adds complexity to our understanding of how imperialism worked. But if one accepts the general argument about the centrality of violence to empire, at the end of the day, how much of a difference did this make? Was the criminal violence of the tea planter not part of the colonial order? The blurry line dividing the crimes of individual colonizers from the crime of colonialism as a system was illuminated by anti-colonial nationalists and post-colonial theorists around the world who, like Aimé Cesaire, argued that colonialism was a "crime against man."[56] The perceived illegitimacy of the colonial regime led nationalists to advocate the violent and non-violent violation of its laws.

Violent Britons invariably saw their Indian victims in some way as inferior and sometimes as sub-human. As one Indian commentator observed, the innumerable cases of racial violence proved that "Europeans have no regard for the lives of the Indians. They rank them with the beasts."[57] There is evidence in this book to suggest that the self-perceptions of Britons in India were forged in the crucible of chattel slavery and linked to its discourses of race. The identity and behavior of the British in colonial India were informed by knowledge of the dynamics and representations that defined slavery. Britons saw themselves as "the lords of human kind," a master race and a race of masters.[58] As Catherine Hall argues, "the identity of coloniser is a constitutive part of Englishness."[59] Ideas about the colonizing ruling race were linked to the master/slave relationship and, sometimes, to the language of white/black. And even if there were shifts and slippages between the cultural and biological connotations inherent in the concept of the colonial master race, the salience of race itself never slipped away.

Tony Ballantyne argues that colonial ideas about race were mobile and moved through imperial circuits across time and space.[60] Knowledge

---

[55] Letter from C. Dowding, February 25, 1902, BL, IOR, L/PJ/6/595, File 403.

[56] A. Cesaire, *Discourse on Colonialism* (reprint New York: Monthly Review Press, 2000), p. 14.

[57] *Surodaya Prakasika*, January 7, 1903, BL, IOR, L/R/5/111.

[58] V. Kiernan, *The Lords of Human Kind: European Attitudes Towards the Outside World in the Imperial Age* (London: Weidenfeld and Nicholson, 1969).

[59] Hall, *Civilising Subjects*, p. 12.

[60] Tony Ballantyne, "Race and the Webs of Empire Aryanism from India to the Pacific," *Journal of Colonialism and Colonial History*, e-journal, 2, 3 (2001); and Nicholas Canny, "The Ideology of English Colonization: From Ireland to America," *The William & Mary Quarterly*, 30 (1973), 575–598.

about colonized others could also be learned at home through the consumption of newspapers, literature, theater, trips to imperial exhibitions,
church sermons, the purchase of exotic goods, and stories learned from
family, friends, and neighbors.[61] But did ordinary Britons who went out
into the empire act within a framework of representations that finely
distinguished between the civilizational standing of different peoples
and their place in a global imperial hierarchy? Or did they look through
a less nuanced lens that saw superior (white) selves and inferior (black)
others? The cases examined in this study suggest that the violent and
lawless behavior of whites in colonial India had a precedent in Britain's
Caribbean slave plantations. That is, there was a pre-existing discourse
about how slaves and "niggers" could and should be treated, and that
discourse, even after the emancipation of slaves, was revealed by the brutal
treatment of colonized Indians.

In the period before the abolition of slavery, it is unlikely that Britons
who sailed to Jamaica to work on the sugar plantations came from a
different segment of the population from those who went to the Indian
indigo plantations. Was there a gentler brand of British planter, one who
knew about the ideology of Orientalism and William Jones' claims about
ancient Indian civilization and who chose to go to Calcutta over Montego
Bay for this reason? Probably not. It is more plausible to imagine that the
planter who arrived in the West Indies had a head filled with ideas and
images about race and racial hierarchies that closely resembled those
circulating in the mind of his brother in the East. They saw and described
the African slave in Jamaica and the Indian peasant in lower Bengal in
strikingly similar terms: as "niggers" and "blackies"; in George Trevelyan's
words, as "thin-legged, miserable rice-fed 'missing links.'"[62] After 1833,
when the Indian coolie took the place of the African slave in a "new system
of slavery,"[63] continuities in racial attitudes and racial violence across the
empire were strengthened further still.

The languages and legacies of slavery and race provided the discursive
framework in which the legitimacy and the illegitimacy of British violence
and legal inequality in colonial India were consistently debated and

---

[61] For an excellent overview of how Britons in one English locality (Birmingham) learned
about the colonial order of things, see Hall, *Civilising Subjects*, pp. 267–289. Also see
J. MacKenzie, *Propaganda and Empire: The Manipulation of British Public Opinion, 1880–
1960* (Manchester: Manchester University Press, 1984); and J. Walvin, *Fruits of Empire:
Exotic Produce and British Taste, 1660–1800* (London: Macmillan, 1997).

[62] G. O. Trevelyan, *The Competition Wallah* (reprint New Delhi: HarperCollins, 1992), p. 62.

[63] H. Tinker, *A New System of Slavery: The Export of Indian Labour Overseas, 1830–1920*
(London: Oxford University Press, 1974).

discussed. British criticism and support of slavery always had imperial implications.[64] Moral concerns raised by abolitionists in the 1830s about the treatment of African slaves resonated in contemporary debates about the rights of aborigines in Australia and the brutal behavior of white planters in India. Long after slavery had been abolished, those in the empire who longed for the continuation of a system of white domination mourned what had been lost in emancipation and pressed for the preservation of their privileges. During the infamous Ilbert Bill controversy of 1883, Calcutta barrister H. A. Branson warned his fellow Englishmen of the dangers of a law that would subject them to the criminal jurisdiction of Indian judges by drawing a historical analogy to the post-bellum American South: "We who have read history know what happened when the niggers of the Southern States of America got privileges over their white brethren."[65]

Recorded cases of British violence also signal the racial attitudes and motives of perpetrators. Private Frank Richards recalled in his memoir that the physical abuse of Indians by British soldiers was often presaged by racially abusive language. When the *punkhawallah* took a momentary break from pulling the fan, someone in the barracks would shout, "'Cinch, you black bastard, or I'll come out and kick hell out of you.'"[66] It was commonplace for Britons of all classes to refer to Indians as "blacks" and "niggers" and to treat them accordingly. As a mid-nineteenth-century British observer noted,

Cases of violence towards natives leading to their death are always sadly too common...This springs chiefly from the vulgar conceit that the "Saheb," no matter what his character or position, is immeasurably above the "nigger," and that indeed the latter, poor soulless wretch, exists but to serve the master race and to be cursed or cuffed as though he were really no more than a pariah dog.[67]

In 1874, a series of articles in the *Hindoo Patriot* documenting the trial of George Meares, a planter who bound a postal (*dak*) runner to a pillar and flogged him to death, was printed under the headline, "The Saheb and the Nigger."[68]

In North America, contemptuous attitudes towards natives resulted in "Indian-killing" being perpetrated and treated in the courts as "a kind of

[64] C. L. Brown, *Moral Capital: Foundations of British Abolitionism* (Chapel Hill, NC: University of North Carolina Press, 2006).
[65] *PP*, 1884, vol. LX, c. 3952.
[66] F. Richards, *Old Soldier Sahib* (London: Faber and Faber, 1936), pp. 239–240.
[67] Undated piece from the *Bombay Gazette* cited in Mookherji, *Selections*, pp. 299–300.
[68] *Hindoo Patriot*, August–September 1874.

sport."[69] The same could be said for Indian-killing in India. As an Indian journalist observed: "The English are the ruling race in this country and India is their sporting ground. Englishmen come to India to make money and to make themselves merry. Here shooting of tigers and bears is not sufficient sport; there can be no full sporting without occasional indulgence in native shooting."[70] There could be no clearer expression of colonial racism than the literal taking (and shooting) of Indians for animals.

In the 1830s, non-officials threatened to "lynch" Thomas Macaulay for drafting legislation that subjected them to the jurisdiction of the ordinary civil courts. They disparagingly dubbed Macaulay's laws the "Black Acts." In response, Macaulay sardonically commented that "We were enemies of freedom, because we would not suffer a small white aristocracy to domineer over millions."[71] In 1850, Nizamut Adalat Judge J. Dunbar related the specious argument of those who resisted criminal jurisdiction to the moral bankruptcy of American slave-holders: "The obstinacy with which persons even of liberal education cling to the idea of an actual and indefeasible right to exemption appears to be little less surprising than that perversion of mind which leads the white race in the Southern States of America to claim a right of property in their unhappy slaves."[72] In 1860, Hurrish Chunder Mookherji reported about a factory in Joyrampore that produced leather instruments for planters who tortured their workers: "We trust this leather will be forwarded to Government and through it to England for the satisfaction of those gentlemen that believe the indigo planter in Bengal very much different from the cotton planter of Carolina."[73]

In 1907, the Reverend Charles Dowding expressed his horror at the indentured labor system in Assam and the private powers of planters to arrest and imprison workers for breach of contract by comparing "coolie-catching" to the practices of American slave-owners.[74] He kept clippings of advertisements from local newspapers that offered rewards for the return of runaway workers (5 rupees a head), and noted how this practice led to the arbitrary detention of people in the area. One clipping read:

DEAR SIR – Two men, one very tall, over six feet, two women, and a child in arms, have been caught here, evidently runaways, but appear to be old coolies, if

---

[69] W. Churchill, *Perversions of Justice: Indigenous Peoples and Angloamerican Law* (San Francisco: City Lights Books, 2003), p. 268.

[70] *Sulabh Dainik*, July 6, 1893, BL, IOR, L/R/5/148.

[71] Legislative Consultations of October 3, 1836, No. 5, BL, IOR. P/206/84.

[72] Minute, March 8, 1850, in the Legislative Consultations of May 10, 1850, No. 67, BL, IOR, P/207/60.

[73] *Hindoo Patriot*, July 25, 1860.

[74] Dowding's many letters in BL, IOR, L/PJ/6/417, File 575 and L/PJ/6/832, File 3639.

you should know of any garden who have lost any people tallying to the above description, kindly inform the manager without delay. Yours faithfully —

Dowding remarked upon how closely this resembled the discourse on runaway slaves in the American South:

Readers of the "Key to Uncle Tom's Cabin" will remember that advertisements of similar import were common in the Southern States, before the war, generally followed by the words, "If not claimed in 14 days, will be sold to defray expenses"...Freedom of subjects counts for little in Assam. Whoever they were, it was the kindly thing to catch them, on the chance of doing a neighbour a good turn.[75]

The list of such instances goes on and on. The essential point is that contemporary critics in India condemned the views and behavior of the "mean whites" precisely because of their echoes of slavery in the Americas.

Our consideration of the role of race brings us inevitably to the question of class. The figures predominantly found in cases of white violence – planters, soldiers, seamen – were all members of the "lower orders" of British colonial society, disparagingly referred to by elite administrators as "mean whites." This term of contempt, which had historical roots in the slave-holding societies of the American South where it referred to poor whites or "white trash,"[76] itself connoted both race and class. From the seventeenth century, the identity of the Briton in the empire was defined against a racialized working other who could be treated violently. Citing Englishman Edward Boscawen's observation that "'A Roman ought not to be beaten,'" Peter Linebaugh and Marcus Rediker explain that "By this he meant that Englishness should be a global citizenship that protected its owners against violence. If Parliament failed to act on this petition, he solemnly explained, 'our lives will be as cheap as those Negroes.' Sir Arthur Hesilrige 'could hardly hold weeping' when forced to think of Englishmen working alongside Africans."[77] It was, in other words, the Englishman's job to lord over rather than work alongside the African. It was also his prerogative to beat but not be beaten.

This brings us back to Hall and raises a critical question about what exactly constituted the Englishman's identity as a colonizer: to what extent did the Englishman as colonizer perceive it to be his right to strike colonized subjects in the empire? The empire beckoned Britons as a site of possibility, riches, and opportunity, a place where one could be one's own

[75] BL, IOR, L/PJ/6/832, File 3639.

[76] J. R. Gilmore, "The 'Poor Whites' of the South," *Harper's New Monthly Magazine*, 29 (1864), p. 115.

[77] P. Linebaugh and M. B. Rediker, *The Many-Headed Hydra: Sailors, Slaves, Commoners, and the Hidden History of the Revolutionary Atlantic* (Boston: Beacon Press, 2001), p. 134.

master.[78] In class terms, being one's own master implied life of economic self-sufficiency. But what did this mean in terms of how Britons treated people overseas? Many Britons with little economic opportunity at home went off into the empire for "adventure." And there, it appears, a decivilization occurred. A dehumanization. An emboldened sense of the right to maim and murder with impunity set in. As Cesaire instructs in his searing critique of colonialism: "colonization works to *decivilize* the colonizer, to *brutalize* him in the true sense of the word, to awaken him to buried instincts, to covetousness, violence, race hatred and moral relativism."[79]

The question is, how and why did this happen? Were working-class whites particularly prone to the exercise of physical brutality? Were they tempted to violent excess by the promise that in the empire they were not meant to work "by the side of the black man" but to "to govern and to war, to instruct, direct, and educate, to root out the baneful superstitions and noxious errors of the native mind"?[80] Or did their criminal violence flow from the founding violence of conquest and the enabling conditions of colonialism itself?

Due to the emphasis on power, prestige, and civility, Britons in the empire were expected to control their behavior as a means of maintaining the boundary that distinguished the ruler from the ruled.[81] Thomas Macaulay stressed the need for every Englishman in India to represent the honesty and integrity of English governance, warning of the dangers posed by "Englishmen of lawless habits and blasted character." Macaulay wrote: "Every Englishman participates in the power of Government, though he holds no office. His vices reflect disgrace on the Government, though the Government gives him no countenance."[82] The notoriously brutal tea planters were, in fact, given "countenance" by the government to the extent that their labor and recruitment laws were established by the state. The "brutal planter" lorded over a plantation system based on fear, force, and coercion and, as novelist J. M. Coetzee has vividly demonstrated, an imperialist will do terrible things while "waiting for the barbarians."[83]

White soldiers and sailors and planters, however, certainly did not have an exclusive preserve over the exercise of brutality and racial violence in

---

[78] Hall, *Civilising Subjects*, p. 27. [79] Cesaire, *Discourse on Colonialism*, pp. 35–36.

[80] "Colonization in India," *The Calcutta Review* 30 (1858), pp. 177–178.

[81] On upper-class morals and racial prestige, see K. Ballhatchet, *Race, Sex and Class under the Raj: Imperial Attitudes and Policies and Their Critics* (London: Weidenfeld and Nicolson, 1980).

[82] T. Macaulay, *The Miscellaneous Writings and Speeches of Lord Macaulay* (London, 1880), p. 28.

[83] J. M. Coetzee, *Waiting for the Barbarians* (London: Penguin, 1980).

India. Racism extended across the entire spectrum of British colonial society, and it is likely that we know more about their violence because of the evidence offered in the archival record. In the case of "nigger-bashing"[84] soldiers, this can be partially explained by the fact that they constituted the largest segment of the British population in India and because the army had a disciplinary structure and a system of courts-martial that offered a framework for reporting and accountability. It is also worth acknowledging the brutalization poor whites were subject to on ships, in the army barracks, and elsewhere. While these experiences may have made them more brutal towards others, they probably appear more frequently in the official record because they were prosecuted more often. This can be read not as evidence of any particular "meanness," but as a reflection of their limited political, legal, and social capital as compared with the more powerful members of colonial society who were better positioned to manipulate the law in their own interests.

In thinking about the role of class in explaining racial violence we must consider how physical force was used to sustain the imperial economy. On the indigo plantations of lower Bengal and on the tea plantations of Assam, assaults on workers were endemic to the system of production. Here, much of the violence was regarded as disciplinary. It was used to keep workers working, to intimidate them, and to punish them. As the Reverend Dowding wrote, "there were 'whips' who were famous for getting out of a horse the last 'pound of work' it was capable of performing, so there were, in these days in Assam, those who almost pride themselves on doing the same with their labour-force."[85]

Mechanisms used to discipline and punish labor in the colony, as the literature on master and servant law in the British empire demonstrates, departed from contemporary practice at home.[86] Whereas laborers in nineteenth-century Britain progressively gained protection from injury and exploitation under the state's regulatory laws, workers on the tea plantations of colonial Assam continued to labor under a law of indentured servitude and labor recruitment that made breach of contract a crime and provided planters with the power to arrest and punish workers. Floggings, canings, and imprisonment were widespread and well-known practices on the tea gardens, and relations between European managers and coolies were considered to be something other than "as between man

---

[84] Curzon to the Secretary of State, March 12, 1903, BL, IOR, Mss Eur/F111/162.

[85] C. Dowding, "Assam Coolie Recruiting," in J. Buckingham, *Tea-Garden Coolies in Assam: Replying to a Communication on the Subject which appeared in the "Indian Churchman"; Reprinted with an Introduction and an Answer by the Rev. Charles Dowding* (London, 1894).

[86] D. Hay and P. Craven (eds.), *Masters, Servants, and Magistrates in Britain and the Empire, 1562–1955* (Chapel Hill, NC: University of North Carolina Press, 2004).

and man."[87] The penal provisions of contract law in India outlived their predecessor in Britain by over half a century.

This, finally, brings us back to the question of law. Formal legislation that authorized the exercise of violence, such as the labor law in Assam, would obviously have encouraged its use. And yet, much of the racial violence in colonial India was committed beyond and not within the bounds of law. Although colonial law did not exactly produce white violence, it did not effectively prohibit it either. In large measure, law protected and normalized violence by placing most Europeans in India above the law and by extending special protections to the strong that it denied to the weak. Over most of the period under review in this book, criminal Britons in India were aware of and emboldened by the limited jurisdiction of the criminal law, the feeble power of local authorities, and the failure of the courts to secure convictions. In short, they could and did commit violence because they knew they could get away with it. As an Indian commentator noted, the failure of colonial justice promoted beastly acts of brutality: "Though a large number of such offences has been committed, in none of them have the delinquents been punished adequately. It is this that encourages the Europeans to deal with the Indians as if they were no better than beasts."[88]

Chapter overview

Chapter 1 focuses on the moral, legal, and political problems posed by a neglected but crucial third element in colonial society beginning in 1766 (one year after the British took control in Bengal) and ending in 1833 (when Thomas Macaulay commenced the codification process). Non-official whites made the task of ruling India more difficult by presenting a practical law-and-order problem that challenged the Company in its critical phase of expansion. Original case law of the period provides a window onto the wild and lawless behavior of Europeans in early colonial India, revealing that the expansion of empire and the absence of law opened up new spaces of violence and criminal opportunity.

Chapter 2 demonstrates that the official response to the menace of European misconduct was the codification of law. A codified rule of law was designed to provide the colonial state with a mechanism to discipline a growing population of white settlers, capitalists, and planters in India who were immune from local criminal jurisdiction and therefore outside the

---

[87] P. G. Melitus, Secretary to the Chief Commission of Assam, "Report on Labor Emigration into the Province of Assam for the Year 1900," BL, IOR, V/24/1223.

[88] *Surodaya Prakasika*, January 7, 1903, BL, IOR, L/R/5/111.

bounds of law. By the mid-nineteenth century, the non-official community that had once been a threat to colonial authority emerged as a powerful
and effective lobbying group. They viewed legal equality as the subversion, rather than fulfillment, of justice and successfully pressured the
government not to put them under the jurisdiction of laws framed for a
subject population. The Code of Criminal Procedure provides a case
study through which to examine the causes and consequences of how
legal codification promised uniformity but delivered something different.
By according special legal entitlements and exemptions to the dominant
group, the new law exacerbated the very problem it was designed to solve
as the privileges granted by the state created a zone of illegality inside of
which Britons in India could literally get away with murder.

The race-based distinctions made in the Code not only contradicted
imperial pledges of legal equality, they also posed a practical challenge to
the state's ability to maintain law and order, especially as the ranks and
rogue behavior of whites in India grew. Colonial lawmakers were deeply
troubled by and conflicted about the problem of British brutality but were
stymied in the ability and willingness to act. The judicial consequences of
these colonial inversions – where unequal laws were redefined as equal
and appropriate, given the special conditions in the colony – were not lost
on critics of the system, who noted that distinctions in the letter and
practice of the law produced discriminatory decisions. As one Indian
observed:

The accounts we now receive of oppressions in law courts make us ask, how is it, O
English Government, that you have given the name of *dharmadhikaran* [abodes of
justice] to your law courts and how is it that you require people to call your Judges
dharmavatar [incarnations of justice]? Why do you call your law courts abodes of
justice when they have become markets of injustice?[89]

Chapter 3 argues that while the non-official community's insistence on
maintaining legal privileges delayed and derailed the establishment of a
uniform law of criminal procedure, prevalent ideas about native mendacity
and Indian cultural difference hastened codification of the law of
evidence. The theory of evidence in India was founded on the colonial
assumption that native witnesses and their statements were not to be
believed. This chapter examines the efforts of nineteenth-century colonial
administrators to elicit the truth from an Indian populace perceived to be
teeming with forgerers, professional witnesses, and a general population
that could not distinguish fact from fiction. This chapter traces the development of various "truth technologies" designed to elicit reliable evidence

---

[89] *Sulabh Dainik*, July 19, 1893, BL, IOR, L/R/5/19.

from an unreliable people, including the judicial oath, the field of Indian medical jurisprudence, and the figure of the medico-legal expert. The belief that scientific facts were infinitely more trustworthy than oral evidence made the use of science in law particularly important in colonial criminal inquiries and proceedings, as it allowed oral testimony to be displaced by physical evidence. Colonial ideas about Indian people, bodies, and culture produced a medico-legal literature grounded in an ethnographic idiom that contradicted the claims of an objective scientific method. This had an important impact on cases of violent whites, as a medical discourse about the peculiar vulnerabilities of Indian bodies helped ensure that European murderers got off the hook.

Chapter 4 situates the book's examination of the tension between law, violence, and empire on the tea plantations of colonial Assam. If, in India, they managed things "differently," in Assam the politics of law and violence appeared in their barest and darkest form. Perched at the northeast frontier of British India, Assam sat on the geo-political edge of empire and possibly beyond the pale of justice. Colonial Assam was dominated by British tea planters and a system of indentured servitude that made breach of contract a crime and provided employers with the power to punish. The delegation of disciplinary powers under the penal contract indicates that the colonial state was prepared to extend its monopoly over the use of physical force to keep the plantations going. Planter violence and the lack of impartiality associated with *safed insaaf* (white justice) reveal the use of law as an instrument of colonial control and oppression. At the same time, there is also evidence that tea workers sometimes used law in clever and strategic ways that did not simply reinforce the power of the colonial state.

Chapter 5 brings the contests over law and violence squarely into the field of anti-colonial politics. By the late nineteenth century, the scourge of planter violence and the failure of the state to convict in several highly publicized cases became symbolic of the injustice of empire itself. The situation in Assam occupied a prominent place in the columns of Indian newspapers and on the agendas of nationalist organizations as the planters' *zulm* offered a graphic example of the violent basis of colonial rule and the miscarriages of justice associated with its system of administering "one rule for the black man and another for the white."[90] Stark inequalities in legal rights – from racially stacked juries to exemption from local criminal courts to, in the case of Assam, exemption from justice altogether – produced biased legal decisions and the general perception that "no justice is to be had in our courts where Europeans are charged with acts

---

[90] Legislative Council Member W. Bird's Minute of August 26, 1844, NAI, Legislative Proceedings, October – December 1844, October 12, 1844, No. 4.

of violence done to the natives of India."[91] Indian nationalists and anti-imperialists abroad brought daily attention to the perverse verdicts delivered by white juries in racial cases where Britons almost invariably got off. The mounting legal and political claims that were instigated by various well-publicized cases of European violence in the late nineteenth century culminated in the appointment of the Racial Distinctions Committee (1921), which sought to remove the color bar in Indian law and to redress "the color of the law" in the wider imperial system.[92]

---

[91] R. G. Sanyal, *Record of Criminal Cases as Between Europeans and Natives for the Last Hundred Years* (Calcutta, 1896), pp. 159–160.

[92] G. W. O'Brien, *The Color of the Law: Race, Violence, and Justice in the Post-World War II South* (Chapel Hill, NC: University of North Carolina Press, 1999).

1 White peril: law and lawlessness in early colonial India

In July 1809, James Tickborne, a timber dealer in Sarun district, was tried in the Calcutta Supreme Court for the murder of his servant, Mungrah Aheer. The facts of the case are roughly as follows. On August 22, 1808, Tickborne summoned Mungrah to come before him. When Tickborne's messengers informed him that Mungrah was too ill to appear, Tickborne bound and beat them severely and dispatched them again to bring Mungrah. Too weak and ill to walk on his own, that evening Mungrah was carried before Tickborne, who immediately confined him within a detached building referred to by witnesses as a "necessary house." Mungrah there remained for fourteen days without food or water. On the fifteenth day, he died. Soon afterwards, a large group of local men and women surrounded the *cutcherry* (local court), shouting loudly that Tickborne was the murderer of Mungrah Aheer. The following week, Tickborne placed another servant in confinement, prompting the local magistrate, J. Ahmuty, to request in writing that Tickborne release the man and "desist in future from detaining any person (not a menial servant) within your premises from sun set to sun rise."

After conducting a preliminary investigation, Ahmuty determined that the allegations were true. Following standard procedure, Ahmuty sent for further orders from Calcutta.[1] In his letter, Ahmuty described Tickborne as a man with a "violent temper" who was "held always in great terror by the Natives in his service" towards whom he acts in a "virulent and acrimonious" fashion. Ahmuty also linked Tickborne's criminal and insubordinate behavior to the "insurmountable difficulties and impediments" presented by the existing legal system: "Fully sensible of and confident in his exemption from the immediate effects of my limited jurisdiction over him, he has not only in a great measure defied my authority but has latterly conducted himself in a manner highly disrespectful to the Court."[2]

---

[1] Regulation XV, Section 2 of 1806 required local magistrates to send for orders from Calcutta when they deemed a European liable to criminal prosecution in the Supreme Court.

[2] Ahmuty's letter of December 3, 1808, in the case of James Tickborne, BL, IOR, O/5/9.

In response to Ahmuty's recommendation, the Governor-General moved to prosecute Tickborne in the Supreme Court at the East India Company's expense. A European justice of the peace, W. Cracroft, was dispatched from Benares with a warrant for Tickborne's arrest. When Cracroft attempted to take him into custody, however, Tickborne (who was intoxicated on a boat) refused to cooperate, calling to his servants for swords and pistols, and exclaiming "*Maroo! Maroo!*" ("Kill him! Kill him!"). A violent scuffle ensued, with Tickborne knocking Cracroft into the water. Then, when Cracroft tried to put Tickborne into his *palanquin*, Tickborne punched him in the face and the chest and kicked out a panel of the *palanquin*. Ultimately, Tickborne was subdued by a group of locals "collected on the spot," who tied his hands and legs down, strapped him to a *charpoy* (bed), and carried him on their heads. After Tickborne had calmed down a bit, Cracroft offered to remove the ropes if he would peaceably enter the *palanquin*. Once untied, Tickborne bit two native officers and attempted to seize their swords.

The Calcutta Supreme Court ultimately convicted Tickborne of manslaughter in the death of Mungrah Aheer, sentencing him to twelve months, imprisonment and a 400-rupee fine. Tickborne was also convicted of aggravated assault and false imprisonment of another servant, Rugbunse Lal, whom he had severely beaten and confined for eight days. For this, he was sentenced to an additional twelve months in prison and a 100-rupee fine. In July 1811, as his two-year prison term was set to expire, the government passed an order forbidding Tickborne from living outside the Town of Calcutta. Disobeying the order, Tickborne fled upcountry to Soonapure beyond the Company's frontiers, where a warrant could not be served on him. Four years later, Tickborne got his come-uppance when the *Subahdar* (governor) of the Morung, who had "some grounds of resentment or hostility against Tickborne and had long threatened him with vengeance," executed him within the limits of his domain.

Tickborne's case was one of many to come to the attention of the colonial authorities in the early nineteenth century. The problems posed by such a man were multiple. On the one hand, as the Governor-General noted, the gross violence and criminal oppressions committed by Tickborne were "equally injurious to the English character and to the peace and happiness of our native subjects."[3] On the other hand, as Ahmuty pointed out, it was difficult to control such men, because the Company's legal system provided local officials with limited authority over Europeans who committed violence against Indians. The Tickbornes of early colonial India also posed a

---

[3] Circular order of July 10, 1810, ibid.

political problem to the extent that they infringed upon the state's exclusive power to exert "pain-related power."[4] Colonial officials were not opposed on humanitarian grounds to Tickborne's flogging and confinement of his servants per se, for the state regularly imposed far more brutal punishments.[5] What bothered them was the way in which men like James Tickborne challenged their exclusive authority by wrongfully assuming the state's power to punish.

The problem of white violence had a major impact on law, society, and state formation in early colonial India. Whereas scholarship on criminal law in colonial India has skillfully interrogated the connections between colonial crimes of culture and British efforts to control Indian society, comparatively little has been written about colonial efforts to control "white peril." The historical impact of non-officials in India – Europeans who worked neither for Company nor Crown – more generally has been both understudied and underestimated.[6] Non-officials, private traders, and free-merchants, pejoratively referred to as "interlopers" in the eighteenth century, played an extremely important part in the history of colonial law precisely because of the legal, political, and moral challenges they posed to colonial authority and stability.

This chapter challenges the view that British law and order swept across and transformed a chaotic pre-colonial legal landscape by revealing the disorder and lawlessness at the very center of the colonial project itself. With the everyday acts of violence committed by a mostly forgotten cast of European characters brought to the fore, it becomes clear that physical

---

[4] The phrase is borrowed from D. Paton, *No Bond but the Law: Punishment, Race, Gender and Jamaican State Formation, 1780–1870* (Durham, NC: Duke University Press, 2004), p. 12.

[5] J. Fisch, *Cheap Lives and Dear Limbs: The British Transformation of the Bengal Criminal Law 1769–1817* (Wiesbaden: Franz Steiner Verlag, 1983).

[6] Recent studies of non-officials and poor whites in India include D. Arnold, "European Orphans and Vagrants in India in the Nineteenth Century," *Journal of Imperial and Commonwealth History*, 7, 2 (1979), 104–127; D. Arnold, "White Colonization and Labor in 19th Century India," *Journal of Imperial and Commonwealth History*, 11 (1983), 133–158; Harald Fischer-Tiné, *Low and Licentious Europeans: Race, Class and White Subalternity in Colonial India* (Delhi: Orient BlackSwan, 2009); S. Mizutani, "A 'Scandal to the English Name and English Government': European Pauperism in Colonial Calcutta, 1858 – the 1920s," unpublished paper presented at the European Association for South Asian Studies (2004); and R. K. Renford, *The Non-Official British in India to 1920* (Delhi: Oxford University Press, 1987). There is also a growing literature on mixed race communities. See, for example, E. Buettner, *Empire Families: Britons and Late Imperial India* (Oxford: Oxford University Press, 2004); D. Ghosh, *Sex and the Family in Colonial India: The Making of Empire* (Cambridge: Cambridge University Press, 2006); C. J. Hawes, *Poor Relations: The Making of a Eurasian Community in British India 1773–1833* (London: Curzon, 1996); and S. Mizutani, "Rethinking Inclusion and Exclusion: The Question of Mixed-Race Presence in Late Colonial India," *University of Sussex Journal of Contemporary History*, 5 (2002), 1–22.

violence did not simply play a limited and episodic role in the conquest of India. In fact, not only was physical violence a persistent and integral feature of British rule in India, law was its most reliable and consistent accomplice.

Colonialism and the absence of law

The problem of white violence in India emerged and endured as a problem of law.[7] This is a meaningful and significant point, given the foundational role of law in the construction of the British colonial state. From the first royal trading charter issued by Queen Elizabeth in 1600 to the Indian Independence Act of 1947, law defined the territorial boundaries of the empire, legitimized its authority, and facilitated the daily routines of governance. As a global empire, Britain linked the legitimacy and lawfulness of its power to promises of law and order. In contrast to the Spanish *conquistadores*, who were seen by Britons as illegitimate and forceful usurpers of native rights, Britain's early colonization of the Americas in the seventeenth and eighteenth centuries was understood by Britons to be lawful and consensual. As Britain expanded into Africa and Asia, the promise of law and order remained a central pillar of the empire.

In India, the practices of the British colonial state tended to fall short of its rhetorical promises of even-handed and impartial justice. This is not surprising, given that colonial politics consist of a system of exclusion that is contingent upon constructing categories that differentiate colonizers from colonized. Was it even possible for Britain to control India so long as Britons and Indians stood on an equal footing before the law, or did imperial domination require legal differentiation? By tracing how the Company developed an unequal system of law, we can see how this system created an absence of law, which enabled European crime and lawlessness in the early colonial period.

The East India Company was initially authorized by the Crown to make laws to govern only its official representatives in India. As the Company's power and influence spread, so did the sway of its legal authority. The Charter Act of 1661 permitted the Company to exercise civil and criminal jurisdiction over all residents within the boundaries of its factories according to the laws of England. The legislative theory supporting the Company's right to prosecute and punish both Europeans and Indians in its territories was confirmed by the case of *The Indian Chief* (1800), according to which Company settlements were conceptualized as English territories governed

---

[7] On the notion of absence of law, see G. Agamben, *The State of Exception* (Chicago: University of Chicago Press, 2005).

by English law.[8] Reimagining India's geography as English territory, Company law effectively transformed Indians into aliens in their own lands.

The Company's early legal system, which rested on a sharp line of distinction between Company servants and native Indians, had no means to deal with non-Company Europeans in India. Indeed, the very presence of these "interlopers" was a violation of the Company's royal trade monopoly, which authorized only servants of the Company to do business in India. Although at least one early interloper, Thomas Pitt, went on to assume an official position of power as the Governor of Fort George, the Company generally looked upon these men as criminals.[9] The Company's fifth Charter of 1683 was specifically framed to suppress the interlopers by expanding its powers to seize illicit persons, ships, and merchandise found within the limits of the Company's exclusive trade, to try the interlopers as pirates by martial law, and to execute them upon conviction.[10]

In the eighteenth century, the Company established a parallel system of laws and law courts. In the Presidencies of Bengal, Madras, and Bombay were the Crown Courts – initially these were Mayor's Courts, which were supplanted by Supreme Courts in 1773 (see Figure 1.1). The Crown Courts were tribunals of English law with jurisdiction over everyone within the limits of the Presidency and in all cases involving Britons anywhere on the subcontinent. The jurisdiction of the Crown Courts even extended into the seas, as the Port Jackson Regulations required that when anyone belonging to a colony of New South Wales appeared illegally on a boat leaving the coast, they were to be delivered to a magistrate at the first port where the ship arrived, which was most often Calcutta.[11] The Supreme Courts were presided over by a chief justice and three other judges, all of whom were British barristers with no less than five years' standing, appointed by Parliament. In the interior of the country, called the *mofussil*, was a hierarchical arrangement of Company Courts that administered a plurality of laws and, for the most part, had jurisdiction only over Indians and non-British Europeans. Judges in the Company Courts were judicial officers in the Company's service, many of whom had no prior legal training or experience.

---

[8] Cited in B. K. Acharyya, *Codification in British India* (Calcutta: S. K. Banerji & Sons, 1914), Lecture 1.

[9] "Documentary Contributions to a Biography of Thomas Pitt, Interloper, Governor of Fort George, and Progenitor of an Illustrious Family," in H. Yule (ed.), *The Diary of W. Hedges*, vol. III (London, 1887).

[10] J. Kaye, *The Administration of the East India Company* (London, 1853); and J. Keay, *The Honourable Company: A History of the English East India Company* (London: HarperCollins, 1991).

[11] Case of Michael Tracy and Mary McDonald, BL, IOR, O/5/10.

Figure 1.1 **Calcutta Supreme Court, 1787**
Established by Lord North's Regulating Act of 1773, the Supreme Court
replaced the Mayor's Court in Calcutta. The Court was presided over by a
Chief Justice and three Puisne Judges appointed by the Crown from
barristers with at least five years of experience. The Supreme Court had
jurisdiction over all British subjects resident in Bengal, Bihar, and Orissa.
However, the cost and inconvenience associated with bringing witnesses
and evidence to Calcutta for a trial, meant that Britons in the *mofussil* were
largely immune from prosecution and punishment in most criminal matters.

The development of the Company's legal system accompanied its territorial and commercial expansion, as well as an increase in the size of the
official and non-official populations. In the mid-eighteenth century, the
Company had approximately 76 civil servants in Bengal, 260 European
officers and soldiers at Fort William, and another 260 military men in the
mofussil. In addition, there were about 100 non-officials in Bengal. By 1793,
the entire European community in Bengal had grown, especially the
Company's military (which now exceeded 5,000 European troops) and the
non-official population of Calcutta (which now consisted of 225 people).[12]

---

[12] S. C. Ghosh, *The Social Condition of the British Community in Bengal, 1757–1800* (Leiden:
E. J. Brill, 1970).

Until 1793, European British subjects could not be tried in the Company Courts in most civil and criminal matters. Although a European British subject could sue an Indian in a *mofussil* court, Indians had to take their grievances against European British subjects to the Crown Courts in the Presidency. Depending on where you were in India, this could be upwards of 1,000 miles away. Magistrates were authorized to make allowance for witnesses and prosecutors to travel to Calcutta at a daily rate of 2 annas (one-eighth of a rupee). The Supreme Court held sessions only quarterly, which further exacerbated the inefficiency of the system by presenting prolonged waiting periods on top of long-distance travel. For financial and other logistical reasons (including time spent away from work and the difficulty of transporting witnesses), Indians in the interior were generally unable to bear the burden of bringing their cases to trial in the Presidency and were therefore extremely vulnerable to abuses by European British subjects in both civil and criminal matters. A Bengal Regulation passed in 1796 slightly alleviated this burden by making all Europeans who were not British subjects amenable to the magistrates and circuit courts within whatever district they were apprehended and subject to trial as natives.[13]

The Company's policy of sending Britons to the Presidency for trial could have unexpected consequences. R. G. Wallace described an incident in which members of His Majesty's 17th Regiment stationed 1,000 miles from Calcutta and desperate to return to the Presidency conspired to murder an Indian by reasoning that "only one of them would be hanged for the crime; and that in the meantime they would all have a pleasant trip to Calcutta."[14] All seven soldiers were indeed sent to Calcutta for trial. However, five of them were convicted of murder and executed.

In 1793, the Bengal Government passed two Regulations designed to address the problem of British misconduct in civil matters in the *mofussil*. The first prohibited all non-official European British subjects from living further than 10 miles outside of Calcutta without a license and required that they agree to make themselves amenable to the local civil courts.[15] The second required Europeans not in the Company's service to report their names, professions, and application for licenses to remain in the country to the Governor-General and to provide two securities for good conduct and testimonials of good character. Licensed Europeans found more than 10 miles outside of the Presidency without written permission could have their licenses withdrawn, have their property seized "with

[13] Bengal Regulation II of 1796.
[14] R. G. Wallace, *Fifteen Years in India; or, Sketches of a Soldier's Life* (London, 1822), p. 105.
[15] Bengal Regulation IX, section XIX of 1793.

double the value thereof," and be deported from India.[16] In 1813, when the Company's trade monopoly was abolished, European British subjects in the *mofussil* were placed under the local jurisdiction of all civil courts higher than the *zillah* (district) level (courts of first instance with European judges).[17] Even so, Indians could appeal only to the Sadr Diwani Adalat, while Britons could appeal directly to the Calcutta Supreme Court.

In criminal matters, the Company's local judicial officers had extremely limited authority and control over Britons in the *mofussil*. This was a source of great frustration to them and a topic of frequent complaint. In 1796, Patna Circuit Court Judge Charles Keating wrote to Calcutta condemning the criminal law as "a prohibition to the obtaining of redress." Earlier that year, Judge Keating heard the case of an indigo planter named Richard Johnson who had initially appeared before the civil court in Tirhoot to sue his bearer, Bhola, and the bearer's wife, Bussiah, for stealing a writing box containing 481 rupees and 1,200 pice.[18] In the course of the trial it was discovered – and attested to by Johnson's own witnesses! – that Johnson had engaged in "an undue arrogation and illegal exertion of magisterial authority." In plain terms, Johnson had tortured Bhola and Bussiah in an effort to elicit their confession to an alleged theft.

Johnson began by alternately having Bhola hold a red-hot piece of iron in his hands and then stand on it, repeatedly asking him who had taken his money. As Bhola continued to profess his innocence, Johnson chained his legs and arms in irons, suspended him to a triangle, and beat him twenty-five times with a cane. After threatening at gunpoint to kill Bhola, Johnson stripped his wife, Bussiah, naked and chained the two together in the stocks using irons around their necks, threatening to throw their infant child into the water. (The stocks were torture and detention facilities constructed by British indigo planters to extract payment of debt, confessions, and so forth.) Johnson then mounted their naked bodies facing backwards on donkeys, and as a *dowl* (drum) was sounded, the couple was paraded publicly through three neighboring villages, with "a great mob of men and children assembled and making a noise." Finally, after affixing bamboo and irons to their necks, Johnson sent for the *thanadar* (police officer).

As no proof whatsoever was presented by Johnson in support of his claim, what began as a civil suit soon led to criminal charges being lodged against him in the Supreme Court. In committing the case to Calcutta,

---

[16] J. Crawfurd, *Notes on the Settlement of British Subjects in India* (London, 1833), p. 40; and Regulation XXVIII of 1793.
[17] Charter Act of 1813, section 107.   [18] BL, IOR, O/5/4.

Judge Keating noted that Indian subjects in the *mofussil* faced "insuperable impediments" to obtaining justice in criminal complaints against Europeans:

I have deemed it my duty to submit the case to your Honourable Court with a view to the drawing of your attention towards the future protection and welfare of a description of people who at present have no prospect of redress, from their worldly circumstances and distant residence from the Presidency against European British subjects in matters of a criminal nature.[19]

Keating beseeched the Calcutta authorities to protect their Indian subjects from his own British countrymen. Richard Johnson was convicted of assault and denied permission to ever return to Tirhoot.

Non-official violence was represented in official discourse as a menace external to the emerging Company state. The problem of British brutality, however, was not simply an affront to the better class of Englishman or an unambiguously outside threat: *the law itself was part of the structure of violence.* The jurisdictional exemptions provided by law gave men like Richard Johnson practical impunity from prosecution and punishment in the *mofussil*, enshrining a place of lawlessness at the center of law's empire in India. Contrary to the imagined vision of British law and order sweeping across a pre-colonial landscape of mayhem and arbitrary authority, the expansion of empire itself opened up new spaces of violence and criminal opportunity for non-officials in the Indian interior.

One way the Company dealt with this problem of white lawlessness was by a license system that forbade Europeans from proceeding to or residing in India without a license from the Court of Directors. Violation of the license requirement was a "high crime and misdemeanor" punishable by fine and/or imprisonment. The license system, which remained in place until 1833, was designed to provide some measure of official oversight over the free-merchants, interlopers, and adventurers in India who challenged the profitability of the Company's trade monopoly and its legal powers. From 1814 to 1831, the Court of Directors approved 1,253 applications for licenses to proceed to India.[20] Non-officials who wished to move to the *mofussil* needed a second license authorizing them to live more than 10 miles outside of the Presidency.

In practice, the Company found it extremely difficult to enforce its license system. Hard as it was to control the oceanic passage to India, there was little way for the Company to control the movement and behavior

---

[19] Patna Court of Circuit Senior Judge Charles Keating to Sir John Short Baronet, President, and members of the Nizamut Adalat, April 28, 1796, BL, IOR, O/5/4.

[20] "Statement of the Number of Licenses to Proceed to and Reside in India," *Papers Relating to the Settlement of Europeans in India* (1854), Appendix No. I, BL, IOR, V 3244.

of both licensed and unlicensed Europeans once they left the Presidency. After all, the dual legal system, by definition, exempted Britons from local authority. In 1789, Michael MacNamara filed a charge of theft against his servants. An inquiry by the Magistrate of Dacca, Samuel Middleton, found MacNamara to be "a most worthless character and a drunken vagrant" who never in the first place possessed the property he claimed was stolen from him. Middleton advised that MacNamara "does not merit any support whatever," or the protection of government, and requested "some measures being adopted to prevent these low Europeans travelling the country in the manner they now do. Wherever they go, they plunder."[21] The license system also opened up opportunities for fraud. In 1794, William Hill attempted to pass through the Mahratta country en route to Persia using an old pass granted in 1791 to Richard Mathews. The "infamous and notorious Doctor Hill" was apprehended and ordered home to Europe. He reappeared in India and was again deported in 1799.[22]

Although class prejudices undoubtedly underscored the scornful attitudes of Company officials towards "low Europeans" like Michael MacNamara – P. J. Marshall notes that most of the Company's servants in late eighteenth-century Bengal were described as "'gentlemen or the sons of gentlemen'"[23] – the problem was not simply a question of class. It was also a question of law. In an essay titled "Two Faces of Colonialism," David Washbrook defines the colonial rule of law as one where "the state may make law for its subjects, [but] posits itself as above that law and as unaccountable to it."[24] What about the third face of colonialism – that of a Richard Johnson? Johnson, and the many other criminal Britons like him in India, complicated the Janus-faced nature of colonial rule by entering India under the aegis of a new political order and threatening it from within. Even if the colonial state posited itself as above the law, ordinary Britons like Richard Johnson were not meant to be. Johnson's dastardly behavior threatened imperial stability by exposing to Indians a dark side of the British character. As Henry Dundas noted in 1793, "upon this feeling of the superiority of the Europeans the preservation of our empire depends."[25]

[margin annotation: Class + race]

[21] BL, IOR, O/5/2.   [22] BL, IOR, O/5/3.

[23] P. J. Marshall, *East Indian Fortunes: The British in Bengal in the Eighteenth Century* (Oxford: Clarendon Press, 1976), p. 13. In his important and wide-ranging body of work on British colonial society in India, Marshall largely overlooks the problem of European criminality and its impact on colonial law and policy.

[24] D. A. Washbrook, "India, 1818–1860: The Two Faces of Colonialism," in A. Porter (ed.), *Oxford History of the British Empire*, vol. III (Oxford: Oxford University Press, 1999), p. 407.

[25] T. C. Hansard, *The Parliamentary History of England from the Earliest Period to the Year 1803*, vol. XXX (London, 1817), p. 676.

Johnson's actions also threatened the exclusive nature of colonial authority. By taking the law into his own hands, Johnson encroached upon the state's monopoly of legitimate violence and pain-related power. Richard Johnson exemplified to British officials what could happen when the wrong sort of European took part in the powers and privileges of Company sovereignty. It was not appropriate, Warren Hastings sharply remarked, for such men to confuse their national origin with a right to dominate, to speak in the language of "'Since *we* became masters of the country,' '*our* native subjects.'"[26] In Hastings' view, it was government's duty to provide protection to its colonial subjects.

In 1808, a group of European soldiers were convicted of arson for setting fire to a small Indian home in Calcutta. All of the men were discharged from their military service and deported. The perceived ringleader of the group, John Grant, was sentenced to death for willfully and deliberately setting the fire. (His punishment was commuted to transportation to New South Wales for seven years.) In his decision, Calcutta Supreme Court Judge Henry Russell observed:

The hut of the poor man is equally entitled to the protection of the law as the mansion of the rich and stands much more in need of it. The natives are entitled to have their characters, property and lives protected and as long as they enjoy that protection from us they give their affection and allegiance in return; but should the day ever arrive, God forbid, that they should be denied that protection then I fear that as we should no longer deserve so we should no longer enjoy their allegiance and attachment.[27]

If the colonial government could not even control Britons in India, then how could it stabilize its authority, much less sustain any broad claim to be the fountainhead of law and order across the subcontinent?

Commanding India, commanding themselves

All Europeans who are permitted to remain in the interior must be taught, practically, that obedience to the law is an indispensable condition of their licence to reside there.

Court of Directors (1832)[28]

---

[26] Hastings' testimony before the Lords' Committee on European Colonization and Settlement, cited in D. Basu, *The Colonization of India by Europeans* (Calcutta: R. Chatterjee, 1925), p. 31.

[27] Case of Hardwick and others, BL, IOR, O/5/8.

[28] Court of Directors to the Governor-General, April 10, 1832, *Papers Relating to the Settlement of Europeans in India*, BL, IOR, V 3244.

mmm

Concern about the behavior of non-officials and the lack of local criminal jurisdiction over them was a consistent theme in the ongoing debate about the opening of free trade and the prospects of a permanent white settlement in India. From 1764 to 1813, there was steady opposition in London and Calcutta to the open colonization of Indian land by European settlers. In 1794, Lord Cornwallis noted that "it will be of essential importance to the interests of Britain that Europeans should be discouraged and prevented as much as possible from colonizing and settling in our possessions of India."[29] In 1818, John Bebb and James Pattison warned the Board of Control (a parliamentary oversight committee) about "the impolicy and danger of allowing Europeans (not in the King's or Company's Service) in any considerable number to resort to and settle in India."[30] Official anxiety that, in Charles Grant's words, "multitudes of the needy and the idle…[the] low and licentious" would "domineer over the natives, harass, extrude, exasperate them" restricted would-be white settlers and merchants from freely entering India.[31] The opinion shared by administrators in England and India was that non-officials would oppress the natives, offend their religious sensibilities, degrade the imperial image by their drunkenness and misconduct, and weaken local confidence in the benefits of British governance.

The Company, however, had a hard time controlling both its borders and the movement of Europeans within India (see Map 1.1). In May 1765, shortly after assuming formal control of Bengal, the Company recalled "all free merchants and other Europeans who reside up the country" to Calcutta within the month "as the only means of securing the necessary authority of Government and protection of individuals."[32] As the Company's territorial power expanded, a series of treaties was made with Indian potentates that explicitly required them not to retain any other Europeans in their service or to permit Europeans from settling in their dominions without the permission of the Company's government. Many of the treaties asked local rulers to "deliver up to the English Company such of their servants who have deserted or may desert in case of his apprehending him."[33] This suggests that the establishment of Company sovereignty was not only ill-defined and insecure vis-à-vis competing Indian potentates, its power was also disputed in relation to

---

[29] Extract of letter from Cornwallis to Henry Dundas, November 7, 1794, ibid.

[30] Letter of February 27, 1818, ibid.

[31] Basu, *The Colonization of India by Europeans*, p. 22.

[32] Order of May 14, 1765, in extract of letter from Bengal, November 28, 1766, cited in the case of Vernon Duffield, *et al.*, BL, IOR, O/5/1.

[33] See the Treaty of 1775 between the Government of Bengal and Asuf Ul Dowlah, Nabob of Oude, BL, IOR, 2440 *Papers Relating to East India Affairs* (1813).

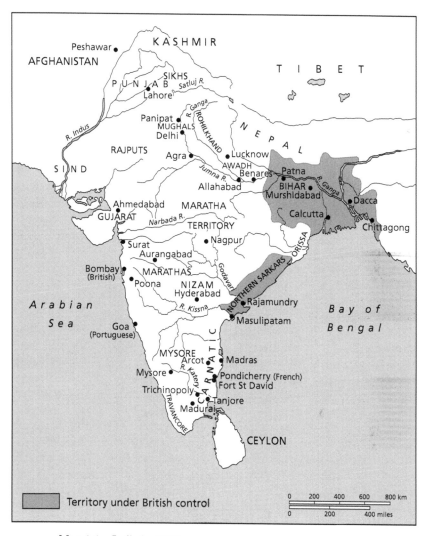

Map 1.1   India in 1765

Ycholt

non-official white rivals in India.[34] A series of incidents involving Europeans who provided arms and military training to Indian authorities underscored this anxiety.[35]

In addition to the license system, regulations passed in the late eighteenth century restricted the ability of Europeans to hold long-term leases on land in the *mofussil*. The reluctance to allow whites to settle in India was linked both to the Company's will to maintain exclusive control over "our possessions of India"[36] and to a particular view of Indian civilization. Early colonial administrators regarded India as "a country rich, populous and powerful in itself," inhabited by agriculturalists who possessed land rights and useful knowledge.[37] Philip Francis insisted that "The soil of right belongs to the Natives."[38] Many administrators, including Francis, worried that a population of white settlers could lead to a revolution, a fear greatly exacerbated by the loss of the American colonies. In 1801, the Court of Directors explicitly resolved that "It is equally in the interests of the nation and the duty of the Company to guard against colonization."[39]

There was also the issue of their unseemly and disorderly conduct. White settlers were seen as a threat to the Company's power and profits because they made it more difficult "to maintain order and subordination" and also because of the destabilizing effect of their behavior: "by gradually lessening the deference and respect in which Europeans are held, [they] tend to shake the opinion entertained by the Natives of the superiority of our character, and might excite them to an effort for the subversion and utter extinction of our power."[40] Officials feared that the settlers might themselves revolt against the Company. They also worried that they might inspire Indians to revolt.

The conduct of non-officials was unbecoming for a variety of reasons, including: their "excesses disgusting to the Natives, which frequently lead to acts of violence and outrage"; their inclination to "domineer over and oppress the Natives from a sense of their own personal and national superiority";[41] and the general fact that their "uncontrollable manners

---

[34] This point extends the argument of S. Sen, *Distant Sovereignty: National Imperialism and the Origins of British India* (New York: Routledge, 2002).
[35] See the cases of Frederick Maitland Arnott, J. H. Bellasis, Thomas Martin, Joseph Straussenberg, and Steven Raymond, BL, IOR, O/5/4.
[36] Extract of letter from Cornwallis to Henry Dundas, November 7, 1794, *Papers Relating to the Settlement of Europeans in India*, BL, IOR, V 3244.
[37] John Bebb and James Pattison to George Canning, February 27, 1818, ibid.
[38] Extract from Bengal Revenue Consultations, May 12, 1775, Minute of Philip Francis, ibid.
[39] Resolution of Court of Directors, February 4, 1801, ibid.
[40] Bebb and Pattison to Canning, ibid.   [41] Ibid.

expose[d] the Company's valuable privileges to the greatest detriment and hazard."[42] While there are obvious class biases in these official observations, it is important to stress that the strength of official condemnation of their conduct related to the weakness of law to control it.

In 1813, the Company's trade monopoly was terminated. This was largely determined by the Company's financial distress, by changed conditions in the world market, and by shifts in the ideological terrain of empire. The American Revolution and the switch from indigo cultivation to sugar and coffee cultivation in the West Indies provided a huge boom to the indigo market in India. In turn, the indigo planters and merchants of Lower Bengal – some of whom arrived from Britain's Caribbean plantations – became important players in the political economy of Calcutta, even as they heightened longstanding anxieties in London about the potential consequences of their bad behavior. Non-officials remained subject to many of the same regulations and restrictions, including the license system and the prohibition on landholding. Although India's borders were now open, official opinion was still divided on the question of whether white settlers would ultimately undermine Company authority or expand its prospective profits.

In London, trepidation about the character and habits of "Englishmen of the worst description" persisted in the face of a legal system that provided no adequate mechanism of local control.[43] Warren Hastings, for example, remained strongly opposed to an unrestricted white settlement. He feared that such men "would insult, plunder and oppress the natives; and no laws enacted from home could prevent them from committing acts of licentiousness of every kind with impunity."[44] Opening the floodgates to such profligate characters, Hastings warned, would lead to "the ruin of the country" and the collapse of the empire.

The termination of the Company's monopoly, however, did not cause a massive influx of non-officials. Between 1813 and 1833, the population increased by fewer than 300 people, from 1,881 to 2,149.[45] Nonetheless, before the Company's charter came up for renewal in 1833, questions were again raised in London about the problems and possibilities of an unrestricted white settlement. Concern about white settlers' treatment of native people in India coincided with inquiries into the treatment of aborigines in Australia and the debate on the abolition of slavery.[46]

[42] Court of Directors to Bengal, February 8, 1764, BL, IOR, O/5/1.
[43] T. Macaulay, *Speeches and Poems with the Report and Notes on the Indian Penal Code* (New York, 1867).
[44] Evidence given on April 5, 1815, before the House of Lords, *Hansard's*, vol. XXV, p. 554.
[45] Crawfurd, *Notes on the Settlement of British Subjects in India*, pp. 19–20.
[46] J. Evans, P. Grimshaw, D. Philips, and S. Swain, *Equal Subjects, Unequal Rights: Indigenous Peoples in British Settler Colonies, 1830–1910* (Manchester: Manchester University Press, 2003).

A memorandum sent to officials in India in 1832 solicited feedback on a host of issues related to European colonization: "whether it has of late years been promoted or discouraged. What particular classes of persons should be particularly encouraged to proceed to India. What are the dangers to be guarded against in the admission without licence of British settlers, and under what conditions Europeans should be allowed to settle in India."[47] The responses that came back were mixed. One Company official anonymously responded that "with a view to preserve our empire there, no European should be encouraged to settle in India."[48] Others advised that the government should prevent only "improper persons" from entering India. The optimists insisted that European settlement posed no great danger "because it is evidently the interest of persons who go thither for commercial objects to conciliate the natives."[49] Ardent supporters of colonization, such as Charles Metcalfe, a Member of the Supreme Council, insisted that European settlement was necessary to civilize the *mofussil* and provide much-needed remittances at little cost to government. Contrary to earlier apprehensions about the "lower orders" of European society compromising Indians' respect for and obedience to government, Metcalfe insisted that imperial stability and Indian development depended upon the circulation of European knowledge, morals, capital, skill, and personnel:

I am further convinced that our possession of India must always be precarious unless we take root by having an influential portion of the population attached to our Government by common interests and sympathies. Every measure, therefore, which is calculated to facilitate the settlement of our countrymen in India, and to remove the obstructions by which it is impeded, must, I conceive, conduce to the stability of our rule, and to the welfare of the people subject to our dominion.[50]

Elite Indians also supported the idea, though for different reasons. Ram Mohun Roy argued that a permanent white settlement would benefit India by stopping the flow of bullion back to England. Roy observed that "As a large sum of money is now annually drawn from India by Europeans retiring from it with the fortunes realized there, a system which would encourage Europeans of capital to become permanent settlers with their

---

[47] Circular from T. Hyde Villiers, Esq., Secretary to the India Board, February 11, 1832, *Appendix to the Report from the Select Committee of the House of Commons on the Affairs of the East India Company*, Appendix I (A).

[48] Letter to T. Hyde Villiers, Esq., Secretary to the India Board, February 1832, ibid., Appendix I (A), Answers to Circular (2), 3.

[49] John Sullivan, Esq. of the Madras Civil Service, to T. Hyde Villiers, Esq., Secretary to the India Board, February 21, 1832, ibid., Appendix I (A), Answers to Circular (2).

[50] Metcalfe, "Memorandum of European Settlement," February 19, 1829, *Papers Relating to the Settlement of Europeans in India*, BL, IOR, V 3244.

families would necessarily greatly improve the resources of the country."[51] He was, however, quick to recommend that an expanded white settlement required "the enactment of equal laws."[52]

Departing from the position of his predecessors, Governor-General William Bentinck asserted that India's improvement could only be achieved through an extensive European settlement.[53] Bentinck dismissed older fears that white settlers would oppress Indians, become hostile to government, and ultimately stage (or cause) a revolution. In Bentinck's view, the only way the government could maximize and encourage "the productive powers of the country" was through the diffusion of European capital, skill, and example.[54] For a variety of reasons, including the tropical climate, the warlike nature of certain native classes, and the indigenous rights of private property, Bentinck assured his colleagues at home that the "hazard of evil" was minimal.[55] For those Britons who came to settle in India, Bentinck confidently declared there was "no scope for wild adventure."[56]

On this last point, Bentinck was wildly off base. There was, in fact, enormous scope for wild adventure, menacing misconduct, and grotesque violence, as is abundantly demonstrated by the historical record. Even after India's borders were opened to free traders, the Company's legal control over Britons in the interior in criminal matters remained narrowly circumscribed. Local magistrates could try European British subjects in cases of assault and trespass, but those charged with felonies and gross misdemeanors had to be committed for trial at the Supreme Courts in the Presidencies. Concerned about the potential for abuse and misbehavior, and miffed by Calcutta's growing sympathy with the non-official population of Bengal, the Board of Control ordered an account of all Europeans and "persons passing as Europeans in India" removed from or ordered to quit India since 1766. This resulted in an official record titled "European Misconduct in India 1766–1824," comprising twenty-five large, handwritten volumes that run for nearly 20,000 pages.[57]

---

[51] Ram Mohun Roy to the Board of Control, "On the Revenue System of India," August 19, 1831, *Report from the Select Committee on the Affairs of the East India Company*, vol. II, pp. 716–722.

[52] Remarks by Ram Mohun Roy of July 14, 1832, *Minutes of Evidence Taken before the Select Committee of the House of Commons on the Affairs of the East India Company*, Appendix V, p. 467.

[53] William Bentinck, "Minute on European Settlement," May 30, 1829, *Papers Relating to the Settlement of Europeans in India*, BL, IOR, V 3244.

[54] Ibid.   [55] Ibid.   [56] Ibid.

[57] A few cases from this series are briefly considered in P. Spear, *Nabobs: A Study of the Social Life of the English in 18th Century India* (London: Oxford University Press, 1963), pp. 60–61 and 192–194.

Captors: European misconduct in early colonial Bengal

In her study, Linda Colley offers two parables about "the making and meanings of the British empire."[58] The first, portrayed by Daniel Defoe's *Robinson Crusoe*, is the imperialist as warrior: seizing and settling land, conquering and colonizing natives. The second, manifest in Jonathan Swift's *Gulliver's Travels*, is the colonizer as captive: oppressed, bound, and dominated by native people. This second story provides the starting-point for Colley's book, which argues that "overseas venturing brings no conquests, or riches, or easy complacencies: only terror, vulnerability, and repeated captivities."[59] I would argue that just as there is a third face of colonialism, so too there is a third parable about the meaning and making of the British empire, this one featuring a cast of in-between characters who were captors but not conquerors. Their story is the subject of the remainder of this chapter.

The official record of "European Misconduct in India, 1766–1824" presents an unfamiliar picture of British power and society in early colonial Bengal (the accounts from Bombay and Madras were never sent to London). Here we see the terror and desperation of the many European vagabonds, imposters, robbers, burglars, beggars, frauds, planters, loafers, escaped convicts, and absconding soldiers and seamen who wandered about the Town of Calcutta and the Indian interior inebriated, diseased, insane, misbehaved, and unwilling or unable to hold down steady work. Their "general misconduct, constant intoxication, bad character and acts of disgraceful vagrancy," along with their confederacy against the government, resistance to authority, and murderous violence, made them a menace to each other, to Indians, and to the Company, which prosecuted, punished, and deported them at its own expense.[60] These men – and the few women among them, too – threatened a cornerstone of imperial power: its system for administering justice.

What makes the cases in this record so interesting is not only the individual stories of mayhem and misconduct but also what they reveal about the insecurity of early Company power and the uncertain status and ineffective nature of its laws. Neither rulers nor ruled, the unruly figures we find here presented a third face of colonialism that made the task of ruling India more difficult. In narrating the details of a small selection of these cases, my intention is to bear witness to a largely suppressed, if not

---

[58] L. Colley, *Captives: Britain, Empire, and the World, 1600–1850* (London: Jonathan Cape, 2002), p. i.
[59] Ibid., p. 2.   [60] BL, IOR, O/5/25.

hidden, history and to reflect upon what the cases tell us about the relationship between violence, law, and empire in India.

In December 1767, the Bengal Government wrote home to request "a full exertion of the privileges granted in the Royal Charter...to rid the country" – by force, if necessary – "of a man who endeavours by false reports and representatives to lessen the respect due to the present administration and to destroy the confidence now subsisting between us and the powers of Hindustan." The Bengal authorities insisted that if their request was not granted, "anarchy and confusion must infallibly take place" and British influence in India would be "totally subverted."[61] The very act of making this request reflected the unsure nature of the Company's legal rights as articulated in the royal charters, a point to which we will return shortly.

The man in question was William Bolts, an alderman at the Mayor's Court of Calcutta and a rather infamous character in the Company's history. The alderman appointment was an unpopular one, with an annual salary of a mere £25 and duties that required residence in Calcutta, thereby preventing participation in the lucrative upcountry trade. When Bolts was discovered engaging in a ruthless private trade, he was ordered home to Europe.[62] Defying the Council's order, Bolts fled to Chinmurah, where he wrote a string of provocative missives challenging the Company's "glaring attempt to an infringement of the British liberties."[63] Echoing the critique of many commentators before him who challenged the propriety and constitutionality of the Company's trade monopoly,[64] Bolts disputed the Company's right to dismiss and deport him. He insisted that the alderman appointment was for life and, as an employee of a Crown Court, Bolts held that he should be allowed to remain in India regardless of the Company's wishes. Tapping into an older debate about the constitutional authority of the Company to infringe upon the merchant's right to trade and personal freedom, Bolts argued that it was the custom of the Company's covenanted servants to reside in the country as long as they pleased.[65] The Privy Council sided with Bolts, reversing his dismissal and deportation.

---

[61] Bengal Public Letter, December 10, 1767, in the case of William Bolts, BL, IOR, O/5/1.

[62] W. Bolts, *Considerations on Indian Affairs Respecting the Present State of Bengal* (London, 1772); N. L. Hallward, *William Bolts: A Dutch Adventurer under John Company* (Cambridge: Cambridge University Press, 1920); and W. G. J. Kuiters, *The British in Bengal, 1756–1773: A Society in Transition Seen through the Biography of a Rebel: William Bolts (1739–1808)* (Paris: Indes Savantes, 2002), p. 127.

[63] Bolts to the Court of Directors, October 8, 1767, BL, IOR, O/5/1.

[64] J. Thirsk and J. P. Cooper (eds.), *Seventeenth-Century Economic Documents* (Oxford: Clarendon Press, 1972), pp. 436–444.

[65] Bolts to the Court of Directors, October 9, 1767, BL, IOR, O/5/1.

deportation [handwritten margin note]

Bolts' case is one of many that highlight the Company's contentious relationship with, and unclear legal authority over, Europeans in early colonial India, men whom they felt obligated to protect but powerless to control. The Company's primary method to prevent, restrain, and punish European misconduct was deportation. The famous missionary Bishop Heber called the power of deportation "essential to the public peace," noting that it was the only way to control such "profligates":

> Many of the adventurers who come hither from Europe are the greatest profligates the sun ever saw; men whom nothing but despotism can manage, and who, unless they were really under a despotic rule, would insult, beat, and plunder the natives without shame or pity. Even now, many instances occur of insult and misconduct, for which the prospect of immediate embarkation for Europe is the most effectual precaution or remedy. It is, in fact, the only control which the Company possesses over the tradesmen and ship-builders in Calcutta, and the indigo planters up the country.[66]

Deportation raised critical legal questions, as the forcible removal of Europeans from India often subverted the due process of law. In July 1787, William Duane was discharged from the Company's armed services upon arrival in India. Seven years later, when he was found to still be residing in India without a license, he was ordered home, where he published a series of angry articles in *The World* protesting the "hostile measures taken against me without charge, accusation or trial."[67] The Company's right to deport was enshrined in various laws, including the Charter Act of 1661, which granted the Company "full Power and Lawful Authority, to seize upon the Persons of all such English, or any other of our Subjects, in the said East Indies...and send them to England."[68] However, although the Company vowed to exercise this power "tenderly,"[69] it frequently ran roughshod over its own legal processes.

In certain instances, when officials considered the evidence insufficient to ensure a conviction in the Supreme Court, summary deportations were ordered without any trial whatsoever. In 1796, Conrad Funck, a German who had served the Company for seventeen years, was charged with bribery and robbery in the town of Calcutta. Funck requested a trial, but the Governor-General decided that although the evidence was not

---

[66] P. Auber, *Supplement to an Analysis of the Constitution of the East India Company* (London, 1828), p. 26.

[67] BL, IOR, O/5/3.

[68] F. W. Madden and D. K. Fieldhouse (eds.), *Select Documents on the Constitutional History of the British Empire and Commonwealth*, vol. I (Westport: Greenwood Press, 1985), p. 415.

[69] Opinion of William de Grey, Charles Yorke, and Charles Sayer, August 9, 1796, BL, IOR, L/L/6/1.

sufficient to convict him in a court of law, it was sufficient to justify his deportation, which he ordered summarily.[70] In other cases, "bad characters" were removed from India even *after* being acquitted by the Supreme Court. In 1790, Henry Pyne, an unlicensed Englishman residing in Chittagong, was tried for assault. After his acquittal, the Company decided that on account of his "general bad character and mode of behavior" he was denied permission to remain in the country.[71]

The removal of Europeans from India did not offer a lasting solution to the problem of criminal misconduct, as deportation proceedings were politically and financially costly. The protocol in the interior began with an extensive preliminary investigation by a local magistrate. The magistrate reported his findings to Calcutta for orders as to whether the accused should be sent for prosecution in the Supreme Court. Although unlicensed Europeans could be deported within a few days, licensed Europeans required twelve months' notice, which was ample time for them to disappear back into the *mofussil*. Many of those ordered home were so violent and distasteful that commanders of commercial ships refused to transport them, and arrangements had to be made for a "charter party passage" home at the Company's expense. Not infrequently, these men returned to India, further exposing the vulnerability of the Company's power, ports, and coastlines.[72]

Before examining some of the fascinating cases in this record, a note of caution is warranted. Despite the title, "European Misconduct in India, 1766–1824," the cases are limited to Bengal. Furthermore, the Bengal accounts represent only cases and proceedings relating to people found without a license and those whose licenses and permission to reside in India were revoked. By definition, unlicensed Europeans were already in violation of the law and would have been difficult to apprehend. Beyond this, licensed Europeans who were tried and convicted by the Supreme Court but who did not have their licenses revoked do not appear in this record, nor do soldiers tried by military court-martial. Finally, those who evaded the law altogether are absent from the record. Therefore, as rich and revealing as the record is, it offers only a partial history of European misconduct in early colonial India.

The Company offered five primary reasons for revoking the licenses of and deporting Europeans from India. These were: confederacy against

---

[70] Funck's petition written from New Gaol, March 14, 1795, BL, IOR, O/5/4.

[71] Public Letter from Bengal, November 6, 1790, BL, IOR, O/5/2.

[72] Cases of Europeans deported at least twice include: Vernon Duffield (BL, IOR, O/5/1), Passos de Ferreira (BL, IOR, O/5/2), Michael Macnamara (BL, IOR, O/5/2), John Adams (BL, IOR, O/5/3), William Hill (BL, IOR, O/5/3), Conrad Funck (BL, IOR, O/5/4), and George Greek (BL, IOR, O/5/4).

the government and resistance to authority; violent and murderous conduct towards the natives; interacting with native gangs in acts of burglary within Company territories; "general misconduct, constant intoxication, bad character and acts of disgraceful vagrancy"; and escaped convicts from New South Wales.[73] Analysis of the cases will be presented in three thematic groupings: resistance and confederacy against the government; general misconduct; and violence.

Resistance and confederacy against the government

It is worth noting here that "resistance" is not a category generally used to think through white-on-white relations in colonial India. Resistance is usually a concept we use to think about how colonized populations responded to colonial rule. Thus the very notion of European resistance to European power – that "third face" – requires a shift in how we imagine British colonial society in India. The effort to exclude interlopers, adventurers, deserters, free-merchants, and private traders had long been part and parcel of the Company's will to exclusive power on the subcontinent.[74] Conversely, those Europeans who were the targets of this emergent power fought tooth and nail to resist it.

In 1766, seven young British soldiers resigned their military commissions and applied for residency licenses to remain in the Bengal Presidency.[75] The Company denied their request and ordered them home to Europe. The men refused to leave. When two of the soldiers, Vernon Duffield and Francis Robertson, learned about their involuntary booking home on the vessel *Camden*, they stocked up on supplies, locked themselves in their house, and barricaded the doors. They remained inside for several days until they figured that the *Camden* had left the dock. When they emerged, they were immediately seized by Company guards and sent to Madras to board another ship home.

Two of the other soldiers, James Nicol and Thomas Davie, fled to Benares, which was then within the dominion of Siraj ud-Daulah (ruler of Bengal prior to the British conquest), and began supplying his subjects with fire-arms and military training. Nicol and Davie were ultimately found

---

[73] BL, IOR, O/5/25. In this chapter, I do not address escaped convict cases. See Clare Anderson, "Multiple Border Crossings: Convicts and Other Persons escaped from Botany Bay and Residing in Calcutta," *Journal of Australian Colonial History*, 3, 2 (2001), 1–22.

[74] P. J. Stern, "The Fringes of History: The Seventeenth-Century Origins of the East India Company-State," in S. Agha and E. Kolsky (eds.), *Fringes of Empire: People, Power and Places in Colonial India* (Delhi: Oxford University Press, 2009).

[75] The series of cases is presented in one record, BL, IOR, O/5/1.

living with a Monsieur Gentile – "a Frenchman who resides with the Nabob and is known to be no friend to the English" – and were turned over to Company officials who had them escorted to Calcutta by armed guards. Although Nicol denied the charge of selling arms and pledged never again to enter into the service of an Indian potentate, he was imprisoned for five months at Fort William and then deported without trial.

In England, Nicol filed a lawsuit challenging the legality of the Company's actions in improperly depriving him of his liberty and unlawfully removing him from India. He claimed that he and Davie were left "prisoners deemed to die without trial rather than gentlemen under confinement whose transgression is not yet known."[76] Nicol argued that he had resigned from the Company's army to protest the abolition of the double *batta*, the extra living expenses paid to soldiers in the Company's employ. On January 1, 1766, shortly after assuming the *diwani* of Bengal, the Company stopped paying the double *batta* to the 20,000 men accustomed to receiving it. At the time, a lieutenant-colonel in the Company's service would have earned a base salary of 248 rupees a month. Single *batta* added 620 rupees and double *batta* 1,240 rupees. The abolition of the double *batta* was met with mass resignations by the Company's junior officers.[77] Maintaining that he had moved to the interior simply to engage in trade – an odd defense, given that trading without a license was the very grounds for his removal from India – Nicol argued that his deportation was illegal.

The Court of Common Pleas split the baby in its decision. On the one hand, the Court found that the law granted the Company the exclusive trade to and from India but not the trade *in* India. As Nicol did have a right to trade in India, his seizure and imprisonment were declared illegal. On the other hand, the Court confirmed the Company's right to remove people found to be residing in India without a license, which put the Company in a legal limbo: how could unlicensed persons be deported if they could not first be legally seized, imprisoned, and tried?

The trials of William Bolts, Vernon Duffield, and James Nicol form part of a long series of cases in which British subjects exploited and challenged the Company's uncertain power and dubious legal authority. Rather than offering any real incendiary or conspiratorial threat in and of themselves, these men exposed the tenuous nature of early Company power and the vagueness of law that crippled the Company's ability to act. Even when the Company could get its hands on such elusive and (frequently) armed

---

[76] Nicol to Captain Pearson (Governor's Military Secretary), June 15, 1767, BL, IOR, O/5/1.
[77] R. Holmes, *Sahib: The British Soldier in India, 1750–1914* (London: HarperCollins, 2005), p. 272.

characters, it knew not what to do with them. Did the Company possess
the legal right to deport unlicensed Britons who were subjects of the King
but had no formal relationship to the Company? What would happen
when they applied for *habeas corpus*? Could such persons lawfully be
detained in custody?

Ten years after his first deportation, Vernon Duffield returned to India.
Disguised in "Moorish dress," he and two European accomplices were
caught attempting to enter the dominions of Asaf ud-Daulah. They were
arrested and brought to Patna where, prior to being loaded onto a ship
bound for Calcutta, they barricaded themselves in a bungalow and threatened to commit suicide in protest against their deportation. Aware that
force would be required to physically remove them from the bungalow,
and unsure of his power to use such force, the Company's Chief at Patna
sent for orders from Calcutta.

If the Company was confused about its legal authority over Britons in
India, it was even less certain of its power over non-British Europeans. In
1767, Joseph Pavesy, an Italian who had come to Calcutta as a servant to
an Englishman, moved to Behar, "where he conducted himself with great
violence towards the Natives, assuming judicial power, inflicting corporal
punishment on the Native inhabitants at his own discretion and committing many other outrages." Describing Pavesy as a "straggling European
foreigner," the local Company officer issued a warrant for his arrest.[78]
However, Pavesy publicly flogged the peons sent by the Company to
apprehend him. While a prisoner in Fort William, Pavesy applied to the
Calcutta Supreme Court for a writ of *habeas corpus*, asking why he should
not be set free, as he was not a subject of the King. Pavesy also challenged
the Company's power to deport unlicensed Europeans who were not
British subjects. Although the Company insisted upon "the power inherent in every Government to expel foreign vagabonds who clandestinely
enter the country and commit outrages and disturbances against the peace
of it," the Supreme Court decided in Pavesy's favor and ordered his
immediate release.

One of the strangest cases of resistance to authority in the early colonial
period involved William Tucker, a man whose criminal conduct came to
the notice of the Bengal Government on four different occasions over the
course of more than twenty years. Tucker initially caused trouble in
Assam in 1801 where he effectively shut down the salt trade. Armed
with swords, pistols, muskets, and boatloads of *sepoys*, Tucker attacked
boats passing through Goalparrah and made off with their goods. His

---

[78] Secret Letter from Bengal, January 15, 1776, BL, IOR, O/5/1.

reign of terror brought local business to a complete standstill. Local official B. McCullum warned Bengal that Tucker

shows himself all powerful, no one can control his conduct, he therefore acts as he pleases and everyone here supposes he acts from authority. He sends orders to the Civil Officers of Government by the Company's Sepoys and if he is not obeyed he insults the officers...I have only to repeat that Mr. Tucker's daring oppressions increase daily and if you do not take measures to put a stop to him I should not be surprised soon to see Goalparrah burnt to the ground.

In 1802, Tucker was ordered down to Calcutta, where his license was revoked.[79]

Five years later, Tucker was granted a new license to plant indigo in Dinajpur. By 1810, there were sixty criminal charges lodged against him for plunder, assault, forcing financial advances on *ryots*, and obliging them to enter indigo contracts. In addition to his maniacal physical abuse, Tucker had also assumed judicial authority and was found to be issuing *tullub chittees* and *islah namas* (official letters and notices) that required local people to attend his factory and answer complaints and disputes concerning their debts. His license to reside in Dinajpur was again annulled, and he was ordered to remain in Calcutta.[80]

In 1820, Tucker popped up again, this time as an assistant in the post office in Kedgeree, where he resumed with even greater zeal his "tyranni-cal and oppressive conduct." Various *arzees* (petitions) were lodged against him for beatings, floggings, mistreatment of workers, withholding of wages, illegal use of post office staff for personal purposes, and "illegal and arbitrary assumption of judicial authority."[81] Despite the long list of charges, little was done to prosecute him. As the local magistrate, R. Walpole, noted, this "encouraged Mr. Tucker in his impropriety of conduct and induced a belief in him that his tyranny and oppression might be practised without hindrance and with impunity."

In May 1820, Tucker's assistant, John Williamson, tied two Indian sailors, Haroo and Gareebullah, to the pillars of Tucker's house and punched, kicked, and flogged them with a *rattan*. The men had come on shore from a Company ship to get water from a public tank that Tucker had illegally privatized. Despite direct orders from Walpole, Tucker refused to release the *lascars* (seamen). A month later, Tucker beat and confined three other boatmen who worked for a local shipping agent named Harton. When the local *kotwal* (police chief) brought a letter from Harton demanding the release of his men, Tucker, who was

---

[79] BL, IOR, O/5/6.   [80] BL, IOR, O/5/11.   [81] BL, IOR, O/5/20.

lounging on his verandah, became incensed and ripped the note in pieces without reading it, vowing never to release the boatmen.

In January 1822, Tucker was finally dismissed from his position and ordered back to the Presidency, which he did only after destroying government documents, threatening his European neighbors, and stealing from the local shops. Although Tucker was prohibited from moving beyond the limits of the Supreme Court's jurisdiction, the following year he returned to Kedgeree in the employ of a European fish company. Within six months, the local magistrate was investigating reports that Tucker, armed with pistols, was threatening the local Europeans and stealing goods from shopkeepers in the bazaar.[82]

General misconduct

In 1802, J. Gerard, the Adjutant-General of Allahabad, wrote to Calcutta to express his concern about the limited powers vested in the Company's civil and criminal courts over local Europeans not in the Company's service. He advised the government to restrict the number of licenses it granted to Europeans in the *mofussil*, warning that "many of them are so improper and flagitious characters as cannot fail to create an unfavourable impression of Europeans in general in the minds of natives."[83]

European thieves, vagrants, and vagabonds were a steady presence in early colonial Bengal, both in the port town of Calcutta and upcountry.[84] Some of these so-called "bad characters" were drunk and disorderly misfits with neither any means of subsistence nor any way to return home. The craftier of them sought to cash in on the benefits of empire by impersonating Company officials for personal gain. In this latter group fell Tobias Henry Wagner, a German member of a group of European "banditti" who impersonated Company servants in red coats and robbed and plundered local communities on the Company's frontier in Assam. Another was Arthur Reynolds, who was repeatedly arrested in Calcutta for improper conduct and for disguising himself as an officer of the navy and attempting to extort money.[85]

Others, while not destitute, were adept at both impersonating authority and avoiding apprehension. In 1823, an intoxicated William Davison, who had assumed the alias of Lieutenant Davidson, attempted to climb

---

[82] BL, IOR, O/5/22.
[83] Letter of February 10, 1802, in reference to the case of Redmond Malloy, BL, IOR, O/5/6.
[84] See the 1801 cases of Garatt Missett and Peter Ambrose, BL, ibid.
[85] Wagner's case from 1796 in BL, IOR, O/5/5; and Reynolds' case from 1798 in BL, IOR, O/5/8.

into the covered carriage of a group of Indian women in a market in Farukhabad. When one of the women's relatives tried to stop him, Davison attacked and beat the man. Davison also bit a bystander who attempted to restrain him and struck a police officer who was dispatched to the scene. Davison then proceeded to the *thana*, where he stole a sword and "paraded the town with it drawn and cutting at trees and other objects, terrifying and putting to flight the inhabitants, and slightly wounding a buffalo." The authorities ultimately discovered that Davison had other criminal charges (including assault and homicide) pending against him in other districts. He was deported to England without trial on account of not having a license to reside in India.[86]

One of the things that make William Davison's case particularly interesting is how it inverts our rudimentary assumptions about power and privilege in colonial India. The desperation of a Davison, impersonating a European officer and attacking a carriage of Indian women, challenges our most basic preconceptions about imperial relations. Here the Indian women are the visible "haves" and the British man is the publicly distressed "have-not," literally clawing at them from below. While Davison surely terrorized those at whom he drunkenly waved his stolen sword, he must also have been a foolish and ridiculous sight to behold. Mr. Davison's case was not unique.

In 1789, a Mr. Allen was found by the Collector of Chittagong to be "strolling about the country without any visible means of gaining a livelihood although pretending to be a merchant." Allen was ordered to Calcutta after he was found to have "taken up" with a native woman whom he not only physically abused but also "plundered...of her money, her trinkets and everything she possessed and then turned... ashore." In Calcutta, he was ordered into custody as an unlicensed vagrant European.[87] Three years later in Islamabad, John O'Reilly, John Barton, and Thomas Blythe forced their way into the compound of an Indian woman named Aura Marguard. Armed with blunderbusses, muskets, swords, pistols, and sticks, the men attempted to break into the bungalow where Aura had locked herself in an inner room. In the fracas, they threatened the servants in the compound, shooting and injuring one of them. Before the trial was held, two of the men died and a third escaped from prison.[88]

On the night of December 15, 1814, Mussamaut Mooneah was at home in Cawnpore when two European men knocked on the door of her compound and demanded admittance. When she refused, they climbed on

---

[86] BL, IOR, O/5/22.   [87] BL, IOR, O/5/2.   [88] BL, IOR, O/5/3.

top of a neighbor's house and onto her verandah. One of them crossed the compound and accosted her mother, while the other, whom Mussamaut Mooneah distinctly recognized as a Company private named Thomas Gallagher, pushed her aside, blew out her bedroom lamps, and reached for her jewelry. Gallagher, whose blue army cap was later found in the lane near Mussamaut Mooneah's house, was tried, convicted, and sentenced by the Supreme Court to transportation to New South Wales for seven years.[89] The case of Thomas Gallagher suggests that the race–gender hierarchy that conventionally places white men and brown women on opposite ends of the spectrum of imperial power was sometimes inverted.

Violence

The largest and most disturbing category of cases in the record of European misconduct involves physical violence. While some cases involved European attacks on other Europeans, most European violence was directed against the Indian servants, laborers, and women who served them. To make sense of this large volume of cases, I will analyze them in three groups: first, I consider cases involving European seamen and soldiers. Then I examine incidents involving the abuse of servants and laborers. Finally, I turn to cases of gender violence.

Violent seamen and soldiers In the late eighteenth and early nineteenth centuries, India's port cities had large transient populations of European seamen and soldiers who were essential to the growth and protection of the Company's territories in India, even if they sometimes threatened its sovereignty and stability.[90] Easy access to cheap toddy, arrack, Bengal rum, and other native spirits was related to the high rates of violent crime among European regiments and the profligate behavior that contradicted the imperial image of moral superiority.[91] In April 1789, J. Price, Marine Paymaster at Fort William, complained to the Bengal Government about the wayward behavior of English seamen who deserted the Company's ships and service and "get drunk and lay about the streets and ultimately die in the hospital."[92] An official medical report from 1812 stated that four out of five soldiers in hospital in India died from "the free use of ardent spirits."[93]

---

[89] BL, IOR, O/5/16.

[90] H. Fischer-Tiné, "Flotsam and Jetsam of the Empire? European Seamen and Spaces of Disease and Disorder in Mid-Nineteenth-Century Calcutta," in A. Tambe and H. Fischer-Tiné (eds.), *The Limits of British Colonial Control in South Asia: Spaces of Disorder in the Indian Ocean Region* (New York: Routledge, 2009), pp. 121–154.

[91] Holmes, *Sahib*, pp. 415–435.   [92] BL, IOR, O/5/2.   [93] BL, IOR, O/5/25.

Douglas Peers argues that the Company's garrison state required both the practical capacity to fight as well as the visible appearance of omnipotence and control. As Peers writes, "Image was just as important as ability."[94] The careers of many British soldiers in early colonial India ended before they had even begun. Due to their "ungentlemanlike behavior," indecency, and neglect of duty on the journey over, many soldiers were discharged and deported immediately upon arrival in India.[95] Others deserted the service upon disembarking – at great risk to themselves, as desertion was a capital offense.[96] The drunken and disorderly soldier, like the wandering and wayward seaman, was a symbolic affront to British racial prestige, a practical thorn in the side of local magistrates, a health hazard, and an unruly usurper of military discipline.

The physical violence of British seamen and soldiers was usually directed at either their European comrades or at the Indian cooks, porters, neighbors, *syces*, *sepoys*, and the women who served them sexually. In cases of white-on-white violence, however, the punishments were usually more severe. Although capital punishment of European offenders would become exceedingly rare in the second half of the nineteenth century, in the earlier period many European soldiers were executed for the willful murder of their European comrades. These include James Brannon, who was convicted and hanged in 1811 for the murder of Sergeant William Clarke; Richard Cahill, who was convicted and executed in 1812 for murdering another artillery man, Francis Moran, by repeatedly stabbing him with a bayonet; and Private Benjamin Danks, who was convicted and executed in 1816 for the willful murder of Sergeant Joseph Read, by repeatedly striking him on the head with a hammer and slitting his throat.[97]

In cases where European seamen and soldiers attacked their Indian subordinates, the consequences were far more lenient. On March 16, 1815, Philip Charles Hogan, commander of the British trading ship *Maria*, was tried in the Supreme Court on its Admiralty side for the murder of Muhammad Ruza. Ruza's son, Bhikoo Khan, an eye-witness to the incident, testified that in August 1814, while sailing on the high seas

[94] D. M. Peers, *Between Mars and Mammon: Colonial Armies and the Garrison State in India, 1819–1835* (London: Tauris, 1995), p. 63.

[95] Case of John Gillon (1797), BL, IOR, O/5/5.

[96] "An Act for Punishing Mutiny and Desertion of Officers and Soldiers in the Service of the United Company of Merchants Trading to the East Indies and for the Punishment of Offenses Committed in the East Indies or at the Island of St. Helena," April 17, 1761, BL, IOR, L/MIL/5/457.

[97] Brannon's case in BL, IOR, O/5/11; Cahill's case in BL, IOR, O/5/13; and Dank's case in BL, IOR, O/5/17.

off the Andamans, Hogan ordered Ruza to scrape the exterior of the ship. When Ruza answered that stormy weather and high-breaking waves temporarily prevented him from working on the side of the boat, Hogan commanded another staff member to "beat him, tie him and throw him over." Several witnesses testified that Ruza was suspended by a rope 1 cubit above the water for five days and nights with nothing to eat or drink. It rained the entire time and the swollen sea barely kept Ruza's body afloat. However, Hogan prevented anyone from assisting or even looking at Ruza by threatening them with like treatment. On the fifth day, Bhikoo saw his father lying speechless on the deck, where he subsequently died. At trial, the defense argued that "there was a general order that men that did not work should have no food." Hogan was acquitted.[98]

In 1816, a military court of enquiry was assembled in Delhi to investigate the death of a bearer named Bunder. According to an artillery captain, Robert Granshaw, Bunder accidentally knocked his hat off while raising the *chatta* (umbrella) over Granshaw's head. An irritated Granshaw struck Bunder once on the left side of his head and once on the left side of his body, leaving Bunder unable to walk or speak. Granshaw carried Bunder to the house of a European surgeon, where he died within thirty minutes. The Governor-General decided not to prosecute Granshaw, reasoning that it was a case of manslaughter at worst and not worth the expense of prosecution.[99]

On September 5, 1820, Charles Hodges and Chase Bracken appeared before a military court of enquiry in connection with the death of Bracken's *syce*, Kokrah, in Berhampore. The beating occurred after Bracken ordered Kokrah to fetch his saddle. When Kokrah replied, "I have nothing to eat," Bracken, interpreting the comment as a request for a salary advance, slapped him in the face and punched him in the shoulder. Hodges then punched Kokrah several times under his ribs. Kokrah fainted several times as Hodges and Bracken stood over him, whipped him on the backside, and exclaimed, "You are shamming." Within fifteen minutes Kokrah was dead. The Attorney-General advised the government not to try Bracken, as he "had a right of correction." That is to say that Bracken, as Kokrah's master, had the right of corporal punishment. At Hodges' trial, the Calcutta Supreme Court rejected the defense's argument that Kokrah's pre-existing health condition relieved Hodges of criminal culpability: "The fact that the man was in an infirm state of health could in no way affect the case for if a person strikes a child or a sick person when but a slight blow might effect death, he is equally

---

[98] BL, IOR, O/5/16; and *Calcutta Gazette*, March 15, 1814.   [99] BL, IOR, O/5/17.

liable. The law was that whoever should strike another person unlawfully must abide the consequence." Charles Hodges was convicted of manslaughter and sentenced to one year in the Common Jail of Calcutta.[100]

Labor violence Economic violence against Indian labor was the *sine qua non* of the colonial experience. The economic exploitation of laborers went hand in hand with a brutal and constant physical violence, which was noticeably extreme on the tea and indigo plantations where the notoriously "brutal planter" flogged, confined, and killed his workers with virtual impunity. Measuring the magnitude and frequency of physical violence is an imprecise, if not futile, task, as most violent encounters between employers and workers were neither reported nor prosecuted. Circumstances inherent in the colonial experience make it likely that the cases of labor violence that do appear in the historical record represent but a small fraction of the actual incidents of violence.

The inability of the Indian laborer to seek justice for the violence committed upon his/her body was often linked to the near-death state caused by economic deprivation. In 1810, when the Calcutta Supreme Court asked an indigo cultivator named Ali why he did not lodge a formal complaint against planter J. W. K. Looker, who had confined him and his son in the stocks without food or water for nine days, Ali replied that for want of food, he could not make the journey to Court.[101]

Mortal beatings of Indian servants raised legal questions about the master's right to strike and medical ruminations on how much violence was too much for an Indian body to bear. The near-instant death of many laborers at the hands of their employers – death within fifteen to thirty minutes, if not less – often evoked commentary on the pre-existing health of the deceased rather than the deadly brutality of the abuser. Over the course of the nineteenth century, claims about the weak and moribund Indian body would become standard in mitigating charges and punishments of Europeans accused of murdering natives (more on this in Chapter 3).

In early colonial Bengal, European defendants were more likely to be acquitted or convicted of lesser crimes (manslaughter instead of murder) based on their good character rather than on medical claims about the vulnerable Indian body. On July 15, 1796, Francis Jones, superintendent of a salt factory in Chittagong, was tried in Calcutta for the murder of one of his employees. Jones struck the worker on the head three times with a stick 3.5 cubits long and 6–7 inches in circumference, knocking him off

[100] BL, IOR, O/5/20.   [101] BL, IOR, O/5/10.

the steps of the bungalow and breaking his jaw and teeth. The laborer took three breaths and died on the spot. The jury found Jones to be a man of "general good character" who bore no malice against the deceased and convicted him of the lesser charge of manslaughter. Jones was sentenced to be burned in the hand.[102]

In July 1816, Malcolm MacKenzie, a ship-builder in Chittagong, was charged with beating and illegally confining his worker Abdoolla. MacKenzie admitted to whipping Abdoolla ten times with a *rattan* before placing him in leg irons weighing 10 seers (approx. 10 kg) and confining him for one day and one night. MacKenzie maintained that his behavior was justifiable because Abdoolla had gone to work for another factory without giving proper notice. In committing the case to Calcutta, Chittagong Magistrate W. Pechele described MacKenzie's actions as "tyrannical, unjust and entirely at variance with the principles on which the dealings of Europeans with the Natives ought to be regulated, as well as with the laws enacted by the British Government for the maintenance of justice in India." MacKenzie was convicted and fined 100 rupees, 20 of which were given to Abdoolla as compensation for the injury he had received.[103]

The most troublesome group of violent European offenders in colonial Bengal was undoubtedly the indigo planters of lower Bengal, who brutalized each other, their workers, and the local magistrates, whose authority they openly defied. From its inception the system of indigo production was, in the words of Faridpur Magistrate E. De-Latour, a "system of bloodshed": "Not a chest of indigo reached England without being stained with human blood."[104] The violence of the indigo planters lashed out in all directions, with affrays and brutal conflicts transpiring between European planters and Indian *zamindars*, between European planters and other European planters, and between European planters and their Indian cultivators.[105]

Until the mid-nineteenth century, indigo was one of Bengal's most important exports, second only to opium. Dependent on the financial returns from indigo, the Bengal Government struggled unsuccessfully to subject the planters to the restraints of law.[106] Official inquiries into their

---

[102] BL, IOR, O/5/4.   [103] BL, IOR, O/5/17.

[104] J. Long, *Strike but Hear! Evidence Explanatory of the Indigo System in Lower Bengal* (Calcutta, 1861), p. 68.

[105] W. Dampier, Superintendent of Police in the Lower Provinces, May 23, 1844, and G. F. Cockburn, Officiating Magistrate in Howrah, May 23, 1844, NAI, Legislative Proceedings, October – December 1844, October 12, 1844, No. 1.

[106] Extract from Court of Director's Judicial Despatch to Bengal, August 6, 1828, *Papers Relating to the Settlement of Europeans in India*, BL, IOR, V 3244.

conduct and orders from the Court of Directors did little to stop the planters from forcing *ryots* to cultivate or from torturing them when they refused. In July 1810, the government ordered local magistrates to bring all incidents of indigo-related violence to its attention.[107] A decade later, another order was issued directing the police to collect more accurate information "regarding the general conduct of merchants, indigo planters, or others being European British subjects or foreign Europeans who may reside in the interior of the country."[108] Magistrates were required to send quarterly reports to Calcutta documenting all instances in which merchants, indigo planters, and other Europeans were convicted of acts of violence and oppression and of offenses or misconduct of a serious nature.

The physical violence associated with indigo cultivation was often related to restrictions on land-holding.[109] Until 1837, European planters were prohibited from holding long-term leases on land, as the Company's policy was to tax Indians rather than dispossess them of their lands.[110] The prohibition was also linked to concern about extending legal rights to Europeans in places where the government lacked legal control over them. This gave rise to the illicit practice of Europeans holding leases in other people's names and also to an advance system that was used by planters to "encourage" Indian peasants to cultivate. The advance system effectively turned the *ryots* into indentured servants who were physically forced to accept advance money and then to work it off.[111]

In July 1809, Thomas Clark, an indigo planter in Purneah, was charged in the Supreme Court with homicide in the death of a *ryot* named Munpur Biswas. Because Munpur refused to accept an advance to sow indigo, Clark punched him ten times in the ears, nose, and neck, and kicked him with his boots repeatedly in the groin and thighs. Even after Munpur fell to the ground bleeding from his nose and mouth, Clark continued to kick him. The next morning, Munpur was dead. Clark was convicted of manslaughter and sentenced to twelve months' imprisonment and a 400-rupee fine. Although Clark's license to reside in the interior was withdrawn, the following year he moved back to Nuddea.[112] A similar case involved John Lathbury Turner, an indigo planter charged in the

---

[107] *Papers Relating to East India Affairs* (1813), BL, IOR, 2440, p. 39.

[108] Order of March 1821 cited in the case of Alan Dunlop, BL, IOR, O/5/20.

[109] J. Crawfurd, *Letters from British Settlers in the Interior of India Descriptive of their own Condition, and that of the Native Inhabitants under the Government of the East India Company* (London, 1831).

[110] Extract from Bengal Revenue Consultations, May 12, 1775, BL, IOR, V 3244.

[111] R. P. Behal and P. P. Mohapatra, "'Tea and Money versus Human Life': The Rise and Fall of the Indenture System in the Assam Tea Plantations, 1840–1908," *Journal of Peasant Studies*, 19 (1992), 142–172.

[112] BL, IOR, O/5/9.

death of a *ryot* named Mootee Roy. Turner punched and kicked Roy for failing to sow indigo "according to their engagements." After the beating, Roy and two other *ryots* were sent to the stocks, where Roy died. Turner was acquitted and discharged when it was determined that a snake-bite wound found on Roy's hand had been the probable cause of death. Although Turner's license to reside in the interior was initially withdrawn, he was later granted a new license.[113]

Blair Kling argues that the indigo industry of Lower Bengal "ultimately rested on a foundation of coercion and intimidation." And yet Kling hesitates to judge the planters by universal moral standards, suggesting that "accounts of oppression by the planters should be viewed in relation to prevalent *mufassal* morality. The planters were probably no more oppressive than the Indian *zamindars* though they may have seemed so to a peasantry who were unaccustomed to their novel demands."[114] Whether the planters' *zulm* was quantitatively or qualitatively different from the *zamindars' zulm* is uncertain, but clearly the purpose of opening India's borders to European capitalists was not to extend indigenous modes of tyranny and oppression. After all, confidence in the transformative powers of capitalism and the moral and cultural superiority of Europeans is what brought colonial administrators around to the benefits of private industry and white settlement.[115] Furthermore, it seems untenable to argue that anyone could become "accustomed" to abuse by large bands of *latteals* (bludgeon-men), vicious corporal punishment, and illegal confinement in the stocks.

The stories of torture and cruelty in the indigo districts were both consistent and consistently horrific. In the early nineteenth century, local officials constantly reminded the government about their powerlessness in the face of the planters' mortal misconduct and wild lawlessness. In 1829, Sadr Diwani Adalat Judge Turnbull informed the Court of Directors that indigo production had turned his region into a "state of ferment":

From the moment of ploughing the land and sowing the seed, to the season of reaping the crop, the whole district is thrown into a state of ferment. The most daring breaches of the peace are committed in the face of our police officers, and even the magistrate himself. In utter defiance of all law and authority, large bodies of armed men are avowedly entertained for the express purpose of taking or retaining forcible possession of lands or crops. Violent affrays, or rather regular pitched battles, ensue, attended with bloodshed and homicide. Our police

[113] Ibid.
[114] B. B. Kling, *The Blue Mutiny: The Indigo Disturbances in Bengal, 1859–1862* (Philadelphia: University of Pennsylvania Press, 1966).
[115] Governor General Bentinck's "Minute on European Settlement," May 30, 1829, *Papers Relating to the Settlement of Europeans in India*, BL, IOR, V 3244.

establishments are corrupted, and the *darogahs* [village constables] are notoriously to be in the pay of the planters to secure their good offices...It is certainly high time that decisive measures should be adopted to put down evils of such magnitude.[116]

Rather than analyzing indigo violence in relation to a pre-existing *mofussil* morality, it is more useful to understand the "brutal planter" as a figure created, enabled, and normalized by the empire and its laws.

European indigo planters knew that so long as the Bengal Government needed them, local authorities had little power to control them, and they conducted themselves accordingly. As the Board of Control noted in a paper on "Conduct of Europeans in India":

Whatever be the ground of any dispute which arises between an indigo planter and Natives, or between two planters, force appears to be appealed to, in most instances, for its decision. The explanation for this fact is not to be found in any particular turbulence of character, either on the part of the planters or of the Natives, but in the *impotence* of the law to protect either. [Emphasis in the original text.][117]

A few examples of planter violence – against other Europeans and against Indians – will suffice to illustrate Judge Turnbull's point about the "state of ferment" in the indigo districts.

In 1805, Mrs. Elizabeth Caulfield appealed to the government for assistance in prosecuting John Gourley, who had murdered her husband, Thomas Caulfield, an indigo planter in Jessore. On June 27, 1805, Caulfield spotted Gourley (superintendent of his neighbor James Goldie's factory) and his servants cutting down his indigo plant and carrying it to their boat. When Caulfield reprimanded Gourley for "doing wrong," Gourley struck him in the face and drew his sword. Caulfield backed off. Two days later, Gourley returned with several ships, landed near Caulfield's factory, and sent a note to his bungalow summoning him. Caulfield advised Gourley to return to his own field and threatened to sue him in court. Armed with a double-barreled gun, Gourley and 300 armed men entered Caulfield's factory and surrounded him and his son. Gourley wrestled Caulfield to the ground and strangled him while the others beat Caulfield's son with canes, clubs, and other weapons. Gourley then stepped back and shot Caulfield at point-blank range, yelling "Hurrah" as his men charged Caulfield's bungalow, where they shot Elizabeth Caulfield and stole some household items. Thomas Caulfield was dead within three hours, and John Gourley, who took

---

[116] Turnbull's Minute of July 2, 1829, ibid.
[117] *General Appendix to the Report from the Select Committee of the House of Commons on the Affairs of the East India Company*, Appendix V (77), p. 484.

shelter in the Danish Settlement of Serampore beyond the Company's jurisdiction, was never apprehended.[118]

Incidents of European indigo planters leading vicious attacks on their European neighbors with private militias of up to 1,000 armed men were alarmingly common. On June 4, 1808, Robert Scott Douglas, an indigo planter in Sarun, sent a mob of 1,000 men armed with swords, sticks, and other weapons to attack his neighbor Matthew Moran's factory. The armed mob surrounded the bungalow before rushing in, beating the European superintendent, Thomas Clark, unconscious, plundering his belongings, and setting the granary on fire. Douglas and two of his Indian servants were charged with arson in the Supreme Court. Douglas, who was found an accessory to the crime, was imprisoned for one year and fined 1,000 rupees.[119]

Emboldened by the feeble nature of local authority, European indigo planters such as Gourley and Douglas constantly abused each other and their employees. Some had thick rap sheets but never faced the law, because they intimidated plaintiffs from persevering in legal proceedings or they bought off the local police or they simply defied government orders. Alan Dunlop was a particularly notorious planter in Jessore with a long list of civil and criminal charges, including affrays, forcibly entering the house of a neighboring planter and beating his servants, plundering of boats, forcible seizure, illegal confinement, theft, and so on. For years, he exercised an "arbitrary and oppressive" authority over his Indian servants, which the law was either unable or unwilling to prevent. In 1813, a superintendent in one of his factories seized and imprisoned one of the cultivators. When two *darogahs* (village constables) were sent to release the *ryot*, Dunlop's servant beat the imprisoned *ryot* in front of them and refused to release him.[120]

In 1828, the Court of Directors ordered a special report on the indigo planters, including "a list and summary of all cases recorded in the civil and criminal courts since 1810, in which they, or their principal or armed servants, have been concerned as plaintiffs or defendants."[121] The report, which touched on the behavior of 473 European planters and their assistants across 32 districts in Bengal (220,000 square miles), was dubiously favorable. The planters were described by a variety of local officials as "honorable and upright," "kind and conciliatory," and generally responsible for the nice clothes, growing riches, and learned industriousness of their laborers.[122] The Court of Directors was deeply suspicious of these findings, which stood

[118] BL, IOR, O/5/7.   [119] BL, IOR, O/5/9 and *Calcutta Gazette*, June 28, 1810.
[120] BL, IOR, O/5/20.
[121] Extract from Court of Director's Judicial Despatch to Bengal, August 6, 1828, *Papers Relating to the Settlement of Europeans in India*, BL, IOR, V 3244.
[122] Ibid., Appendix Nos. II and III.

in stark contrast to the constant stream of violent incidents reported back to them over the previous thirty years.[123]

Gender violence Although the Company did not recognize gender violence as constituting a special category of European misconduct, an enormous number of cases in the record involves violence against women. The British in India vigilantly addressed scandalous and sensational forms of gender violence (such as *sati* [widow immolation]). However, they were less interested in controlling those forms of violence against women with which they were more familiar (such as domestic violence).[124] The backwardness, inferiority, and different-ness of Indian society were supposedly proven by the extraordinary cultural practices of female infanticide, child marriage, *purdah* (female seclusion), and caste-prostitution. By contrast, cross-culturally common forms of gender violence, like rape and wife-murder, produced no "moral panics," imperial scandals, or parliamentary inquiries. In fact, despite their prevalence, they were hardly noticed at all.

European men inflicted violence on Indian, European, and mixed-race women of all backgrounds and ages in early colonial Bengal. Examples includes James Biron, a master in the Pilot Service, who was convicted of manslaughter in the death of two female infants on two separate occasions (for which he was imprisoned for four years total), and Lieutenant William Leach, whose European wife requested that he be deported from India to protect her from his abusiveness.[125] In 1811, artilleryman John Gilliard was convicted of the rape and attempted murder of Heera, an Indian woman in Agra whom he confined, repeatedly raped, and then stabbed with a bayonet in the stomach, belly, and back.[126] The following year, another artilleryman, Andrew Masberg, brutally stabbed Hannah Myers, an Indian widow with a small child. Myers had inherited a small sum of money from her deceased husband, which she invested in jewels and ornaments. When Hannah moved in with Masberg, he pawned several of her ornaments and beat her whenever she suggested that they settle their accounts. Hannah ultimately left Masberg and "entered the service" of another European artilleryman, which infuriated him. One evening, Hannah and some friends were shopping at the local bazaar when she ran into Masberg. Enraged by the discovery that she had taken up with another European soldier, Masberg threw Hannah and the 2-year-old

[123] Court of Directors to the Governor-General, April 10, 1832, ibid.
[124] E. Kolsky, "'The Body Evidencing the Crime': Rape on Trial in Colonial India, 1861–1947," *Gender and History*, 22, 1 (March 2010); and E. Kolsky, "Rape on Trial in Early Colonial India, 1805–1857," *The Journal of Asian Studies*, 69, 4 (November 2010).
[125] BL, IOR, O/5/8.   [126] BL, IOR, O/5/11.

child sleeping in her arms to the ground, slit her throat, and stabbed her on both sides of her body. He threatened to stab anyone who approached to help her and again struck her on the forehead. Masberg was convicted by the Supreme Court of assault with intent to commit murder and sentenced to three years' imprisonment and a fine of 1 rupee.[127]

In 1813, Patrick O'Neal, a private who had deserted from a European artillery regiment at Berhampore, assumed the alias of Captain Chalk, an Officer of Engineers. O'Neal conned his way onto a boat owned by a private European merchant named Chisholm that was transporting European goods into the *mofussil*. O'Neal tricked the Indian boatman in charge of the shipment into letting him take possession of the boat by pretending he was an intimate friend of Chisholm's. As O'Neal made his way down the river, he caused "such various acts of violence and did cause such alarm among the natives at the different places he stopped at that the villagers along the banks deserted their habitations and fled into the interior of the country." At some point during his journey, O'Neal sold several boxes of the stolen goods to an upcountry European trader named Nix. After sharing several meals with Mr. Nix and his wife, things started to go south. O'Neal "addressed the most indecent propositions to Mrs. Nix" and, when she rejected his advances, he assaulted her, stabbed Mr. Nix twice in the back of his head, stole Mrs. Nix's gold wedding ring, snatched the earrings from her ears, and "otherwise mistreated her." Mr. and Mrs. Nix escaped from O'Neal only by jumping into the river. O'Neal was charged in the Supreme Court with assault and robbery on Mrs. Nix. Appalled by O'Neal's unruly behavior, Chief Justice Edward Hyde East reminded the Grand Jury about the role of justice in securing and stabilizing the empire:

The native inhabitants of those extensive regions which are placed under the East India Company's dominion have long had certain experience that this Court in its dispensation of Justice, knows of no distinction between European and Native. The foundations of their confidence have been and must continue to be placed on British justice no less than on British valour – the two certain supports of the empire. The robbery planned and executed by this man, if you give credit to the witnesses, was committed in the face of day, by means of an authority which he assumed as a European over the simplicity and humility of the native servants employed by the owner to protect his property. Under the pretense of being an Officer of Engineers and a friend of the owner of the goods, he converted that superiority and deference which justly belongs to the character he assumed into an engine of rapine oppression and fiasco, the excess of which at last betrayed the imposter.

Patrick O'Neal was convicted and executed on July 22, 1813.[128]

---

[127] BL, IOR, O/5/13.
[128] BL, IOR, O/5/14; and supplement to *Calcutta Gazette*, December 9 and 16, 1813.

In 1814, shoemaker William Dupont was charged in the Calcutta Supreme Court with the murder of Elizabeth Manning, a "half-caste female" with whom he had lived for five years. Thomas Polton, his neighbor, testified that one day, Dupont and Polton returned home in the late afternoon to find Elizabeth Manning "very much intoxicated, lying on a mat with her clothes nearly up to her chin." Dupont "fell into a great passion and beat the deceased with a round ruler which he found in the house." Polton interfered, took the ruler away, and went home. The next morning, a servant found Dupont drunk on the couch with Manning lying dead on the floor beside him in a pool of blood, her head split open, her brain visible. Although Dupont told police that Manning had fallen off the bed, the coroner's examination concluded that:

The head and face were covered with bruises and wounded; there was an extensive lacerated wound from the crown of the head to the forehead, another above the brows, and a third with a very extensive bruise at the back of the head at that place the bone was fractured and depressed, one of the eyes was closed by a bruise and blood flowed from the nose and ears. The brain was much injured by the blows sufficient to have caused death, a fall from a bed could not have produced such injuries.

The jury convicted Dupont but pleaded with the chief justice for mercy as they thought he "accidentally found the ruler and did not seem to have premeditated the assault." Dupont was burned in the hand and imprisoned for twelve months.[129]

Undoubtedly, the most appallingly brutal and revolting instance of gender violence in the entire record of "European Misconduct in India, 1766–1824" is the case of William Orby Hunter. In 1796, Hunter, an indigo planter in Tirhoot, was charged with "great cruelty and oppression" committed against three low-caste slave girls, Punnah, Kunoovey, and Ajanassee, who worked for Hunter's live-in mistress, Bhaugwannah Khowar. Hunter was initially sent to the Calcutta Supreme Court on charges of maiming the girls, who were discovered with their noses, ears, and hair cut off, their genitals mutilated, and their feet fettered in iron chains. One of the girls also had her tongue cut out. All three suffered from venereal disease, and before the trial began one of them (Kunoovey) died. Given the varying accounts of the witnesses, it is hard to get at the truth of what happened. What follows is my piecing together of the widely opposed and contradictory testimony of the trial's two main protagonists (Hunter and Bhaugwannah) and their witnesses.

---

[129] BL, IOR, O/5/15.

HUNTER: Bhaugwannah Khowar (Bibi) came to live with me seven years ago as my mistress. Although she always quarrelled with me, I was good to her. I gave her clothes, money, a *palanquin*, and a monthly salary. In January 1795, Bibi brought home a naked, filthy, starving girl of a tolerable colour whom she found on the streets of Patna. Every day since she entered my house, the girl (Punnah) crept into my bed while I slept and prostituted herself to me. A year later, in January 1796, another slave girl (Ajanassee) also came to my house. She prostituted herself to me within thirty minutes of arrival. She daily paid me visits in my apartment, sometimes totally naked. The girls came to me to escape the barbarity of Bibi. Bibi used to send the girls to me three or four times a day to make use of them as I wished. Bibi had command of these women and she also used to send them to me to disgrace and forcibly ravish them when they stole from her. After sixteen months of this, why should I have to use force on them?

One day last May, Bibi informed me that Punnah had stolen some gold and silver jewellery and that she would probably steal again. Under her directions, I ordered my blacksmith to make iron fetters for her, unacquainted as I am with the laws and customs of the country and the authority the natives possess over their slaves. The next day, I was in the men's quarters when I heard screams and cries and rushed over to find Bibi severely correcting one of her servants. It was then that I saw a "patch" on one of their noses. I immediately turned Bibi out of my home.

Bibi had a violent temper and no respect for the lives of her slaves. She once proudly told me that they would eat her excrement if she ordered them to do so. I used to see her five servants laying totally naked in her quarters with that part which modesty forbids me to name placed immediately opposite to the door way. One day, I almost blush to recount it, Bibi called me into her quarters to show me how her slave servants passed the night. I then saw two women naked one upon the other with some felicitous instrument made of cloth bound round with string doing as fathers and others do. As I am the master of my *zenana* [women's quarters], no male witness but me can testify to the visions I here recount. I am vulnerable to the revenge, jealousy, fury and passion of women in the *zenana*. It was Bibi who, jealous of my noticing the girls in preference to herself, thus mutilated these unfortunate wretches in order to render them disgusting instead of desirable objects. She was constantly beating the girls.

I understand that on her way to Patna, Bibi beat the slaves with bamboo and ordered Kunoovey to be thrown into the well due to the putrid smell emanating from her venereal sores. She warned the other servants that she would murder anyone who tried to save Kunoovey as she was her slave and she could do with her as she pleased. When the other servants pulled Kunoovey from the well, Bibi had all three girls cast into the jungle. I deny all of the charges lodged against me. It was Bibi who was cruel and violent with the girls. How often have I forgiven her faults and stood as her friend, and now she comes and makes a false complaint against me.

BIBI: In May 1796, Sahib locked one of my slave girls (Ajanassee) in his room and forcibly ravished her. To restore her honour, Ajanassee went out back to the well to drown herself. Hunter summoned her before him and had her legs chained in irons and her nose cut off. He also locked Punnah up to prevent her from escaping. He cut off her nose too when he found her trying to drown herself in the well.

Hunter regularly had forced connection with the three girls at different times, disgracing them. When I demanded he stop and told him that I planned to lodge a complaint against him, he threatened to flog me with a whip. Sahib claimed that the girls were encouraging him to lust. He ordered me to cut off their hair and noses and said that he would ruin my character if I didn't obey him by charging me with having sex with a 7-year-old boy. Sahib often kept a penknife in his hand to mutilate the servants. I refused to do it, so he took me into a private room and flogged me with a horse whip. I finally ordered my servant Mogulaunnee to do as the sahib demanded and cut the girls' noses, though again I threatened to lodge a charge against him. Sahib replied, I am not the least afraid of your complaining against me. I am afraid of no one. I have twenty-five people to watch over you. How can you get away to inform against me?

Hunter was constantly disgracing himself with the common women, and we quarrelled all day, every day. When he was at home he shut me in and only let me out at breakfast and at dinner time, locking the doors at all other times. He ultimately turned me and the girls out of his house and we proceeded to Patna. On the way, Kunoovey, who was on fire from her disease, took her clothes off and dangled her feet in a nearby well. Somehow, she fell in.

Hunter was ordered to stand trial in the Supreme Court at Calcutta. On October 16, 1796, one day before his trial was scheduled to begin, Bibi sent Hunter a letter admitting her guilt and exculpating him of all blame, offering to live with him as a slave until she died. The following day, Bibi told the authorities that "he was my Saheb for seven years and a half. If I had committed any fault he was equally guilty and that if he had committed any fault, I was also culpable, whatever disgrace he had suffered." In December 1796, Hunter and Bibi stood trial jointly for false imprisonment and assault on the three slave girls. Hunter was convicted of all counts against him; Bibi was convicted of three. Observing "the miserable condition of the two poor women who had been the objects of acts so atrocious and cruel" – the third girl, Kunoovey, was by then deceased – the chief justice decided that he would follow the practice of the criminal courts in England and allow the victims to demand pecuniary compensation. The parties congressed and agreed that Hunter would pay 1,000 rupees to each of the two women and a fine of 100 rupees to the King. Hunter paid immediately and was set free. Bibi was imprisoned for six months and fined 1 rupee.[130]

Conclusion

In its selection of officers, the East India Company sought out men with "good character, honesty, and sobriety," requiring them to sign a

[130] BL, IOR, O/5/4.

covenant and enter into penalty bonds for good behavior before sailing to the subcontinent.[131] Representing what I have called the "third face" of colonialism, William Orby Hunter was certainly not the sort of Englishman the Company was prepared to deal with in India. Neither ruler nor ruled, unruly non-officials like Hunter complicated the colonial situation and made the task of ruling India that much more difficult.

Taken together, the cases in the record of "European Misconduct in India, 1766–1824" demonstrate a simple but important point: white crime was a serious and widespread problem in early colonial India. European criminals challenged the Company state in its critical phase of territorial expansion by presenting a practical law-and-order problem and by undermining the ideology of moral and cultural superiority that sustained Britain's self-described right to rule. In contradiction to the rhetorical claims of imperial law and order, the many white vagabonds, imposters, stragglers, burglars, beggars, frauds, planters, imposters, loafers, escaped convicts, seamen, and soldiers who menaced the Town of Calcutta and wandered wildly about the Indian interior vividly exposed the disorder and violence brought by colonial contact itself. The moral, legal, and political challenges posed by this third group offer a sober reminder of the fact that the line dividing the rulers from the ruled was neither self-evident nor easily maintained. Britons in early colonial India did not constitute a monolithic ruling class, and the efforts of the emerging Company state to exert its power were directed not only at competing Indian powers and territories but also at these non-official and non-conforming others within white society.

---

[131] Ghosh, *Social Condition*, p. 9.

2 Citizens, subjects, and subjection to law: codification and the legal construction of racial difference

In the summer of 1831, amidst debates about the impending renewal of the East India Company's royal charter, a motion was passed in the House of Commons at Westminster for a Select Committee to be appointed to inquire into the Company's operations in India. Of particular concern to Parliament was the Company's excessively complex system for administering justice. As the judges of the Calcutta Supreme Court noted in frustration, the system was so vague and dysfunctional that

> no one can pronounce an opinion or form a judgment, however sound, upon any disputed right of persons respecting which doubt and confusion cannot be raised by those who choose to call it in question; for very few of the public or persons in office at home, not even the law officers, can be expected to have so comprehensive and clear a view of the Indian system, as to know readily and familiarly the bearings of each part of it on the rest.[1]

There were many problems plaguing the Company's judicial system, including its dual structure of laws and law courts, overlapping and unpublished legislation, and a cadre of untrained and inexperienced judicial officers. But the biggest problem of all was the menace of European misconduct and the failure of law to control it.

The following year, the Court of Directors sent a stinging missive to the Governor-General reminding him "that all Europeans who are permitted to remain in the interior must be taught, practically, that obedience to the law is an indispensable condition of their licence to reside there."[2] The insistence that Europeans be taught "obedience" to the law was reinforced by Thomas Macaulay in his famous parliamentary speech of July 10, 1833. As he stood before Parliament to present his views about the future role of British governance in India, Macaulay vividly emphasized the importance of protecting Indians from "a new breed of Brahmins":

[1] *Hansard's*, 3rd Series, vol. XVIII, p. 729.
[2] Despatch from the Court of Directors to the Governor-General, April 10, 1832, *Papers Relating to the Settlement of Europeans in India*, BL, IOR, V 3244.

Unless, therefore, we mean to leave the natives exposed to the tyranny and insolence of every profligate adventurer who may visit the east, we must place the European under the same power which legislates for the Hindoo...India has suffered enough already from the distinctions of caste and from the deeply rooted prejudices which those distinctions have engendered. God forbid that we should inflict on her the curse of a new caste, that we should send her a new breed of Brahmins, authorized to treat all the native population as Parias.[3]

In Macaulay's view, the duty of the British was "to give good government to a people to whom we cannot give a free government."[4] At the core of Macaulay's good but not free government stood what he saw as one of England's greatest potential gifts to the people of India: a codified rule of law.

Macaulay soon set sail for the subcontinent charged with the monumental task of creating "one great and entire work symmetrical in all its parts and pervaded by one spirit."[5] At the time, the Company administered a plurality of laws, including regional Regulations, Acts of Parliament, Hindu and Islámic law, English common and statutory law, and the principle of justice, equity, and good conscience. In place of this confusing and uncertain system, codification offered a simple and uniform law to which all inhabitants of India (including non-Indians) would be made subject. According to Macaulay, the principle underlying his codification scheme was "uniformity when you can have it; diversity when you must have it; but in all cases certainty."[6]

Around this same time, the Royal Commission on the Criminal Law attempted to codify the criminal law of England.[7] Although codification failed to progress in England, colonial codifiers radically transformed the Indian legal landscape in a fashion that outlasted the end of empire. The significance of the colonial context has been largely ignored by legal historians despite the fact that codification was an imperial and an international endeavor that linked legislators around the world. In India, legislators consulted contemporary American codes, including Edward Livingston's Louisiana Code and David Dudley Field's New York

---

[3] Macaulay's speech of July 10, 1833, in *Hansard's*, 3rd Series, vol. XIX, p. 527.

[4] A. C. Banerjee, *Indian Constitutional Documents, 1757–1947* (Calcutta: A. Mukherjee, 1961), p. 248.

[5] Minute of January 2, 1837, in C. D. Dharker, *Lord Macaulay's Legislative Minutes* (New York: Oxford University Press, 1946).

[6] T. B. Macaulay, *Speeches and Poems with the Report and Notes on the Indian Penal Code* (New York, 1867), p. 200.

[7] L. Farmer, "Reconstructing the English Codification Debate: the Criminal Law Commissioners," *Law and History Review*, 18, 2 (2000), 397–426; M. Lobban, "How Benthamic was the Criminal Law Commission?," *Law and History Review*, 18, 2 (2000), 427–432; and M. D. Dubber, "The Historical Analysis of Criminal Codes," *Law and History Review*, 18, 2 (2000), 433–440.

Code, as they sought to create a codified criminal law for the whole empire.[8] Whitley Stokes dedicated his book, *The Anglo-Indian Codes: Substantive Law*, "to all who take an interest in the efforts of English statesmen to confer on India the blessings of a wise, clear, and ascertainable law, and especially to those who are interested in what is still, in London and New York, the burning question of Codification."[9]

When the movement to codify English law faltered, many pinned their hopes on the possibility that the success of the Anglo-Indian Codes would "re-act upon England herself."[10] In a fascinating analogy that reversed the political economy of empire, James Fitzjames Stephen observed that "The Indian Penal Code is to the English criminal law what a manufactured article ready for use is to the materials out of which it is made."[11] In 1877, Stephen was invited by Parliament to bring his experience to bear upon efforts to codify English law. (He was unsuccessful.)

In late nineteenth-century India, by contrast, the enactment of codes had become so prolific that many criticized its expense and utility. Law Member Courtenay Ilbert remarked that "India is a poor country. How far are we justified in compelling the Indian taxpayer to spend Indian money on objects for which we ourselves grudge expenditure?"[12] Calcutta High Court Judge C. D. Field questioned the purpose of "these calligraphic proceedings in high places,"[13] and members of the Indian press mocked the facility with which new laws were passed and amended: "although the word *law* denotes something permanent and lasting, with the Indian Legislative Council it has quite a different meaning. In such a rapid succession are Laws and Regulations framed and repealed that they might be compared to the earthen-houses children make for play, which are no sooner made than they are destroyed."[14]

From the perspective of imperial stability, colonial codification also posed an unavoidable dilemma. By promising a uniform system of law that placed colonizer and colonized on an equal legal footing, codification threatened to up-end colonialism's fundamentally unequal politics. In E. P. Thompson's famous formulation, a codified rule of law would turn

---

[8] Macaulay's Minute of June 4, 1835, in Stokes, *English Utilitarians*, p. 221.
[9] W. Stokes, *The Anglo-Indian Codes: Substantive Law* (Oxford, 1887), p. x.
[10] "Preface to the Second Edition," C. D. Field, *The Law of Evidence in British India* (2nd edn. Calcutta, 1873).
[11] G. O. Trevelyan, *The Life and Letters of Lord Macaulay* (London: Lowe and Brydone, 1959), p. 387.
[12] C. Ilbert, "Codification," *The Law Quarterly Review*, 5, 20 (1889), 360–366.
[13] C. D. Field, *Some Observations on Codification in India* (Calcutta, 1880), p. 19.
[14] *Nur-ul-Absar*, October 1, 1872, *Selections from the Vernacular Newspapers Published in the Punjab, North-Western Provinces, Oudh, and Central Provinces* (Delhi, 1872).

the colonizers into "the prisoners of their own rhetoric."[15] This raises a vexing historical question: why did law reformers like Macaulay opt to reform the Indian legal system along lines that endangered the empire's political existence?

Eric Stokes argues that India offered English Utilitarians an opportunity to experiment with a legal institution that they could not implement so easily at home. The colony provided a particularly valuable laboratory for the codification of law, a process that historically has been most successful in undemocratic environments.[16] As Macaulay observed, "It is a work, which cannot be well performed in an age of barbarism. It is a work which especially belongs to a government like that of India – to an enlightened and paternal despotism."[17]

The fact that English codifiers in colonial India had more room to maneuver, however, does not alone explain why they chose to do so. Colonial officials were also desperate to establish legal means to restrain Europeans in the *mofussil* – Macaulay's "new breed of Brahmins" – who committed crimes with impunity. While other institutional problems such as overlapping legislation, untrained officers, and unclear legal sources were important reasons to reform the law, it was the menace of European misconduct that stood at the center of the case for codifying the law. By filling in the spaces where there was no law and replacing a dual system of laws and law courts with a uniform one, codification offered the colonial government the legal authority it required to control *all* inhabitants in India, including non-official Britons.

Soon after arriving in India, Macaulay discovered that many of his countrymen were unwilling to submit to the implications of having a black man and a white man stand on equal footing in court. Non-officials rallied loudly around the rights of the "freeborn Englishman" and protested all measures to subject them to laws framed for a subject population. Although colonial administrators had decided to codify the law in order to control the non-officials, they were ultimately ambivalent in their efforts to bring the punishing power of the law to bear upon their sometimes unruly countrymen. As a result, rather than creating a non-discriminating and universal law, the codified law of India delivered something different.

Modern liberal political ideas and institutions were frequently distorted in their application in the colonies, where "special conditions" were said

---

[15] Thompson, *Whigs and Hunters*, p. 263.
[16] Farmer, "Reconstructing the English Codification Debate"; and G. A. Weiss, "The Enchantment of Codification in the Common-Law World," *The Yale Journal of International Law*, 25, 2 (2000), 435–532.
[17] *Hansard's*, 3rd Series, vol. XIX, p. 531.

to require procedures and practices that differed from those implemented at home. Partha Chatterjee calls this particular form of governance the "rule of colonial difference."[18] The case of legal codification offers an unusual illustration and complication of Chatterjee's theory. The Anglo-Indian Codes were clearly marked by difference in, for example, their provision of special legal privileges for Britons. The rules of jurisdiction as elaborated in the Code of Criminal Procedure (1861) expanded legal distinctions, exceptions, and inequalities, and thereby exacerbated and normalized the very problems of white violence and lawlessness that the codified law was supposed to solve. Although a codified law was meant to subordinate the non-official and teach him "obedience" to the law, the Code of Criminal Procedure formally secured to him an elevated status in law to which special benefits accrued. The legal recognition of different rights within the realm of a supposedly universal law was justified by arguments that special circumstances required special legislation. Abstract principles, that is, could not safely be carried to their logical conclusion in colonial India.[19]

Bentham in India

Our discussion of codification begins with Jeremy Bentham. Although Bentham introduced the word "codification" into the English language, by the time he began to write about it in the early nineteenth century, code-making was already underway in continental Europe. Still, Bentham described his comprehensive code – the pannomion – as something new. Positioned as a radical break from the English common-law tradition, the pannomion was a systematically structured and comprehensive code of laws founded on universal and scientific principles. Bentham was an outspoken critic of what he disparagingly called "judge-made law" and insisted that the law should be clear, certain, and easily known to the common person.[20] He condemned his contemporary William Blackstone's effort to consolidate the common law as an attempt "to create one large pile of rubbish."[21]

---

[18] P. Chatterjee, *The Nation and Its Fragments: Colonial and Postcolonial Histories* (Princeton: Princeton University Press, 1993), p. 16.

[19] Non-official Legislative Council Member G. H. P. Evans, debates of March 9, 1883, NAI, Legislative Council Proceedings, 1883.

[20] The scholarly literature on Bentham is vast. For a good introduction, see W. Twining (ed.), *Bentham: Selected Writings of John Dinwiddy* (Stanford: Stanford University Press, 2003).

[21] Philip Schofield, "Jeremy Bentham and Nineteenth-Century English Jurisprudence," *Journal of Legal History*, 12, 1 (1991), 58–88.

The project to codify the Indian law posthumously fulfilled Bentham's stated ambition to become the great law-giver of India.[22] Although Bentham never worked for the East India Company, his ideas were instituted in its government through the efforts of his protégés, such as William Bentinck and Thomas Macaulay. In July 1833, when Macaulay proudly claimed that the British had "established order where we found confusion," he spoke in concert with a chorus of colonial figures who argued that Britain had rescued India from the ravages of the Oriental despot who ruled by personal discretion rather than by rule of law.[23] In England, Bentham's codes promised liberation from the burdensome weight of the common-law tradition. In India, the codes were staged as tools that would free Indians from the historical stagnation caused by arbitrary indigenous rule.

From a Benthamite perspective, the Company's laws were not only unclear: they also provided too much room for the will and whimsy of individual judges. As Macaulay remarked,

What is administered is not law, but a kind of rude and capricious equity. I asked an able and excellent Judge lately returned from India how one of our Zillah Courts would decide several questions of great importance...He told me, that it was a mere lottery. He knew how he should himself decide them. But he knew nothing more...The whole is a mere matter of chance. Everything depends on the temper of the individual judge.

As Macaulay saw it, judge-made law was "a curse and a scandal" not to be tolerated, particularly where people lived under an absolute government, such as the Government of India.[24]

In India, not only was the law unknown to ordinary people, but the majority of the Company's judicial officers had no legal education, no prior legal experience, no knowledge of English or Indian statutory law, no access to published legal decisions or commentaries, and little to no familiarity with Indian languages – including Persian, the official court language in the *mofussil*. Ram Mohun Roy cited the twin problems of language and legal training as the primary impediments to the Company's administration of justice, referring to the Company's officers themselves as "the main causes of obstruction in the dispatch of the judicial business."[25]

---

[22] Jennifer Pitts questions Bentham's imperial ambitions. See J. Pitts, *A Turn to Empire: The Rise of Imperial Liberalism in Britain and France* (Princeton: Princeton University Press, 2005).

[23] Macaulay, *Miscellaneous Writings*, p. 138.

[24] *Hansard's*, 3rd Series, vol. XIX, pp. 531–533.

[25] Ram Mohun Roy's Communication with the Board of Control on the Judicial System of India, September 19, 1831, *PP*, 1831, vol. V, p. 727.

Thomas Macaulay's legal work in India was enabled by the Charter Act of 1833, which instituted major structural, substantive, and procedural reforms.[26] In place of regional legislatures, a centralized Legislative Council was created to make laws for all the inhabitants of India.[27] Comprised of the Governor-General's Executive Council and the newly created position of Law Member, the Legislative Council was empowered to pass laws designated "Acts of India." This reform deprived the provincial governments of their legislative authority and ended the Regulation period in which the Bengal, Bombay, and Madras Presidencies passed separate and often conflicting rules and regulations. Macaulay served on the Council as India's first Law Member and head of the first Indian Law Commission, convened at Parliament's expense to examine, reform, and codify the law.[28]

"Mr. Macaulay ought to be lynched at the very least": the Black Act of 1836

On December 10, 1834, shortly after Macaulay's arrival, the Court of Directors directed the Government of India to pass temporary legislation to expand the jurisdiction of the Company's civil and criminal courts over Europeans in all cases except those involving capital punishment. Legal protection for natives was deemed to be critical in light of the anticipated increase in European settlers following the abolition of the license system. Warning that "eagerness for some temporary advantage, the consciousness of their power, the pride of a fancied superiority of race, the absence of any adequate check from public opinion" could lead to "acts of outrage or insolence," the Court of Directors insisted that Europeans must share equally in the civil rights and judicial liabilities of Indians. In a poetic phrase that would be repeated for years to come they affirmed: "There can be no equality of protection where justice is not equally and on equal terms accessible to all."[29]

The task of codifying the Indian law was enormously arduous. Not only did colonial legislators struggle to fulfill Bentham's philosophical aim of creating "one great and entire work symmetrical in all its parts and pervaded by one spirit,"[30] they also had to contend with the fierce resistance of local Britons who steadfastly opposed the notion that "the

---

[26] 3&4 Will. IV c. 85 section 55. In A. C. Banerjee (ed.), *Indian Constitutional Documents, 1757–1947*, vol. I (Calcutta: A. Mukherjee & Co., 3rd edn., 1961), pp. 221–284.

[27] 3&4 Will. IV c. 85 section 43. In ibid.   [28] 3&4 Will. IV c. 85 section 55. In ibid.

[29] Letter No. 44 from the Court of Directors to the Government of India, NAI, Home (Public), Letters from Court of Directors (1834), No. 98.

[30] Minute of January 2, 1837, in Dharker, *Lord Macaulay's Legislative Minutes*.

conqueror [should] submit himself to the conquered."[31] The first major confrontation between Macaulay and the non-official community surrounded the issue of civil jurisdiction.

On February 1, 1836, Macaulay introduced a Bill into the Legislative Council that divested Europeans in the *mofussil* of their exclusive appeal to the Supreme Courts in the Presidencies in civil matters.[32] Dubbed the "Black Act" by its detractors, Macaulay's Bill gave European British subjects a right of appeal to the Sadr Diwani Adalat, as all other people in the *mofussil* had. The Bill elicited enormous controversy, especially in Calcutta, where raucous meetings and strident articles gave voice to the growing power and privilege of the non-official community.

Many of the local newspapers, which were run by non-officials, attacked Macaulay's Bill by questioning both the authority of the Government of India to legislate for them (being subjects of the Crown, not servants of the Company) and the constitutional power of Parliament to deprive them of their purported right to be tried according to the laws of England.[33] Denouncing Macaulay as a "Public Liar," barrister Theodore Dickens called a public meeting in the Calcutta Town Hall, where he blasted the "torrent of arbitrary power [that] has been passed over us, levelling all distinctions, all institutions, and leaving nothing upright but a Colossus of despotism."[34] Pitting the inviolable rights of freeborn Englishmen against the illegitimacy of a despotic colonial regime, Dickens insisted that the laws of England were the birthright of all Englishmen everywhere in the world, and that neither Parliament nor the Government of India had the power to deny them that right.[35]

A "Petition of Right" signed by seventy-six British-born inhabitants of India was sent to Governor-General Auckland, arguing that they were "entitled as their birth right to the enjoyment of the protection of British Laws and Institutions in whatsoever part of the British Territories they may be placed."[36] Although no residents of Calcutta would have been affected by the proposed legislation, this did not stop them from expressing dramatic fears about the imagined consequences of the "Black Act." At a public meeting in Calcutta, one non-official commented upon the

---

[31] Note by H. L. Johnson, Deputy Commissioner, Silhat, NAI, *Extra Supplement to the Gazette of India*, July–December 1883.

[32] Legislative Consultations of February 1, 1836, No. 20, BL, IOR, P/206/81.

[33] See the many newspaper editorials and letters to the editor from February to October 1836 in *The Englishman and Military Chronicle* and the *Bengal Hurkaru*, BL.

[34] Quoted in R. G. Ghose, "Remarks on the 'Black Acts,'" reprinted in *Nineteenth-Century Studies* (Calcutta), 12 (1975), p. 408.

[35] *The Englishman and Military Chronicle*, February 6, 1836.

[36] "Petition of Right," Legislative Consultations of March 28, 1836, Nos. 8–9, BL, IOR, P/206/81.

dangerousness of subjecting an Englishman to the judicial authority of a Hindu:

I have seen at a Hindu festival, a naked dishevelled figure, his face painted with grotesque colours, and his long hair besmeared with dirt and ashes. His tongue was pierced with an iron bar, and his breast was scorched by the fire from the burning altar which rested on his stomach. This revolting figure, covered with ashes, dirt, and bleeding voluntary wounds, may the next moment ascend the Sudder [Sadr] bench, and in a suit between a Hindu and an Englishman, think it an act of sanctity to decide against law in favour of a professor of the true faith.[37]

Macaulay was quick to condemn the protesters – "500 persons who have no interest, feeling, or taste in common with the 50 millions among whom they live" – and their self-serving concept of liberty: "We were enemies of freedom, because we would not suffer a small white aristocracy to domineer over millions."[38] He pressed the Council to ratify his Bill without hesitation in order to protect the native population from the European settler and to prove the Company's commitment to administering equal justice:

The least flinching, the least wavering, at this crisis would give a serious, perhaps a fatal check to good legislation in India. It was always clear that this battle must sooner or later be fought…The real question before us is whether from fear of the outcry of a small and noisy section of the society of Calcutta, we will abdicate all those high functions with which Parliament has entrusted us for the purpose of restraining the European Settler and of protecting the native population…I think that the Act before us is in itself a good Act, I think that by passing it we shall give a signal proof of our determination to do justice to all races and classes.[39]

On May 9, 1836, Macaulay's Bill was passed.[40]

The non-official community was enraged by the violation of what they viewed as their inalienable rights and privileges. Some, like Thomas Turton and Samuel Smith, unsuccessfully took up the matter in the House of Commons, where a petition to inquire into the constitutional rights of Englishmen in India was dismissed.[41] William Tayler later recalled the force of anti-Macaulay sentiment in Calcutta at the time: "The Black Act was the cause of an agitation which may fairly be said to have convulsed Indian society for a time. Several barristers took the lead; public meetings

---

[37] NAI, *Opinions in Favor of the Ilbert Bill*, p. 12.
[38] Legislative Consultations of October 3, 1836, No. 5, BL, IOR, P/206/84.
[39] Undated Minute in the Legislative Consultations of March 28, 1836, No. 13, BL, IOR, P/206/81.
[40] Acts III of 1839 and VI of 1843, collectively known as the "Black Acts," further extended the jurisdiction of the lower civil courts over British subjects.
[41] Memorial from Thomas Turton and Samuel Smith, May 2, 1836, Legislative Consultations of May 9, 1836, No. 6, BL, IOR, P/206/82.

were convened; scurrilous articles filled the columns of the daily journals. One impassioned orator hinted that Mr. Macaulay ought to be lynched at the very least."[42] The fierce protest against the "Black Act" would serve as the historical benchmark for all future opposition to uniform legal jurisdiction in India.

The "doctrine of equal rights" v. the "actual state of things": the Code of Criminal Procedure

The most intense phase of codification in India lasted for roughly fifty years, from 1833 to 1882. The Code of Criminal Procedure (1861) provides an apt case study to explore the colonial subversion of legal equality and the legal construction of racial difference. Instead of establishing formal legal equality, the Code of Criminal Procedure institutionalized racial inequality by delineating race-based rights and privileges, including: juries with European majorities for Europeans, but not for Indians; Presidency trials for Europeans, but local trials for Indians; and a racially differentiated schedule of punishments. Amendments to the Code in the following decades confirmed and expanded these racial distinctions under pressure from non-officials who insisted that formal legal equality was impossible in a caste-saturated and backward place like India.

In 1834, an Indian master mariner named George Bladen Taylor was violently assaulted by three Europeans in Cochin. Although Taylor had been bludgeoned so severely that eye-witnesses discovered him bloodied and screaming, "I am murdered, I am murdered," the three European defendants were punished with a fine of only 500 rupees.[43] Referring to Taylor's case, the Court of Directors sharply reminded the Government of India of its duty to prevent such miscarriages of justice.[44]

Seven years later, the Court of Directors was informed of another disturbing murder case. In Lower Bengal, a European indigo planter named Wyatt claimed he was shooting sheep on his property when he accidentally shot and killed his servant Fuqueerah.[45] More than thirty eye-witnesses to the incident testified that there were no sheep anywhere in the vicinity when Fuqueerah was shot. The local European magistrate performed a preliminary inquiry before sending the case up to Calcutta for further orders. After reviewing the papers, Advocate-General John

---

[42] Quoted by Council Member Hunter, March 9, 1883, NAI, Legislative Proceedings, 1883.

[43] Legislative Proceedings, October 10, 1836, Nos. 20–21, BL, IOR, P/206/84.

[44] Judicial despatch from the Court of Directors, No. 6, September 30, 1835, Legislative Proceedings, October 10, 1836, Nos. 20–21, ibid.

[45] NAI, Legislative Department, November 29, 1841, Nos. 14–18.

Pearson decided it was a case of "accidental death" and ordered no additional steps be taken to prosecute Wyatt. The Court of Directors cited the Fuqueerah case when they reiterated their insistence on a system of uniform criminal jurisdiction: "The unsatisfactory manner in which this case was disposed of affords an additional instance of the urgent want of Tribunals for the trials of British-born subjects in the *Mofussil* charged with heinous offences. We trust that at no distant period this defect may be supplied [sic]."[46]

Local judicial officers in India shared London's concern about the tyrannical and lawless behavior of non-officials if for no other reason than it threatened their ability to do their jobs. In 1838, the Bird Committee Report on police reform in Bengal recommended that British-born subjects in the *mofussil* be placed under the jurisdiction of the local courts due to "innumerable instances" of abuse.[47]

Successive Indian Law Commissions repeatedly tried but failed to extend the criminal jurisdiction of the *mofussil* courts. In 1843, the second Indian Law Commission presented the Government of India with a "Jurisdiction Bill" specifically crafted to offer equal legal protection to all the inhabitants of India. The Preamble to the Bill read:

The principle is that the persons and properties of all the inhabitants of the country shall be under the same protection – that every one injured in his person or his property shall be equally able to obtain redress – that every one having a demand or complaint, civil or criminal, against another shall be equally able to bring it to a judicial determination.[48]

Yet, despite its stated principle of legal equality, the Jurisdiction Bill preserved existing inequalities (such as the right of a British-born subject charged with a capital crime to be tried in the Calcutta Supreme Court) and proposed new privileges (such as giving British-born subjects the choice of being tried by a judge alone or aided by three assessors,[49] one of which had to be a European).

One of the more interesting proposals for new distinctions came from Legislative Member Herbert Maddock, who also happened to be a strong supporter of expanding local jurisdiction. Maddock proposed that Europeans should receive lesser prison sentences, insisting that

---

[46] Court of Directors, Letter No. 9 of 1841, August 18, 1841.
[47] Bengal Police (Bird) Committee Report (1837–1838), BL, IOR, V/26/150/1.
[48] Law Commissioners' Report (1843), *Jurisdiction over European British Subjects and Draft Act*, NAI.
[49] Assessors acted as non-binding advisors to the judge on issues of fact. Unlike juries, which delivered a joint and binding opinion, the opinions of the assessors were given individually in open court, and the judge could ignore the assessors' opinions if he wished.

it would be even absurd to sentence an Englishman and an Indian to the same term of confinement in a jail. Such confinement is of itself a very slight evil to the native and the heat of a crowded building surrounded by high walls is not at all injurious to his health. In regard to Europeans the case is very different; deprived of exercise and exposed to all the heat of the climate within the walls of a jail his suffering must be great.[50]

Maddock did not explain why an Indian would not also suffer from being placed in a hot building with high walls and deprived of exercise.[51] In any event, the Law Commission's Jurisdiction Bill was shelved.

Five years later, Law Member Drinkwater Bethune circulated a second set of Jurisdiction Bills. Many high-ranking officials, including Nizamut Adalat Judge W. B. Jackson, strongly supported Bethune's Bills for both principled and practical reasons:

The intolerable evil of a privileged and dominant class living in the caste peninsula of India being held exempt from the operation of the criminal law of the country is too evident to require comment. In theory such a state of things is anomalous and opposed to all legal principle; in practice it has been found extremely inconvenient, and embarrassing and productive of many evils; and as a matter of policy, such distinction, in the eye of the law admits of no defence...If it is good enough for the Native subjects of the Crown, it is good enough for their white brethren who are engaged with them jointly in all the pursuits of life, in commerce, and agriculture. If it is defective, the insistence of the Europeans will accelerate its amendment.[52]

The Bill's supporters, however, were drowned out by the loud opposition voiced by the non-official community.

Opponents condemned Bethune's Jurisdiction Bills as a second round of "Black Acts," denouncing their "illegality, injustice, and impolicy."[53] Without a uniform criminal code in place in the *mofussil*, many non-officials complained that they would be subject to Islamic criminal law, a law they considered to be "a barbarous and proselytizing law unsuited to

---

[50] Maddock's Minute of September 4, 1844, NAI, Legislative Proceedings, October–December 1844, No. 5.

[51] On the different treatment of European and Indian prisoners, see Fischer-Tiné, *Low and Licentious Europeans.*

[52] Judge W. B. Jackson's Minute of March 27, 1850, and Judge J. R. Colvin's Minute of February 28, 1850, in the Legislative Consultations of May 10, 1850, No. 67, BL, IOR, P/207/60.

[53] Petition of non-official British subjects to the House of Commons, BL, IOR, *Report from the Select Committee on Colonization and Settlement (India) with the Minutes of Evidence Taken Before Them* (1858), Appendix No. 1, pp. 236–238; Annexure 15 to Tindall's Minute, *Racial Distinctions: Main Correspondence*, vol. I, NAI; and A. Hope, *The "Black Acts": A Dialogue between a Free-Born-Briton-Indigo-Planter and an Impartial Man* (Calcutta, 1850).

Christian or civilized men."[54] In a polemical tract titled "Tyranny in India!," the Earl of Ellenborough argued that it was "the maximum of bad taste to make British-born subjects bow the knee to laws built upon the imposture of Mahomet, derived from so impure a source as the Koran, which is regarded by all Christians as a tissue of revolting lies and absurdities."[55] Indigo planter George MacNair expressed the widely held view that "dread of these Black Acts" scared off British capitalists who would otherwise bring their business to India.[56]

By the mid-nineteenth century, non-officials – and especially the planters – exerted significant influence over government policy (see Map 2.1). The political clout of the planters grew as a result of their increasing significance to the colonial economy. At its peak in 1842, indigo accounted for 46 percent of the total value of exports from Calcutta.[57] Although the authorities in London had always viewed the expansion of local jurisdiction as the precondition for an expanded white settlement, the Government of India's lukewarm will to alter its system of criminal procedure reflected a conflicted set of political and economic commitments. Like preceding proposals, Bethune's Jurisdiction Bills were shelved.

Until 1850, the system of exemptions was supported by many wealthy Bengalis who stood to benefit financially from European business and settlement in India. Standing side by side with men like Theodore Dickens during the Black Act controversy of 1836, Bengali elites opposed the Government's effort to "level down" the legal status of their European friends. The shelving of Bethune's Bills, however, caused a rift in this alliance and was a primary cause for the formation of the British Indian Association in 1851. One of the founding grievances of this proto-nationalist organization concerned the failure of the government to establish a system of uniform criminal jurisdiction.

In 1857, when Law Member Barnes Peacock introduced a third Jurisdiction Bill that explicitly preserved certain racial distinctions, the Indian elites of Calcutta publicly protested.[58] Speakers at the "Great

---

[54] "Memorial of the undersigned persons of English, Scottish and Irish birth or descent, inhabitants of the territories of the Crown of India at present under the Government of the East India Company," January 22, 1850, Legislative Consultations of May 10, 1850, No. 44, BL, IOR, P/207/60.

[55] Earl of Ellenborough, *Tyranny in India! Englishmen Robbed of the Blessings of Trial by Jury and English Criminal Law. Christianity Insulted!* (London, 1850).

[56] *Second Report from the Select Committee on Colonization and Settlement (India) with the Minutes of Evidence Taken Before Them* (1858), BL, IOR, W 805.

[57] Kling, *Blue Mutiny*.

[58] "Bill for extending the jurisdiction of the Courts of Criminal Judicature of the East India Company in Bengal, for simplifying the Procedure thereof, and for investing other Courts with Criminal jurisdiction," NAI, Legislative Council Proceedings, 1857, vol. III.

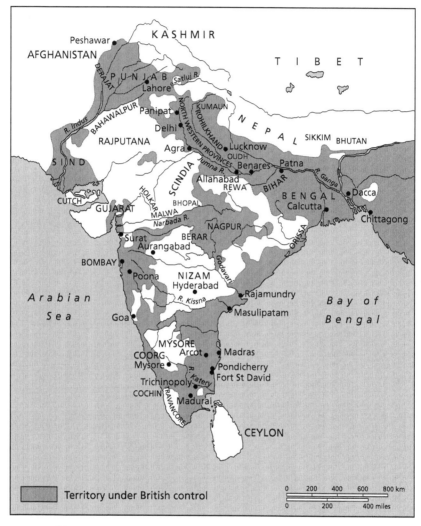

Map 2.1   India in 1857

Exemption Meeting" held at the Calcutta Town Hall in April 1857 pressed the government to deliver on its continued promises of legal equality, condemning "the insults and outrages which the European inflicts with impunity upon his native neighbors whom he emphatically calls the 'Black' or the 'Niggers.'" Deputy Magistrate Kissory Chand Mittra called the exemption of British subjects from the *mofussil* courts "unconstitutional in itself, unjust in principle, and often oppressive in practice."[59] Rajah Kally Krishna insisted that if the courts were good enough for millions of Indians, they were good enough for a small handful of Englishmen, cleverly reminding his listeners that if the English didn't like the local legal system, they could return home: "Englishmen sought India. India did not seek Englishmen. The laws of this country are made for tens of millions of the children of the soil and not for a few hundreds or a few thousands of the conquering race who may please to cast in their lot in the *Mofussil* for their own advantage."[60]

In a widely circulated pamphlet, Ram Gopal Ghose appealed to the principle of justice: "Is it just? Is it fair? Is it honest? – that a hundred million of Her Majesty's native subjects should be taxed that the European delinquent from the most distant corners of the empire may enjoy the benefit of being judged by English laws instead of the East India Company's regulations?" He also highlighted the practical effects of the existing system, which essentially placed the Englishman above the law:

To tell the Hindu *ryot* at any distance from the Presidency that if you want any redress for the Saheb having broken your back-bone, you must go down to Calcutta as prosecutor or witness, and present yourself before the Great Court where the language in use is English, where the laws administered are unknown to your Sudder Cutchery, is to tell him he must bear and be content that the Englishman is a superior being, that he cannot be touched – he cannot be polluted by the contamination of the same laws which govern such animals as you...He is a privileged being.[61]

The non-official community, by contrast, pressed hard for the expansion of exemptions from a government they criticized for being hostile to their interests.[62] Eleven hundred British subjects from Calcutta and the *mofussil* districts of the Bengal Presidency signed a petition expressing their "deep anxiety and alarm" about the proposed abrogation of their rights and privileges. They opposed being leveled down to courts without juries that deprived them of "the inalienable right and surest protection of every Englishman against injustice and error." They bemoaned the purported problem of false evidence and false charges in the *mofussil* and angrily protested being subjected to the jurisdiction of Indian judges who they argued would be steeped in "antagonistic feeling, inveterate

[59] K. C. Mittra, "Great Non-Exemption Meeting," reprinted in *Nineteenth-Century Studies*, 12 (1975), 433–448.
[60] NAI, *Corrected Report of Proceedings of A Public Meeting at the Town Hall, Calcutta, In Favor of the Extension of the Jurisdiction of the Mofussil Criminal Courts* (Calcutta, 1857).
[61] Ghose, "Remarks on the 'Black Acts,'" pp. 412–413, 420.
[62] *Report from the Select Committee on Colonization and Settlement (India) with the Minutes of Evidence Taken Before Them* (1858), BL, IOR, W 805.

prejudice of caste and religion, utter want of independence of mind, and of freedom from improper influence of all kinds."[63]

When Peacock's Bill came before the Legislative Council, Calcutta Supreme Court Justice Arthur Buller opened the session by proposing a compromise solution. Noting that the non-official community "represented the life, the vigour, the best hopes of our Indian possessions," Buller suggested that jurisdiction over European British subjects be extended to the Sessions Courts only and not to the lower courts presided over by Indian officials. In Buller's view, these lower courts would "place them in a worse position than had ever been contemplated by the blackest of previous Acts, and consign them to the tender mercies of a *Moonsiff* [civil judge in lowest-level court]."

In defense of this proposal, Buller contrasted "the doctrine of equal laws for all" with the "actual state of things around him." He contended that "equality was a miserable sham" if it meant that Europeans and Indians would stand as equals before the law. On the one hand, Buller gestured to the European community, "a small but highly civilized community long accustomed to good laws and to a good administration of them." On the other hand, he pointed to the "vast masses but lately emancipated from barbarism, and inspired with no traditional reverence for equal laws or incorruptible justice." If these two groups, one of which looked upon the *mofussil* courts with "horror," and the other which "found in these courts a safeguard far better than any that their forefathers ever dreamed of," were placed under the jurisdiction of the same courts, "equality in appearances" would produce "the grossest inequality."[64] This was not a claim for separate but equal.[65] Rather, it was an assertion that in the colony separate and unequal were fair and just.

The deliberations on Peacock's Bill were cut short by the Uprising of 1857. By the time the Legislative Council returned to the Bill in 1859, the political, social, legal, and ideological terrain of the empire had changed considerably. The Indian Penal Code was near enactment, taking the wind out of the argument that the criminal law in the *mofussil* was unclear and unsuitable. The transfer of power from the Company to the Crown made all of the courts in India Crown Courts, nullifying the Englishman's

---

[63] Annexure 15 to Tindall's Minute, *Racial Distinctions: Main Correspondence,* vol. I, NAI.

[64] Sir Arthur Buller's speech of March 9, 1857, NAI, Legislative Council Proceedings, 1857, vol. III.

[65] In the landmark *Plessy* v. *Ferguson* case (1896), the US Supreme Court upheld the constitutionality of a Louisiana law mandating separate but equal accommodations for blacks and whites on intrastate railroads. This decision introduced into American jurisprudence the doctrine of "separate but equal" as the standard for legalizing racial segregation in public accommodations.

claim to be tried only in English tribunals. Most significantly, Queen Victoria's Proclamation offered yet another imperial promise of equality before the law and governance without distinction of caste, creed, or nationality.[66]

And yet, resistance to legal equality and uniform criminal jurisdiction remained as strong and well entrenched as ever, if not more so. For as a result of the violence of 1857, abstract fears about Indian race hatred had been animated by real visions of mass resistance, and the non-official community was increasingly adamant about their vulnerability to Indian venality, trumped-up charges, and the dangers of being subjected to Indian judges. Furthermore, a shift in the social relations between the non-official and official communities found the two groups coming even closer together to form what Lord Northbrook later described as the "damned nigger party," an alliance founded on fear and hardened racial attitudes.[67]

Law Member Peacock, who only two years earlier had unequivocally stated that "he could not understand on what grounds it could be contended that any one class of persons should be exempt from the jurisdiction of any one of the courts of the country," now gestured to the new "facts and circumstances." Peacock proposed a revised Bill in which only covenanted civil servants and European British subjects were empowered to arrest, hold to bail, or commit any European British to the Sessions Court.[68] Calcutta Supreme Court Chief Justice Charles Jackson suggested that Indian magistrates should have no jurisdiction whatsoever over British subjects.[69] Mobilizing the relative-equality argument, Jackson insisted that Indians had a better judicial system than they had had before and that only Europeans would suffer by the proposal to place them under the criminal jurisdiction of the *mofussil* courts:

The Natives are not worse off, but on the contrary, are much better off as to Courts than they were under the Native Governments. The British subjects, on the other hand, are subject now to Laws and Courts to which they are, more or less, attached, and the real question was, whether European British subjects should be deprived of their own Laws and Courts, and be placed under other Laws and Courts which were deemed by themselves and generally admitted to be of an inferior kind.

---

[66] With her Proclamation of 1858, Queen Victoria took direct control of Britain's territories in India, commencing the period of "Crown Raj" and promising to rule without discriminating along the lines of race or religion.

[67] Quoted in Edwardes, *Bound to Exile*, p. 194.

[68] NAI, Legislative Council Proceedings, 1859, vol. V.   [69] Ibid.

Jackson held that the solution to the problem was "to raise the Native to the position of the British subject, and not to reduce the British subject to the level of the Native."[70]

The Code of Criminal Procedure, when it was finally enacted in 1861, preserved and expanded the existing jurisdictional privileges reserved for European British subjects. It withdrew from Indian magistrates the power to hold any preliminary inquiry into cases of European British subjects, or to arrest, hold to bail, or commit them for any case triable by the Supreme Court. European British subjects suspected of having committed a felony could be arrested, held on bail, or committed for trial at the Supreme Court only by a European British officer, essentially giving total immunity to Britons in districts where the highest judicial officer was an Indian.[71] Jurisdiction over European British subjects shifted to the Indian High Courts in 1865 when they replaced the Supreme Courts (see figure 2.1).[72]

Indian critics were incensed by this "retrograde move in legislation."[73] The British Indian Association registered a lengthy and poignant memorial denouncing the "Exemption Law" for being "opposed to justice and sound policy; that it establishes inequality in the eye of the law, detrimental to the best interests of society; that, in fact, it renders the administration of justice dependent on distinctions of country, colour and creed...What is a privilege for a few thousands, is a source of incalculable injustice and hardship with the many millions."[74] Their critique, however, fell on deaf ears. On January 1, 1862, the Code came into effect in the regulation territories and was gradually extended to all of British India outside the Presidency towns.

European vagrancy: the wild and wandering whites of British India

By the 1860s, a handful of Indians had begun to rise in the ranks of the colonial administration. Indians had technically been permitted to take the entry exam for the Covenanted Civil Service since 1854, but as the exam was administered only in England, it was difficult for them to do so.

---

[70] Ibid.

[71] Act XXV of 1861, section 26. Also see *Hopcroft* v. *Emperor, Criminal Law Journal of India*, 9 (1913), 359.

[72] Indian High Courts Act (1861), 28&29 Vict. c. 315. In Banerjee, *Indian Constitutional Documents*, pp. 64–67.

[73] Report of the Calcutta British Indian Association of September 21, 1859, BL, IOR, *Reports of Meetings of the British Indian Association Calcutta, June 1859–May 1862.*

[74] BL, IOR, Memorial from the British Indian Association of December 31, 1860 (Calcutta, 1860).

Figure 2.1 **Calcutta High Court, 1875**
The Indian High Courts Act of 1861 abolished the power of the Supreme
and Sadr Courts. The High Courts had original and appellate
jurisdiction and were the only courts of record in colonial India. The
Calcutta High Court, established in 1862, inherited from the Calcutta
Supreme Court criminal jurisdiction over European British subjects in
the *mofussil* in most criminal matters.

In 1864, Satendranath Tagore became the first Indian to join the
Covenanted Civil Service. In 1869, Indians who were members of the
Covenanted Civil Service could also be appointed justices of the peace,
and by 1879, one-fifth of all Covenanted Civil Service positions were
reserved for Indians. These administrative reforms were significant both
because they placed the Code of Criminal Procedure's jurisdictional
exemptions in conflict with an expanding corps of Indian judicial officers
and because local administrators had begun to take notice of a growing
problem over which these officers had no authority: white vagrancy.

   Colonial administrators had long been concerned about the negative
impact of "low and licentious" Europeans even when numbers were
relatively small.[75] Despite the loosening of restrictions, large numbers of
non-officials never did migrate to India in the first half of the nineteenth
century: not in 1813 (when the Company's trade monopoly was broken),

---

[75] Charles Grant quoted in Basu, *The Colonization of India by Europeans*, p. 22.

nor in 1833 (when the license system was abolished), nor in 1837 (when British subjects were permitted to hold long-term leases on land). In 1853, a return presented to Parliament found 6,749 British-born subjects in Bengal, most residing in Calcutta, with only 276 in the interior engaged in agriculture or manufacturing.[76]

In 1858, Parliament held a second round of major hearings on European colonization and settlement. Attention, as always, focused on the unruly behavior of non-officials and the government's inability to control it. By that point, a distinction had been drawn between the desirable white settler and the undesirable one. The desirable settlers, as Major-General George Tremenheere told the Select Committee, were capitalists and not laborers.[77] However, despite an interest in attracting desirable settlers, officials across India were noticing a growing population of undesirable whites, including loafers, paupers, petty thieves, discharged seamen, prostitutes, the unemployed, and indigent women and children (see Figure 2.2).[78]

Poor, vagrant, and criminal whites transgressed the empire's racial and sartorial boundaries through their inappropriate dress, drunkenness, and violence. Though somewhat sympathetic to the plight of the "feckless" British loafer, Bombay police official Arthur Travers Crawford insisted that the "truculent and drunken" vagrants were born-and-bred "ruffians":

The record of the ruffian *is* that of a ruffian from start to finish; thief or pickpocket or village ne'er-do-well from his boyhood, he has enlisted, or gone to sea, has been discharged with ignominy, or run away; or worked his way out to the "Injees" on the off-chance of getting employment on the Railways; or he has got employment and been kicked out; drink and dissipation in the large towns have ruined him, body and soul: – desperation finally drives him into the interior where he hopes for peace; and has heard that "niggers" are very kind.[79]

Controlling the widely defined problem of "vagrancy" was seen by all of the local governments as a pressing political and ideological imperative. As the Government of Punjab ominously observed, "the social and political evil is great."[80] A. Money, Commissioner of Bhaugulpore, explained

---

[76] *First Report from the Select Committee on Colonization and Settlement (India) with the Minutes of Evidence Taken Before Them* (1858) BL, IOR, W 805.

[77] Ibid.

[78] See also Arnold, "European Orphans and Vagrants"; Fischer-Tiné, *Low and Licentious Europeans*; A. Ganachari, "'White Man's Embarrassment': European Vagrancy in 19th Century Bombay," *Economic and Political Weekly* (June 22, 2002), 2477–2486; and Mizutani, "A 'Scandal to the English Name and English Government.'"

[79] A. T. Crawford, *Reminiscences of an Indian Police Official* (London, 1894).

[80] W. Kirke, Assistant Secretary to the Government of Punjab, May 4, 1863, NAI, Home, Legislative (A), September 1863, Nos. 7–9.

Figure 2.2 **Loafer makes himself at home**
This drawing of a British loafer appears in T. A. Crawford's *Reminiscences of an Indian Police Official* (London, 1894). Although most of Crawford's book details the "idiosyncrasies of [India's] people," he includes a chapter on "Loafers," which offers a colonial policeman's view of the law-and-order problem posed by this unwanted segment of the European population in India. In Crawford's words, this drawing is a "remarkable illustration of the generosity of natives to poor whites." Photographic images of European loafers and other "mean whites" in India are nearly impossible to find.

that the presence of vagrants threatened imperial stability: "It is very objectionable that numbers of our countrymen should be permitted to roam about with no means of subsistence, except begging and intimidation, and often with no intention of resorting to other means where available. These disreputable white men lower the English character in every bazaar and town which sees them drunk and incapable."[81] Army Commander-in-Chief W. R. Mansfield also noted that their destitute countrymen exposed all Englishmen in India to a loss of prestige and to "shame and inconvenience,"[82] and pressed for a law to control the growing problem.

[81] Money's letter, included with Maine's "Minute on Vagrancy," June 11, 1868, NAI, Home, Legislative (A), October 1868, Nos. 12–15.
[82] Minute of June 6, 1862, NAI, Legislative (A), February 8, 1868, Nos. 1–2.

Legislative efforts to control European vagrancy began in the Bombay Presidency. In June 1862, the Bombay Government appointed a committee to inquire into and report on the "evil" of European destitution and mendicancy.[83] The committee's "Report on European Pauperism" provided a detailed portrait of the causes and condition of European vagrancy in the Bombay Presidency, associating its growth with fluctuations in the labor market and dislocations caused by the events of 1857.[84] In 1857–1858, the Bombay Government added 1,706 men to the navy. Within two years, 43.2 percent of these men had been discharged without pension. Each year between 1859 and 1863, an average of 676 European sailors were discharged from service and thrown into the labor market. In addition, an average of 109 men were annually discharged from the army either without pensions or with pensions inadequate to live on in India. The Report described the political embarrassment caused by these wayward sailors in dramatic terms:

The sailor on arriving in Bombay finds no reputable house in which he can board, and, of necessity, if he leaves his ship, will frequent lodging-houses in which the most degrading vices are practised, and in which he is often robbed of his wages, and speedily becomes a brawler in our streets, and too often a beggar at our doors. The injury to public morals, and the prestige of the British name in this country which this conduct ensures, cannot be over-rated.[85]

The trajectory of European workers in the private labor market was also dire. Whereas the government discharged employees every fourteen years, private companies did so every three years, leaving 33 percent of European railway laborers ("men of improvident habits") unemployed at any given time. The Report estimated that the average annual number of Europeans left destitute in Bombay was 927.

Although the causes of European vagrancy were readily identified, there was disagreement about who bore the financial responsibility for solving the unseemly problem. Was it the government's burden to bear, or should private employers, as Commander Mansfield argued, be required to clean up their own waste?[86] Likening the problem of European vagrancy to an environmental hazard, Mansfield asserted: "vagrancy should be consumed by those who produce it."[87] By contrast, the captains of European

[83] R. West, Under-Secretary to the Government of Bombay, NAI, Legislative (A), February 8, 1868, Nos. 1–2.

[84] "Report on Pauperism," NAI, Legislative (A), February 8, 1868, Nos. 1–2.   [85] Ibid.

[86] Mansfield's second Minute of October 27, 1862, NAI, Home, Legislative (A), September 1863, Nos. 7–9.

[87] Mansfield's "Further Minute," December 23, 1862, NAI, Legislative (A), February 8, 1868, Nos. 1–2.

commerce insisted that private employers were not liable for the future conduct of their dismissed employees.[88]

The authors of the "Report on European Pauperism" assimilated these two positions and proposed that the state should bear the expense of deportation while private employers should be expected to honor their labor contracts. They also proposed that local magistrates in the *mofussil* should be empowered to apprehend and punish vagrants of European or American origin found within their districts with hard labor, imprisonment, and transportation on a third conviction.[89]

The logistical problem of dealing with European vagrants was complicated by their movement across provincial boundaries and by the absence of law in the *mofussil* that gave local authorities little to no jurisdiction over European British subjects. Major S. J. Thorp, Cantonment Magistrate of Sholapure, noted that local officers were reluctant to file charges against European vagrants and criminals in his district because of the great expense that bringing a case to the High Court entailed. Thorp gave a particularly colorful example of the jurisdiction problem:

An instance of this kind took place not many nights since. Two Europeans, without shoes or stockings and in rags, appeared before me, saying they wanted to go to Bareilly. They were informed that no assistance would be given to them to go into the interior. They received a meal ticket and left. The next morning I heard they had been the round of camp, collecting money, and proceeded along the road to Bareilly. That same night, at 11 o'clock, however, I apprehended them in camp, when articles which had been taken from the bungalow of an Officer of the Station were found in their possession. The case would have had to be tried by the High Court; the Officer, aware of the expense he would be subjected to, declined to prosecute, so they were discharged. Another loafer entered the bungalow about 9 o'clock p.m. The lady of the house was seated alone. He had a large bludgeon in his hand, and demanded money, which was given him. The man fortunately walked away, and was not afterwards heard of.[90]

In late 1867, the Bombay Government passed a Judicial Resolution to prevent European vagrants from entering the *mofussil* at all and proposed to the Government of India that European British subjects in the *mofussil*, under Chapter XIX of the Code of Criminal Procedure (which permitted the detention of "persons of suspicious character" unable to find security

---

[88] Bombay Chamber of Commerce Secretary Brooke's Minute of February 10, 1863, NAI, Home, Legislative (A), September 1863, Nos. 7–9.

[89] NAI, Legislative (A), February 8, 1868, Nos. 1–2.

[90] Major S. J. Thorp, Cantonment Magistrate, Sholapure, to the Assistant Quarter Master General, Poona, May 2, 1867, NAI, Home, Legislative (A), January 1868, Nos. 24–26.

for their good conduct), should be committed and prosecuted by magistrates, being justices of the peace.[91]

Around the same time, the Madras Government also appointed a committee to investigate the problem of European vagrancy. The Madras Committee came to similar conclusions, connecting the rise in vagrancy to the private labor market and the discharge of European regiments after 1858. In Madras, it was also found that many vagrants were abandoned Australian grooms who went willingly to prison, demoralized by "the mendicancy, the climate, the want of food and shelter, hopelessness, and…liquor." The Madras Committee recommended a combined system of workhouses and deportation, as well as a law to prohibit "the landing of destitute persons who have no engagement of service on shore, and of time-expired convicts and ticket-of-leave men."[92]

It was not long before the Government of India recognized that the trans-regional problem of European vagrancy could not be solved by regional legislation. In 1868, Law Member Henry Maine introduced a Bill to deal with the "grave political danger" of European vagrancy and the discredit which it "casts on the entire British race."[93] Enacted the following year, the European Vagrancy Act defined a vagrant as "a person of European extraction found asking for alms, or wandering about without any employment or visible means of subsistence."[94] The law empowered the police in the Presidency towns of Calcutta, Madras, and Bombay to bring an "apparently" vagrant person to the magistrate for a summary inquiry and to send him on to a workhouse. Any "apparent vagrant" who refused to go before the police was subject to one month's imprisonment and any "person of European extraction" found asking for alms when he had a means of subsistence or asking for alms in a threatening manner was subject to punishment. Masters of ships who brought convicted felons to India could be fined, and European companies, associations, and private persons who brought persons of European extraction to India were required to pay for their "removal" if they became vagrants one year after their arrival. The amended European Vagrancy Act of 1874 expanded the meaning of "person of European extraction" to include those born in Europe, America, the West Indies, Australia, Tasmania, New Zealand, and Cape Colony, as well as the sons and

---

[91] Resolution No. 3568, NAI, Home, Legislative (A), January 1868, Nos. 24–26.
[92] "Report on European Vagrancy," Proceedings of the Madras Government (Public Department), NAI, Legislative (A), February 8, 1868, Nos. 1–2.
[93] Maine's Minute of June 11, 1868, NAI, Home, Legislative (A), October 1868, Nos. 12–15.
[94] European Vagrancy Act (Act XXI of 1869).

grandsons of such persons, and deprived them of their privileged status under the Code of Criminal Procedure.

Gone native: race-based rights and the Englishman's personal law

The European Vagrancy Act provided local magistrates with increased, though still circumscribed, powers over a small and vaguely defined class of poor, vagrant, and sometimes criminal whites in the *mofussil*. It did not, however, settle the larger problem of having to send European British subjects scattered across the subcontinent to the High and Chief Courts for trials in most criminal cases.[95] Between 1868 and 1870, forty-three such cases were sent to the Bombay High Court from distant parts of the Presidency. The trials involved between five and thirty-two witnesses per case, each of whom were detained for two weeks to three months. The inconvenience associated with this system put legal redress all but out of reach of the ordinary Indian when victimized by a European British subject.[96]

Colonial officials continued to complain that the existing law violated the principle of justice and exposed the government to political danger, as Europeans who committed crimes with impunity lowered the prestige of the ruling race in the eyes of local communities.[97] By 1871, there were three separate proposals on the table to reform criminal procedure.[98] The first, drafted by the North-Western Provinces Government, recommended that justices of the peace and magistrates should have broader local authority to try European British subjects in the *mofussil*.[99] The second, drafted by Law Member James Fitzjames Stephen, proposed to extend the local authority of Sessions judges only.[100] And the third, drafted by the Bengal Government, made European British subjects amenable to all local criminal tribunals.

---

[95] See the Minutes of the Madras and Calcutta High Court Judges, and the Punjab Chief Court Judges, NAI, Home, Judicial (A), February 4, 1871, Nos. 40–41; and NAI, Home, Judicial (A), February 25, 1871, No. 4.

[96] Petition from the Bombay Association, February 1, 1871, NAI, Legislative (A), June 1872, Nos. 141–346.

[97] Maine's Minute, NAI, Home, Legislative (A), August 1864, Nos. 31–33; and Note of May 10, 1866, NAI, Home, Judicial (A), March 25, 1871, Nos. 29–30.

[98] S. C. Bayley, Secretary to the Government of India, to the local governments, December 30, 1871, NAI, Legislative (A), June 1872, Nos. 141–346.

[99] Government of the North-Western Provinces to the Government of India, August 23, 1870, NAI, Legislative (A), June 1872, Nos. 141–346.

[100] NAI, Legislative Council Proceedings, 1870, vol. XVI.

The Bengal proposal was based on the idea that only a uniform and non-discriminating Code of Criminal Procedure

would put an end to the temptation to [Europeans who] bear themselves as a superior and arrogant caste, which the present state of the law holds out to those who are ill-disposed; and it would put an end to a certain antagonism between the authorities of the country and foreigners claiming the privilege of extra territoriality, which must, more or less, prevail wherever such as system obtains.[101]

The Select Committee appointed to review the three proposals concluded that the trial and punishment of European British-born subjects in the High Court was "an expensive and troublesome procedure" that weakened the government's control over the growing non-official population.[102] According to census reports, by 1872, the British population in India had swelled to 142,000, including soldiers.[103] The Select Committee did not, however, believe that the time was "ripe" to go the route of complete legal equality. The Bill that was ultimately introduced into the Legislative Council proposed to extend limited criminal jurisdiction over European British-born subjects in the *mofussil* only to magistrates and Sessions judges who were themselves Europeans. This Bill was drafted in secret consultation with the non-official European community in Bengal.

As was to be expected, a vigorous public debate ensued. The British Indian Association insisted that "the long-looked-for time has arrived" for one set of laws and tribunals, arguing that "Nothing can be more repugnant to the spirit of the English law, English rule, and English character, than the invidious distinction made in British India in the trial of Her Majesty's European subjects and Indian subjects in criminal cases."[104] Indian journalists, who regularly reported incidents of European violence and the failures of justice associated with their trials, pressed for complete legal equality. One proposed that "Government should pass a law declaring that no European shall lay violent hands upon any native and that whoever may infringe this provision shall be fined to the extent of Rs 25,000 or even more."[105] Another called the practice of referring

---

[101] S. C. Bayley, Officiating Secretary to the Government of Bengal in the Judicial Department, November 4, 1871, NAI, Home, Judicial (A), December 30, 1871, Nos. 35–37.

[102] Legislative Council debates of January 30, 1872, NAI, Legislative (A), June 1872, Nos. 141–346. Preliminary Report of the Select Committee in the *Supplement to the Gazette of India*, January–June 1872 (February 3, 1872).

[103] Bose, *Racism, Struggle for Equality and Indian Nationalism*, p. 238.

[104] Memorial of February 29, 1872, NAI, Legislative (A), June 1872, Nos. 141–346.

[105] *Som Prakash*, May 17, 1880, BL, IOR, L/R/5/6 (Bengal, 1880).

Europeans to the High Court "a mockery of justice."[106] Many insisted that as subjects under one sovereign, Europeans and Indians were entitled to the same laws and law courts.[107]

Supporters of legal exemptions were equally passionate in their defense. Whereas non-officials in the 1840s justified the need for exemptions in the language of relative equality – arguing that backward Indians would not be equally oppressed by inferior tribunals as free-born Englishmen – a new argument proposed that Englishmen were entitled to special privileges as a matter of personal law. In January 1872, the Madras Advocate-General held that as criminal cases involved the determination of *mens rea* (the state of mind of the accused), members of different races were ill-equipped to judge each other: "on principle, an Englishman ought not to be tried by one who is wholly alien to him in thoughts and feelings, and who cannot understand his habits of mind or mode of conduct." While an Indian magistrate would be an excellent judge of the state of mind of other Indians, "if he applied to the case of a European his own knowledge of Native character he would err most fatally." To illustrate this point, he gave the example of a bar-room brawl: "a Native adjudicating upon what would appear to him to be a blood-thirsty attempt to murder, but which an Englishman would recognize as an unpremeditated fight between a couple of tipsy soldiers."[108]

This was an interesting and decidedly novel line of reasoning, as consideration of distinct "habits and feelings" had hitherto applied only to natives in the cultural sphere of personal law. Since the late eighteenth century, personal law had applied to Indians in certain civil matters such as women, religion, and inheritance. Here, Britons claimed the Indian's right to personal law in the public sphere of criminal law, a supposedly universal and culture-free space. Arguing that just as women in *purdah* (female seclusion) did not have to appear in court, Englishmen now demanded their own cultural rights and privileges. By demanding his own personal law as other inhabitants of India had, the Briton had, in effect, declared that he was a native.

By 1872, both supporters and opponents of the "compromise" Bill were debating the jurisdiction issue in cultural terms. Should Indian judges and magistrates who did not understand European manners, customs, and

---

[106] *Akhbar-i-Anjuman-i-Punjab*, March 15, 1872, *Selections from the Vernacular Newspapers Published in the Punjab, North-Western Provinces, Oudh, and Central Provinces* (1872), NAI.

[107] *Puttiala Akhbar*, February 12, 1872, ibid.

[108] Madras Advocate-General's letter of January 11, 1872, NAI, Home, Judicial (A), April 1872, No. 79.

habits of thought be allowed to hold criminal powers over Europeans?[109] Some pointed out that Indian judges already sat on the High Courts, where they judged Indians and Europeans alike.[110] Others argued that certain Indians could overcome their cultural provincialism, particularly those who had traveled to Europe and were acquainted with European feelings, ideas, and customs.[111] Hard-liners like Fitzjames Stephen, however, insisted that exemptions were not only part of the Englishman's personal law, they were also the right of the conqueror:

The Muhammadan has his personal law. The Hindu has his personal law. Women, who according to the custom of the country ought not to appear in Court, are excused from appearing in Court. Natives of rank and influence enjoy, in many cases, privileges which stand on precisely the same principle; and are English people to be told that, whilst it is their duty to respect all these laws scrupulously, they are to claim nothing for themselves? that whilst the English Courts are to respect, and even to enforce, a variety of laws which are thoroughly repugnant to all the strongest convictions of Englishmen, Englishmen who settle in this country are to surrender privileges to which, rightly or otherwise, they attach the highest possible importance?[112]

The amended Code of Criminal Procedure (1872) barred Indian judges and magistrates from trying European British-born subjects in the *mofussil*. No magistrate, Sessions judge, or justice of the peace was permitted to inquire into a complaint or try a case against a European British-born subject unless he was himself a European British-born subject. Minor offenses committed by European British-born subjects could be tried by European British-born justices of the peace, more serious charges by European British-born Sessions judges, and all charges against European British-born subjects that carried the death penalty had to be committed to the High Court. European British-born subjects were also given the right to be tried at the Sessions Court level by a mixed jury composed of not less than half European or American jurors and the right of appeal to the High Court. The amended Code collected these privileges in a new chapter titled "Of Criminal Jurisdiction over European British Subjects."

Petitions poured into the government condemning the ever-widening gap between the Briton's and the Indian's legal rights. The British Indian Association denounced the "invidious distinction" introduced by the Act, calling it "repugnant alike to justice and to political ethics...opposed to the principles of enlightened criminal jurisprudence, and to the spirit of

---

[109] Debates of April 16, 1872, NAI, Legislative Council Proceedings, 1872, vol. XVIII.
[110] NAI, *Supplement to the Gazette of India*, May 4, 1872.   [111] Ibid.
[112] Stephen's speech of April 16, 1872, NAI, Legislative Council Proceedings, 1872, vol. XVIII.

civilized rule."[113] The Joyampore Projas Shoba (*Ryots'* Association) charged that the Act was "calculated to defeat the ends of justice and encroach upon the liberty of Her Majesty's Indian subjects."[114] The Jessore Association attacked the "already too inconveniently wide" system that was "foreign to the criminal jurisprudence of any civilized country."[115] The petitions had no immediate effect.

"White Mutiny": the Ilbert Bill crisis

The codification of criminal procedure both constructed and hardened the legal lines of racial distinction in colonial India. Although the establishment of a uniform system of laws and tribunals had been formal imperial policy since 1833, by 1877 there were three separate criminal procedure codes in force in India: the Code of Criminal Procedure (for the *mofussil* courts), the High Courts' Criminal Procedure Act, and the Presidency Magistrates' Act. The Secretary of State called the existence of separate laws and law courts "a wide departure from the settled policy of providing a simple and uniform system of law for India" and implored the Government of India, once and for all, to enact a comprehensive procedure code.[116]

In 1882, fourteen days after the enactment of an amended Code of Criminal Procedure, two letters that would change the course of Indian history were introduced into the Legislative Council.[117] The first was written by Behari Lal Gupta, a covenanted civil servant and Calcutta Presidency magistrate. Gupta called attention to the "anomalous position" of Indian officers in the Covenanted Civil Service, who had less legal authority than their European British subordinates in the *mofussil*. Whereas Indian District magistrates and Sessions judges were prohibited from trying cases against European British subjects in the *mofussil*, European British subjects at the lower rank of joint magistrate were not. Expecting a promotion to Sessions judge in upper Bengal, Gupta implored the Bengal Government to change the law: "If you entrust us with the responsible office of a District magistrate or of a Sessions judge, do not cripple us in our powers."[118] The second letter was from Ashley

---

[113] Memorial from the British Indian Association of Calcutta, July 11, 1872, NAI, Home, Judicial (A), August 1872, Nos. 61–64.
[114] Memorial of November 1, 1872, NAI, Home, Judicial (A), January 1873, Nos. 255–259.
[115] Memorial of November 9, 1872, ibid.
[116] Secretary of State's Despatch (Legislative) No. 44, October 26, 1876, NAI, Home, Judicial (A), October 1878, Nos. 54–56.
[117] The codes were regularly amended every ten years.
[118] NAI, Home, Judicial (A), September 1882, Nos. 219–239.

Eden, Lieutenant-Governor of Bengal. Supporting Gupta, Eden insisted that "the time has now arrived" for Indian members of the Covenanted Civil Service to be relieved of the race-based restrictions of their powers.[119] Eden defended his position on the grounds of administrative expediency, pointing out that as one-fifth of the offices in the Covenanted Civil Service were reserved for Indians, it made little sense to disqualify such a large contingent of the judiciary from trying European British-born subjects.

Initially, the local governments agreed with Eden's call to modify the restrictions placed on Indian magistrates and judges in the interior.[120] Many proposed that jurisdiction over European British subjects should be extended to Indian District magistrates and Sessions judges in the interior who were members of the Covenanted Civil Service. Others argued that only Indians who had spent time in London could be trusted in criminal matters involving Europeans. W. Duthoiut, Officiating Judicial Commissioner of Oudh, reasoned that Indians who took the entrance exam in England were persons who had "overcome the caste and religious prejudices into which they were born [and were] more or less *au courant* with European feelings and customs," whereas those appointed by the Viceroy were "men saturated with caste and religious prejudices, and ignorant of European modes of thought and feeling."[121] On the strength of these local opinions, Law Member Courtenay Ilbert drafted a Bill designed "to remove from the Statute Book, at once and completely, every judicial disqualification which is based merely on race distinctions and the supposed personal privilege of a dominant caste."[122]

Even before Ilbert's Bill was circulated to the local governments, the non-official European community in Calcutta erupted in fury.[123] At a public meeting at the Calcutta Town Hall on February 28, 1883, more than 3,000 Europeans gathered to protest "Mr. Ilbert's scandalous Bill."[124] They described themselves as an oppressed minority whose interests, rights, and privileges were threatened by the "Bengali Babus"

[119] H. A. Cockerell, Secretary to the Government of Bengal, to the Government of India (Home), NAI, *Extra Supplement to the Gazette of India*, July–December 1883.

[120] Confidential Circular to Local Governments and Administrations, Nos. 7–586 to 594, April 28, 1882, NAI, Home, Judicial (A), September 1882, Nos. 219–239.

[121] Duthoiut's letter of May 19, 1882, ibid.

[122] "Statement of Objects and Reasons," January 30, 1883, in NAI, *Extra Supplement to the Gazette of India*, July–December 1883 and BL, IOR, L/P&J/5/40.

[123] See E. Hirschmann, *"White Mutiny": The Ilbert Bill Crisis in India and Genesis of the Indian National Congress* (New Delhi: Heritage, 1980), and Sinha, *Colonial Masculinity*.

[124] "Proceedings of a Public Meeting held in the Town Hall, Calcutta, on the 28th February 1883, in connection with the Criminal Procedure Code Amendment Bill," *PP*, 1884, vol. LX, c. 3952.

and an unsympathetic colonial government.[125] J. Pitt Kennedy, a former member of the Legislative Council, argued that the Viceroy and his Council, "living on the hills, like gods together, careless of mankind," lacked an "intimate acquaintance with the mind of the non-official population." Calcutta barrister H. A. Branson charged that "our rulers live so entirely away from us, when the Viceroy and his select advisors are carried away some 2,000 miles into the hills that they know nothing of what our true wants are." Calcutta businessman J. J. J. Keswith demanded that the non-official community's voice be heeded: "God knows we are heavily enough taxed; that Government never shrinks and never ceases from making demands on us…and yet we are the people on whom an unnecessary law is to be forced."[126]

In their rhetoric, the gulf between officials and non-officials was mapped not only in terms of the physical space dividing the Viceroy in the hills from his white subjects on the plains, but also in terms of the gap between the haughty know-nothing elites and the man on the spot with experience. The man on the spot, Kennedy claimed, knew that abstract principles had no place in India. The covenanted officer knew only what he read in books: "The proposal has its origin in maudlin sentimentalism and presumptuous ignorance, acted on by gentlemen inflamed with the sense of their own importance, which not infrequently takes possession of men who have been successful in examinations."[127]

These self-appointed India hands gestured to the practical realities of racial antagonism, false charges, and ancient caste distinctions to dismiss the possibility that Indians should ever be permitted to stand in judgment of Britons. "Do you think that Native Judges will by three or four years' residence in England become so Europeanized in nature and in character, that they will be able to judge as well in false charges against Europeans as if they themselves were Europeans? Can the Ethiopian change his skin or the leopard his spots?" Keswith asked.[128] Branson insisted that "freedom-loving people" could never be judged "by a nation steeped in the tradition of the conquered": "You cannot suddenly educate a Hindu into a full appreciation of his freedom…Look at the history of India. Here you have a country that has been from all historical times, I say, the victim of one conquering nation or another."[129]

On March 9, 1883, Ilbert's Bill was formally introduced into the Legislative Council.[130] Indian supporters of the Bill, such as Rai Kristodas Pal, called it "a legitimate and logical development of the progressive policy which characterizes British rule in this country."[131] The Bill's British

---

[125] Ibid.   [126] Ibid.   [127] Ibid.   [128] Ibid.   [129] Ibid.   [130] BL, IOR, L/P&J/5/40.
[131] Debates of March 9, 1883, NAI, Legislative Council Proceedings, 1883.

supporters emphasized the ability of a select group of Indians to overcome their cultural backwardness. Council Member Hunter argued that Indian members of the Covenanted Civil Service were "a select body of men" who had overcome the disabilities of caste, class, and climate "by exceptional exertion and by exceptional abilities." Echoing the language of Thomas Macaulay's Minute on Indian Education (1835), Hunter called them "more English in thought and feeling than Englishmen themselves."[132]

The Bill's opponents railed against the prospect of Europeans in India being "leveled down" to the status of Indians. Non-official Member Miller characterized India in dramatic terms as a theater of deceit where witnesses used dress rehearsals and other deliberate machinations to prepare false testimony for their court performances. Miller railed:

When we came to this country, did we find equitable law courts in which Englishmen and Natives could alike obtain equal justice? Did we upset them and introduce this anomaly in favour of our countrymen? No. We found Suraja Dowla [sic], and the Black Hole, and the like of that. There was no such thing as law and justice. The land was a land of violence, of systematic and periodical marauding, of constant blackmail, of daily uncertainty of life and property, in short, of all the many forms of anarchy and misrule and lawlessness which I may not stay to dwell upon. It is a matter of history, and it still lives in proverbs, customs, castes, tenures, structures, which point to the then every-day existence of a state of things for which there was no remedy but to sweep it clean away. It was for us, a mere handful of strangers, to introduce law and order, and to import into this country as much justice as was possible under the circumstances.[133]

Non-official Member G. H. P. Evans pointed to "the danger of carrying abstract principles to their logical conclusion in India, without regard to the consequences." In Evans' view, the problem was not legal inequality: the problem was India. Evans insisted that formal legal equality was impossible in India due to Indian judges' ignorance of the manners, customs, and habits of Englishmen and the widespread problem of native mendacity.[134]

Outside the halls of the Council, public debate over the Ilbert Bill was even more contentious. Indian supporters continued to invoke "the guiding principle of British rule in India…equality in the eye of the law without the invidious distinctions of country, race or religion."[135] At a packed public meeting in the Town Hall of Bombay, Jamsetjee Jejeebhoy announced his commitment to "vindicat[ing] the wise, noble and benevolent policy of

[132] Ibid.   [133] Ibid.   [134] Ibid.
[135] Extract from the Joint Memorial of the British Indian Association, the Indian Association, the Mahommedan Literary Society, the National Mahommedan Association, the East Bengal Association and the Vakils' Association, High Court, Calcutta, BL, IOR, L/P&J/5/40.

the present Government of India from the unreasoning alarms of short-sighted statesmanship." Budruddin Tyabjee reminded the crowd of the repeated imperial pledges of legal equality:

The fundamental principle which has been so often declared and repeated over and over again by successive Viceroys, Ministers, Secretaries of State, Parliaments, and even by Her Gracious Majesty herself – that principle, the recognition of which forms the key-note to the whole of Lord Ripon's policy, that principle on which are based all our political rights, just hopes, and legitimate aspirations; that principle, namely, which declares that the Natives of India are entitled to a just share in the administration of their own country, and that a mere difference in race, colour or creed shall not be just ground for distinction in political treatment... there is no principle better grounded in moral justice or political wisdom.

Pherozeshah Mehta alluded to the "policy of righteousness" and the fact that "England has won India not simply by the sword, but in a large measure by the exercise of high moral and intellectual qualities."[136] Although the problem of European violence was by then occupying the daily attention of Indian newspapers, Indian support of Ilbert's Bill was articulated primarily in abstract rather than material terms.

Non-officials furiously condemned the Bill for a host of familiar reasons. These included: constitutional arguments about the inviolable rights of "freeborn Englishmen;"[137] personal law arguments about the special privileges entitled to Britons as residents of India (how could an Englishwoman be fairly judged by an Indian magistrate raised in a society where "women are ignorant and enslaved"?);[138] and cultural arguments about the inapplicability of the principle of equality in a caste-ridden and socially stratified place like India.[139] By August 1883, petitions opposing the Bill had been signed by 15,000 people, led by the newly formed Anglo-Indian Defence Association.

Despite the fact that only a year earlier all but one of the local governments had advocated the extension of criminal jurisdiction over European British subjects in the interior, by the summer of 1883, most officials had

---

[136] "Humble Memorial of the Native Inhabitants of Bombay at a Public Meeting assembled" and the Report of the Proceedings of April 28, 1883, NAI, *Extra Supplement to the Gazette of India*, July–December 1883.

[137] "Humble Memorial of the Anglo-Indian and European British subjects residing at Mirzapur in Upper India," ibid. Prior cases considering this constitutional question include *Reg.* v. *Edward Reay, Bombay High Court Reports (Criminal)*, vol. VII, p. 6, and *Queen* v. *Gerald Meares, Bengal Law Reports*, vol. XIV, p. 106.

[138] "Memorial of Ladies residing in Bihar," signed by Alice Hudson and 731 other ladies, BL, IOR, L/P&J/5/40.

[139] "Humble Memorial of the undersigned European British subjects and others, residents in India," June 9, 1883, NAI, *Extra Supplement to the Gazette of India*, July–December 1883.

come to the conclusion that "the time is not ripe."[140] The notion that certain Indians could overcome their Indianness was displaced by a hardened belief that "East is East." As the Bengal Government put it, "our thoughts are not their thoughts, nor are their ways our ways."[141]

Ilbert beseeched the Secretary of State to pass the Bill nonetheless.[142] He took on both the personal law argument – "The theory that an Englishman is entitled to the privilege of being tried exclusively by Englishmen has, to the best of my belief, been manufactured expressly for the Indian market. Imagine it being suggested to a Parisian magistrate on behalf of an English pick-pocket"[143] – and the baseless nature of constitutional claims –

in other parts of the world inhabited by men of English race or descent, I am not aware that this argument is ever used or recognized. I have made some inquiries on the subject, and I find that in no British colony is there any distinction between Europeans and Natives with respect to the jurisdiction exercisable over European British subjects, or persons belonging to any similar class.[144]

Ilbert did not prevail.

In December 1883, a "concordat" was privately reached between the Anglo-Indian Defence Association and the Government of India that secured the special privileges provided in the 1882 Code. It slightly expanded local jurisdiction by giving European British subjects in the *mofussil* a right to trial by jury with no less than half European or American jurors on any charge before all District magistrates and Sessions judges.[145] This was designed "to ensure that if the magistrate is an Indian, the European British subject shall have someone who understands his side of the case."[146] On the eve of the Code's enactment, Kristodas Pal lamented that the government was giving with one hand what it took away with the other:

It cannot be denied that while race distinction is removed in one direction, that is to say, as regards a very small class of Native officers, it is deepened in another, that

[140] C. J. Lyall, Officiating Secretary to the Chief Commissioner, Assam, to the Government of India (Legislative Department), June 19, 1883, ibid.
[141] F. B. Peacock, Secretary to the Government of Bengal, to the Government of India (Legislative Department), ibid.
[142] Despatch No. 35 from the Government of India to the Secretary of State, August 10, 1883, PP, 1884, vol. LX, c. 3952.
[143] Ilbert's keepwiths (hand-written notes) accompany Despatch No. 33, from the Government of India (Legislative) to the Secretary of State, September 9, 1882, NAI.
[144] NAI, Legislative Council Proceedings, January 1884.
[145] For the many memorials against the concordat, see PP, 1884, vol. LX, c. 3952; and BL, IOR, L/P&J/5/40.
[146] Tindall's Minute, *Racial Distinctions: Main Correspondence, File No. 105 of 1922*, NAI.

is to say, as regards the Native population at large…Suffice it to say that the nation anxiously looks forward to the establishment of a complete equality in the eye of the law between all classes of Her Majesty's subjects without distinctions of race and religion.[147]

Pal's wish for racial distinctions to be completely removed from the Code of Criminal Procedure would not be fulfilled until after the British empire was itself removed from India.

Whiteness as property: race, law, and imperial identity politics

The special legal rights afforded to European British subjects by the Code of Criminal Procedure reveal the role of colonial law in the construction of racial identities.[148] Ian Haney López defines the formal legal construction of race as "the way in which law as a formal matter, either through legislation or adjudication, directly engages in racial definitions."[149] The Code of Criminal Procedure engaged in this process by creating a line of distinction between European British subjects and everyone else, and by providing European British subjects with certain exclusive privileges. To be a European British subject in the law was to have. As Cheryl Harris notes, this created a "property interest" in Britishness by making it a source of privilege that was "affirmed, legitimated, and protected by the law."[150]

Law gave imperial whiteness a kind of stability. By making race into an object, law was a site that mediated against the porous social boundaries and unstable racial identities found in all European empires. In the Code of Criminal Procedure, you either were or were not a European British subject. And this fact translated either into an immediate claim for certain privileges or a denial of those privileges. Race in the Code was not a repository of shifting ideas about selves and others, civilizers and savages. It was an enduring position of status, a thing to lay claim to, an identity with a vested interest.[151]

The only thing unstable about this racial identity in law and the benefits that accrued to it was the question of entitlement. Who counted as a European British subject? Did children born in India to British parents

---

[147] Speech of January 25, 1884, NAI, Legislative Council Proceedings, 1884.
[148] For a different perspective on the construction of whiteness in colonial India, see S. Mizutani, "Historicizing Whiteness: From the Case of Late Colonial India," *Australian Critical Race and Whiteness Studies Association* e-journal, 2, 1 (2006), 1–15.
[149] López, *White By Law*, p. xv.
[150] C. Harris, "Whiteness as Property," *Harvard Law Review*, 106, 8 (1993), 1713.
[151] My thinking in this paragraph is deeply influenced by Harris, "Whiteness as Property."

qualify for the rights of European British subjects? What about children of mixed-race parentage? Non-whites born in Britain? White settlers from Britain's colonies in Australia and Africa – could they claim the rights of European British subjects in India? What about non-whites from the settler colonies? Stuart Hall argues that "Britishness as a category has always been racialized through and through – when has it connoted anything but 'whiteness'?"[152] Was this true in India – was the "European" in "European British subject" a thinly veiled synonym for "white"?

The terms used in the law to define this privileged identity and its meanings changed over time. In early colonial India, some officials believed that all people born within the territories of the East India Company should legally be considered British subjects, whereas others argued that only natives of the United Kingdom and their legitimate descendants qualified as such.[153] Christianity was sometimes used as a test of Britishness, but the legal transformation of Christians into Britons could cut the wrong way – were Indian Christians entitled to the rights of British subjects? Not according to the Calcutta Supreme Court, which held in *Byjenaut Sing* v. *Reed and others* (1821) that "A native Christian, born of a native Musulman woman, and the illegitimate son of a British father, is not a British subject within the meaning of the term as used in the Charter and in the various Acts of Parliament."[154]

In the first half of the nineteenth century, Parliament offered no precise definition of "British subjects." One Parliamentary Act explicitly stated that Hindus and Muslims were not British subjects (a negative definition),[155] while another held that only natives of the United Kingdom and their descendants were (a positive definition).[156] In 1861, the Code of Criminal Procedure narrowed its legal privileges to "European British subjects" but did not clearly define who was included in this class of persons. The revised Code of 1872 provided some clarity on the meaning of "European British subjects," defining them as:

(1) All subjects of Her Majesty, born, naturalized, or domiciled in the United Kingdom of Great Britain and Ireland or in any of the European, American, or

---

[152] Hall, "The Multi-Cultural Question," p. 222.
[153] "History of the Changes in the Civil and Criminal Jurisdiction Exercised by the Courts in India over European British Subjects," BL, IOR, V/27/140/3.
[154] W. H. Morley, *An Analytical Digest of All the Reported Cases Decided in the Supreme Courts of Judicature in India* (Calcutta, 1850), p. 671.
[155] 9 Geo. IV, c. 33. In *The Statutes of the United Kingdom of Great Britain and Ireland* (London, 1807–1869).
[156] 7 Geo. IV, c. 37. In ibid. A brief legislative history of the East India Company's power to govern British-born subjects in India is recited in *Reg.* v. *Edward Reay, Bombay High Court Reports (Criminal)*, vol. VII, pp. 6–28.

Australian Colonies or possessions of Her Majesty, or in the Colony of New Zealand, or in the Colony of the Cape of Good Hope or Natal. (2) The children or grandchildren of any such person by legitimate consent.[157]

The logic undergirding the 1872 Code was that "European foreigners and Americans accused of offences should be tried by the Courts best acquainted with their feelings and disposition, and therefore more competent to administer effective justice." In *Queen-Empress* v. *Moss and Others* (1891), the Allahabad High Court held that "the word 'European' in s. 451 meant a person born in Europe."[158]

But what did this mean for defendants who were not European British subjects, European foreigners, Americans, or Indians? As Legislative Council Member Harrison put it: "Supposing an accused person in the *Mofussil* were a Malay or a Chinaman; what class of persons would be most nearly of the same race or origin? Would it be Englishmen, Hindoos, or Mahomedans? Supposing the accused were an African negro; who would be considered nearly of the same race or origin?" Given the diversity within India, many questioned whether Indians themselves formed a suitably homogenous racial class to fulfill the Code's intention to have people tried by others "acquainted with their feelings and dispositions." Should a Bengali not be permitted to claim a Bengali-majority jury? Challenging the idea that people should be tried by members of their own race, Bombay High Court Justice John Bucknell recalled a fascinating case from the Straits Settlements that involved "a Danish subject who knocked down with his motor bicycle and killed a Japanese sailor; he was arrested by a Sikh policeman, committed for trial by a West Indian Negro, prosecuted by an Armenian before a jury consisting of two Englishmen, two Chinese, one American, one Eurasian, and one Russian Jew, and was tried before a High Court Judge who was a Ceylon Burgher, he was acquitted and I do not think he had anything to complain of his treatment."[159]

There was also the disputed matter of proving one's racial identity in court. Who bore the burden of proof, and how was proof to be made? In the forgery case of Robert Frederick Charles Mandeville *alias* Robert Frazer *alias* Fergusson (1821), the Nizamut Adalat held that the *onus probandi* rested on the defendant to show he was a British subject.[160] The first Code of Criminal Procedure of 1861 required a committing magistrate to ask an accused person whether he was a European British

---

[157] Act X of 1872, section 71.   [158] *Indian Law Reports – Allahabad Series*, vol. XVI, p. 93.
[159] Bombay High Court Justice John Bucknell to William Vincent, August 18, 1921, NAI *Racial Distinctions: Main Correspondence*, File No. 105 (1922).
[160] *Nizamut Adalat Reports*, 1821, vol. II, pp. 111–121.

subject and to inform him of his rights to be tried by special procedure.[161] The burden of proof was on the person claiming to be a European British subject to prove his identity, and magistrates were empowered to accept or reject the claim, though no clear rules were laid out defining how to do so.

As the law was rather vague, clear standards of proof were worked out in the courts. In *Queen* v. *Thomas Brae* (1865), the Calcutta High Court accepted the following as proof of Thomas Brae's claim to be a European British subject: his personal appearance and an authenticated copy of his parents' marriage certificate, which showed English parentage. The judges concluded that "the person claiming such privileges is bound to prove them. The Court is not to assume such status without proof."[162] In 1867, the Madras High Court decided an accused person could claim exemption as a European British subject from the jurisdiction of a *mofussil* court only by proving both legitimate descent *and* nationality.[163] In 1910, the Oudh Judicial Commissioner's Court accepted Thomas Bradshaw's claim to be a European British subject when he "produce[d] papers which show that he is, through his mother, grandson of one Robert Farrell, who was born in Ireland."[164]

Conclusion

The codification of law formed part of the colonial effort to create a more governable society. It was in large part devised as a solution to the problems posed by the non-official population. Uniformity, in Macaulay's words, was to be its defining feature, by which he meant that a single and certain system of laws and law courts should displace a diverse and confusing one. Although Macaulay insisted that "we must place the European under the same power which legislates for the Hindoo,"[165] the Code of Criminal Procedure did not establish an equal and uniform law of jurisdiction. Instead, it created a racialized and unequal system that provided European British subjects with special privileges and exemptions.

The establishment of a uniform law of criminal jurisdiction was successfully subverted by a small but influential population of whites who refused to allow horizontal legal relations to supplant vertical, imperial ones. In contrast to those who saw legal equality as the great hallmark of colonial justice were others who insisted that legal inequality was

---

[161] *Dawson Downing* v. *Emperor, Criminal Law Journal of India*, 18 (1921), 986; and *Ashley Clarke Harris* v. *Mrs. Peal*, ibid., 21 (1924), 767.
[162] *Sutherland's Weekly Reporter (Criminal)*, vol. III (Calcutta, 1865), p. 64.
[163] *Madras High Court Reporter*, vol. VI (Madras, 1861), p. 7.
[164] *Thomas Bradshaw* v. *Emperor, Criminal Law Journal of India*, 11 (1914), 723.
[165] Macaulay's speech of July 10, 1833, in *Hansard's*, 3rd Series, vol. XIX, 527.

necessary to sustain imperial power and prestige. As Legislative Council Member Thomas observed:

Whether the planter gets justice or not at the hand of the Native Magistrate is rather a secondary consideration; the mere fact of his having, on some trifling charge, had to appear before and be tried by a Native Magistrate, of the same caste and family, perhaps, as one of his own writers or contractors, will so lower him to their own level in the eyes of his two or three hundred coolies, that he will not be able to command their respect any more.[166]

Justifications for why special circumstances required special legislation changed over time. In the early nineteenth century, a constitutional argument about the rights of freeborn Englishmen defined the demand for legal distinctions. This gave way to a relative-equality argument, which posited that equality had no place amidst the peculiar cultural and historical conditions of India. In the final quarter of the nineteenth century, the insistence on special legal privileges was made in the idiom of personal law, which posited that Britons in India, like other indigenous groups, were entitled to special legal dispensations. Arguments in support of legal exemptions were consistently grounded in paradigms that produced conceptual inversions. Equality became inequality or "leveling down." The "doctrine of equal laws for all" was trumped by the "actual state of things." Racial privileges were defined as "safeguards." Equal justice produced grave inequality and injustice.[167]

In the early nineteenth century, there was little official sympathy for the system of having "one rule for the Black Man and another for the White."[168] Thomas Macaulay was totally against it, arguing that Indians had long suffered from subjection to arbitrary despotisms: what was the point of allowing "the curse of a new caste" to continue to oppress the native population? Over time, as the relationship between the official and non-official communities warmed, colonial administrators shied away from this moral and political commitment. In the face of controversy and protest they claimed not here, not now, the time is not ripe. Under the conditions of colonialism, would it ever be? Could it ever be?

---

[166] NAI, Legislative Council Proceedings, 1883 and 1884.

[167] Evidence of Charles Hardless, General Secretary of the Anglo-Indian and Domiciled European Association, submitted to the Racial Distinctions Committee, NAI *Racial Distinctions: Evidence*, File No. 105 (1922).

[168] Legislative Council Member W. Bird's Minute of August 26, 1844, NAI, Legislative Proceedings, October – December 1844, No. 4.

3   "Indian human nature": evidence, experts, and the elusive pursuit of truth

What the horns are to the buffalo, what the paw is to the tiger, what the sting is to the bee, what beauty, according to the Old Greek song, is to woman, deceit is to the Bengali. Large promises, smooth excuses, elaborate tissues of circumstantial falsehood, chicanery, perjury, forgery, are the weapons, offensive and defensive, of the people of the Lower Ganges.

Thomas Macaulay[1]

see also Sath A

The pursuit of truth was a persistent source of anxiety to the British in India. Colonial administrators, Christian missionaries, and a wide range of commentators on Indian society consistently characterized the subcontinent as a place teeming with perjurers, forgers, professional witnesses, and a general population that did not value truth.[2] British ideas about Indian deceptiveness stretched steadily across historical time and the spectrum of political positions. In the late eighteenth century, Governor-General Cornwallis asserted that "Every native of Hindustan, I verily believe, is corrupt."[3] Fifty-odd years later, Calcutta Supreme Court Judge Mordaunt Wells caused a firestorm of public criticism for making repeated remarks from the bench about the unsuitability of Indian jurors and the natives' "disregard for truth."[4] At the turn of the twentieth century, ideas about Indian mendacity were as strong as ever. As Charles Johnston observed in 1911 in the *Atlantic Monthly*:

The dusky folk of Lower Bengal make imaginative witnesses. The inspiration comes upon them suddenly, carrying them away before they realize it. They take some simple fact, some common situation, bathe it in Indian light and drape it

---

[1] T. B. Macaulay, *Critical and Historical Essays Contributed to the Edinburgh Review* (London, 1883), p. 603.

[2] W. Schneider, "'Enfeebling the Arm of Justice': Perjury and Colonial Administration under the East India Company," in M. D. Dubber and L. Farmer (eds.), *Modern Histories of Crime and Punishment* (Stanford: Stanford University Press, 2007), pp. 299–327.

[3] Metcalf, *Ideologies of the Raj*, p. 24.

[4] Quoted in Hume's correspondence of February 8, 1871, NAI, Home, Judicial (A), February 25, 1871, No. 7.

about with Oriental trappings, laying on splashes of gaudy colour and startling ornament, piling splendour on splendour. Relevancy is not great matter. It is the story for the story's sake.[5]

Perceptions of native deceit were so central to colonial understandings of Indian society that it would be impossible to comprehensively trace their emergence or diffusion. Chris Pinney argues that photography and other visual imagery were particularly important to the colonial state where "nothing is as it seems" because "other signs were deemed to be unreliable, mysterious, and deceptive."[6] The "investigative modalities," that Bernard Cohn defines as the means by which British administrators came to know and control facts about native life – from the compilation of religious, legal, and grammatical texts to the decennial census reports – reflect this desire to stabilize the truth about India and Indians.[7] The problem of accessing truth is also a central trope in the fictional literature of empire, most famously in E. M. Forster's *A Passage to India*, where the question of what happened to Ms. Adele Quested in the Marabar cave remains unresolved and perhaps unknowable.

Colonial anxieties about the unreliability of native knowledge took a very literal turn when it came to the administration of justice. In 1827, the Bengal Government complained to the Court of Directors about how the Indian's "notorious disregard for truth" crippled its legal proceedings and obstructed the administration of justice:

It is needless to remark, how much the proceedings of all our tribunals are delayed and embarrassed by the notorious disregard for truth, so generally displayed by the natives in giving evidence, and from their want of moral principle, evils which cannot be mitigated or remedied by any direct or immediate modification of our judicial institutions…The great cause of failure in the administration of criminal as well as of civil justice is the habitual disregard for truth which unhappily pervades the bulk of the native community, and the little security which the obligation of an oath adds to the testimony of witnesses.[8]

During the Ilbert Bill crisis (see pp. 97–103) more than half a century later, Calcutta barrister H. A. Branson pointed to the Bengali's "stilettos of false charges" to justify the demand for the preservation of jurisdictional exemptions: "What the stiletto is to the Italian, a false charge is to the Bengalee. He loves it. It is a weapon he loves, and a facile tongue enables

[5] C. Johnston, "Helping to Govern India," *The Atlantic Monthly*, November 1911, 644.

[6] C. Pinney, *Camera Indica: The Social Life of Indian Photographs* (Chicago: University of Chicago Press, 1997), p. 17.

[7] Cohn, *Colonialism and Its Forms of Knowledge*.

[8] Bengal Government to the Court of Directors, February 22, 1827, *PP*, 1831–1832, vol. XII, Appendix No. II, pp. 236 and 276.

him to use this weapon with the most fatal and truest precision, and we ask that we should not be cast hand and foot among these men with their stilettos of false charges."[9]

The perceived problem of Indian untrustworthiness was not limited to Bengal. In 1831, Richard Clarke, registrar at the Sadr Diwani Adalat in Madras, informed a Parliamentary Select Committee that perjury prosecutions were quite frequent in Madras: "A native will in general give his evidence rather with reference to the consequences of what he may say to his own interest, than from any regard to its truth or falsehood."[10] European members of the Madras Bar later observed that:

Witnesses in this country, *as a rule*, do not come forward to speak the truth, and it is rarer still to find witnesses who are prepared to tell the whole truth without exaggeration or extenuation. Most frequently they appear in the witness-box for the purpose of telling a story of concocted falsehood, and the elucidation of the real facts depends to a large extent on the right of cross-examination.[11]

This chapter examines the codification of the law of evidence and the development of various "truth-technologies," such as the judicial oath and medical jurisprudence, designed to elicit reliable evidence from a people, it was believed, who could not distinguish fact from fiction. Whereas the non-official community's insistence on racial distinctions derailed the establishment of a uniform law of criminal procedure, prevalent ideas about native mendacity and the backwardness of Indian culture hastened the codification of a law of evidence that departed from contemporary evidence rules in England. Over the course of the nineteenth century, the goal of making criminal investigation a science found medical experts and forensic evidence playing an increasingly important role in judicial inquiries and trials.[12] Ideas about Indian people, bodies, and culture produced a medico-legal literature grounded in an ethnographic idiom that contradicted the claims of an objective scientific method. This had an important impact on cases of violent whites, as a medical discourse about the peculiar vulnerabilities of Indian bodies helped ensure that European murderers got off the hook.

Oaths, affirmations, and the hand of man

We began questioning the people as to where the elephant had gone and, as usual, failed to get any definite information. That is invariably the case in the East; a story

---

[9] *PP*, 1884, vol. LX, c. 3952.   [10] Clarke's evidence in *PP*, 1831–1832, vol. XII, pp. 1–12.
[11] Memorial to the Governor-General, the Earl of Mayo, June 24, 1871, NAI, Home, Legislative (A), May 1872, No. 84.
[12] R. Smith and B. Wynne (eds.), *Expert Evidence: Interpreting Science in the Law* (London: Routledge, 1989).

always sounds clear enough at a distance, but the nearer you get to the scene of events the vaguer it becomes.

George Orwell, "Shooting an Elephant" (1936)[13]

In the English legal tradition, the religious oath was a device used to ensure truthful testimony. By swearing on the Bible, a person taking an oath was made to believe that he or she was in the presence of God and would suffer divine punishment in the afterlife for failing to tell the truth. The efficacy of the oath relied on the assumption that the person taking it believed in the Christian God and in life after death. During the colonial period, as Britons increasingly interacted with people who neither believed in their God nor in the Christian concept of divine rewards and punishment, the tradition of the judicial oath underwent a transformation.

By the late eighteenth century, the oath was a largely ritualistic component of English trials.[14] Jeremy Bentham ridiculed the oath's invocation of divine intervention and criticized it as a useless mechanism and an instrument of tyranny.[15] Bentham held that public opinion, not the sanction of religion, secured the truthfulness of testimony.[16] Cross-examination soon displaced the oath as the crucial element in courtroom adjudication in England. In India, by contrast, the oath remained an important instrument for eliciting truth well into the nineteenth century, as colonial administrators were eager to use whatever means they could to secure reliable testimony from a backward people who they believed did not put a premium on truth-telling.

The reform of the judicial oath in England was prompted by an imperial encounter in India. The case of *Omychund* v. *Barker* (1744) involved a Christian, English East India Company servant (Barker) and a Hindu Indian merchant (Omychund). In July 1729, Barker approached Omychund to borrow money, which he did at an interest rate of 12 percent. When the time came to settle his debt, Barker refused. Seven years later, Omychund filed a claim in the Calcutta Mayor's Court to recover his capital. However, before the case was tried, Barker fled on a French East India Company ship bound for Europe. The Mayor's Court determined Barker's departure to be a flight from justice and ordered him to repay Omychund in full plus costs. Barker died during the sea voyage home but

---

[13] G. Orwell, *Shooting an Elephant and Other Essays* (New York: Harcourt, Brace and World, 1966).

[14] J. Oldham, "Truth-Telling in the Eighteenth-Century English Courtroom," *Law and History Review*, 12, 1 (1994), 95–121.

[15] J. Bentham, *"Swear Not At All": Containing an Exposure of the Needlessness and Mischievousness as well as Antichristianity of the Ceremony of an Oath* (London, 1817).

[16] S. Landsman, "From Gilbert to Bentham: The Reconceptualization of Evidence Theory," *The Wayne Law Review*, 36, 3 (1990), 1149–1186.

left behind a will that charged his estate with the payment of his debts. The total amount owed to Omychund was 67,955 rupees.

The case ultimately wound its way to the High Court of Chancery in England, where the defense moved to dismiss the depositions of two Hindu witnesses taken in Calcutta. Rather than solemnly swearing on the Bible, the two men had been sworn in by a Brahman priest in the following manner:

> The several persons being before us, with a bramin or priest of the *Gentoo* religion, the oath prescribed to be taken by the witnesses was interpreted to each witness respectively; after which they did severally with their hands touch the foot of the bramin or priest of the *Gentoo* religion…after which Neenderam Surmah, being himself a priest, did touch the hand of the bramin, the same being the usual and most solemn form in which oaths are most usually administered to witnesses who profess the *Gentoo* religion.

Defense counsel Tracy Atkyns argued that the law of England required a witness to swear on the Bible and that "an Alien Infidel can be no witness." Attorney-General Sir Dudley Rider retorted that the Hindu oath was valid because of its invocation of *a* deity, though not the Christian deity: "They understand an oath in the same manner we do…in swearing, they use an expression equivalent to ours: *So help me God.*" Rider reminded the court of the imperial significance of the issue, pointing out that if during a time of expanding global commerce those who did not believe in Christianity could not be sworn at all, "manifest injustice and manifest inconvenience must follow." The Chancery Court found in Omychund's favor, holding that the sole qualification for giving testimony under oath was belief in a god, though not necessarily the Christian God. Thereafter, the testimony of witnesses sworn according to their own customs could be received as evidence in English courts.[17]

Following *Omychund*, colonial officials in India experimented with different ways of administering oaths according to local custom. Until 1840, the East India Company had a "Gunga Jullee" and "Moolla Koranee" attached to the local courts. The Gunga Jullee generally administered oaths to Hindus by having the witness swear with the sacred *tulsi* (basil) leaves while holding a copper vessel containing water from the Ganges. Hindu witnesses were also permitted to engage in other customary rituals, such as swearing on the heads of their children or "subscribing to a text of the Mitak, expressive of the spiritual consequences of perjury."[18] The Moolla Koranee swore Muslim witnesses in on the Koran even though Islamic

---

[17] 1 *Atk.* 21 (1744). Cited in J. T. Atkyns, *Reports of Cases Argued and Determined in the High Court of Chancery in the Time of Lord Hardwicke*, vol. I (London, 1765–1768), pp. 21–51.

[18] "The Humble Petition of the British Indian Association," February 22, 1872, BL, IOR, L/P&J/5/15.

law in India did not require an oath to give validity to evidence in judicial cases.[19]

The corporal forms of the oath administered by the Company Courts clearly mirrored the corporal form of the Christian oath in which a witness placed his/her hand on the Bible before swearing. This raises the question whether, in fact, these were indigenous customary practices or whether they were invented colonial traditions. Indeed, prior to the interventions of Orientalist scholars in the late eighteenth century, indigenous Hindu and Muslim laws and conventions (including oaths) were neither uniform nor unchanging. The oath taken by the two witnesses in Omychund's case reflects how the colonial state reconstructed Indian society even as it endeavored to rule in a fashion that was congruous with indigenous institutions.[20]

Colonial administrators quickly discovered that these religious oaths were not only ineffective, they were often counterproductive. As William Muir (then Junior Member of the Sadr Board of Revenue and later Lieutenant-Governor of the North-Western Provinces) noted: "The 'Gunga Jullee' and 'Moolla Koranee,' the swearers attached to every Court, thrust their phial of Ganges water or muffled Koran into the hands of witnesses in all cases, no matter how trivial, and the witnesses ordinarily received these symbols as a mere matter of course, and went on unconcernedly to perjure themselves."[21] Bipan Chandra Pal observed that many orthodox Hindus avoided the Company Courts altogether or performed penance after testifying because they objected to the social equality implied in the taking of an oath, as well as its sacrilegious implications:

Our people instinctively saw these dangers and pitfalls of the British system of administration of justice and they tried religiously to avoid these courts, so far as they could, in those days. People who went to a British court of justice ran the risk of losing their souls – that was a very real fear in the mind of our orthodox people in the days of my youth. People with the fear of religion in their heart, would never agree to go to the witness box in a British court of law. They were mortally afraid of telling a falsehood however unwittingly it might be, upon their oath.[22]

Ironically, the *Omychund* decision, which expanded the admissibility of witness testimony in England, had the opposite effect in India, where it

[19] F. L. Beaufort, *A Digest of the Criminal Law of the Presidency of Fort William and a Guide to All Criminal Authorities Therein* (Calcutta, 1849).

[20] Cohn, *Colonialism and Its Forms of Knowledge*.

[21] Muir, "Minute on the Bill concerning Oaths and Affirmations," January 28, 1859, NAI, Home, Legislative (A), May 1872, Nos. 395–444.

[22] B. C. Pal, *Memories of My Life and Times*, vol. I (reprint Calcutta: Bipin Chandra Pal Institute, 1973), p. 117.

deterred people from participating in the legal process and, in the words of the British Indian Association, "frustrated the ends of justice."[23]

In 1793, in accordance with Governor-General Warren Hastings' legal principle of non-interference in religious matters, the Bengal Government permitted witnesses of rank or caste to make a solemn declaration in lieu of an oath.[24] Ten years later, any witness who objected to taking an oath on religious grounds could make a solemn declaration instead.[25] The Nizamut Adalat, Bengal's superior criminal court of revision and reference, continually reminded the lower courts that one of the two – either an oath or a solemn declaration – was indispensable to evidence.[26] The Calcutta Supreme Court examined all Indian witnesses on the solemn declaration provided for Quakers and Moravians.[27]

Colonial authorities in India, and especially in Bengal, remained skeptical about the value and efficacy of the oaths. In 1814, the Bengal Government advocated their elimination altogether.[28] Former Governor-General W. B. Bayley asserted that "the moral sanction of an oath does not, especially among the lower classes, materially add to the value of native testimony." Bayley claimed that penal sanctions were the best means of controlling perjury as "fear of consequences in a future state, or the apprehended loss of character and reputation amongst their countrymen, has little effect in securing truth and honest testimony on the part of those who may be influenced by the bias of fear, favour or affection."[29]

In 1840, a new law revised the Government of India's approach to the problem of eliciting truthful testimony. The Oaths Act, which applied only in the *mofussil* courts, permitted all Hindu and Muslim witnesses to make an affirmation with a religious reference in lieu of an oath: "I solemnly affirm in the presence of Almighty God that what I shall state

---

[23] "The Humble Petition of the British Indian Association," February 22, 1872, BL, IOR L/P&J/5/15.

[24] Bengal Regulation IV of 1793, sections 6 and 14; Bengal Regulation IV of 1797, section 7. Cited in Sir Henry Thomas Colebrooke, *Regulations and Laws Enacted by the Governor-General in Council for the Civil Government of the Whole of Territories under the Presidency of Fort William in Bengal* (Calcutta, 1793–1834).

[25] Bengal Regulation L of 1803, sections 2–4. Ibid.

[26] Circular Order No. 1, February 1, 1828. In J. Carrau, *The Circular Orders of the Court of the Nizamut Adaulut Communicated to the Criminal Authorities from 1796 to 1853* (Calcutta, 1855).

[27] BL, IOR, Despatch from Court of Directors to the Legislative Department, No. 12, September 23, 1840.

[28] BL, IOR, Despatch from the Court of Directors to the Government of Bengal, November 9, 1814; and Letter from the Bengal Government to the Court of Directors, February 22, 1827, given as Evidence before the Select Committee on the Affairs of the East India Company, *PP*, 1831–1832, vol. XII, Appendix No. II, p. 235.

[29] Testimony of April 16, 1832, *PP*, 1831–1832, vol. XII, p. 88.

shall be the truth, the whole truth and nothing but the truth." It was not long, however, before local officials began to complain that the affirmation was as much of a failure as the customary oaths and solemn declarations. An anonymous commentator called the affirmation "meaningless," sardonically reminding the colonial authorities that Indians "do not see anything reminding them of the Almighty God either in the European Judge, the Interpreter, the Prosecuting Counsel, or the persons about the Court house."[30] The editors of the *Khair Khwah-i-Panjab* cleverly linked the disrespect shown towards the affirmation with a more general disrespect for colonial authority: "The oaths which have to be repeated are scarcely more thought of by persons who for a few rupees attend a court to give false evidence than the bow made by them before an officer."[31]

In 1871, the Government of India returned to the elusive task of drafting legislation that would increase truthful testimony. Some officials, like Calcutta High Court Justice Bayley, pressed the government to permit native witnesses to perform whatever form of oath or affirmation was most binding on their conscience, whether "A Hindu by Ganges water and his child's head. A man of the Forest tribe by a tiger's skin. A Ferazee by his beard or the beard of the prophet. Other Muhammadans by a real Koran kept in custody of a Muhammadan Moolah."[32] Citing *Omychund*, Punjab Chief Court Judge C. Boulnois argued for the validity of customary practices: "custom, where a custom exists among the people to whom the witness belongs, should be regarded."[33] Bengal Lieutenant-Governor George Campbell insisted that the government could ill afford to do away with any means of eliciting the truth, especially "amongst a peculiar people with whom the speaking of truth was not in any way the custom."[34]

However, there was another section of official opinion, shored up by India's lawyerly elites, that was disinclined to permit backward native customs into modern colonial courtrooms. Law Member James Fitzjames Stephen condemned these "miserable superstitions," wondering: "How could any European enter into the state of mind of a man who attached some peculiar sanctity to a tiger's skin and a cow's tail?"[35] William Muir warned against "purchas[ing] truth at any price,"[36] and the British Indian

---

[30] C. S., *Hindu Witnesses and the Judicial Oath* (Madras, 1882), p. 6.

[31] NAI, *Selections from the Vernacular Newspapers Published in the Punjab, North-Western Provinces, Oudh, and Central Provinces* (1871), p. 443.

[32] Correspondence of December 19, 1871, NAI, Home, Legislative (A), May 1872, Nos. 395–444.

[33] Memorandum of August 24, 1871, ibid.

[34] Extract from the *Abstract of Legislative Proceedings* of April 2, 1872, ibid.

[35] Stephen's speech of January 2, 1872, ibid.

[36] Muir's "Minute on the Bill concerning Oaths and Affirmations," January 28, 1859, ibid.

Association condemned the inherent barbarism of these customary practices: "Swearing by one's son's head, or over a *salgaram* [a Hindu stone
idol], or by a cow, or by a particular bird, or a village god, is so rude and
barbarous that on those grounds alone it should not find a place in the laws
of a civilized nation."[37] The Bombay High Court proposed the abolition
of all oaths, affirmations, and declarations in favor of an official admonition from the judge that a false witness would be liable to punishment.
Bombay High Court Justice L. H. Bayley argued that fear of prompt
corporal punishment "at the hand of man" was more suitable to India
than fear of a perjury proceeding:

The amount of perjury committed before me week after week of the most trans-
parent character is perfectly frightful, and I doubt if anything short of a knowledge
that the Judge could then and there order his imprisonment or the administration
of fifty lashes or more with the cat-o'-nine-tails would deter a dishonest witness
from telling his falsehoods to the Court. I don't think a mere admonition to tell the
truth, in the language of the Code of 1827, would have any effect upon our
Bombay witnesses, as it is well known that prosecutions for perjury are very rare,
and that the cost, delay, and uncertainty attending them are sufficient to deter
almost everyone from instituting them.[38]

The Legislative Council ultimately determined that the colonial government could not disregard any means for getting at the truth. The
preamble to the new Indian Oaths Act (1873) explicitly noted that the
"peculiar circumstances of India" required a departure, something different, from contemporary English law: "The Indian law relating to oaths
derives its origin from the English Law with such modifications as are
rendered necessary by the peculiar circumstances of India." So long as it
was "not repugnant to justice and decency," Indian witnesses were again
permitted to swear according to their own local forms.[39]

The Indian Evidence Act

The law of oaths and the law of evidence are connected in their concern
with providing rules for the discovery of truth. Like oaths, the development of evidence law in India took its cue from contemporary developments in England, where ideas about evidence and changing standards of
proof underwent dramatic changes in the eighteenth and nineteenth
centuries. The Indian Evidence Act (1872), like the Code of Criminal
Procedure (1861) and the Indian Oaths Act (1873), was also deeply

---

[37] "The Humble Petition of the British Indian Association," February 22, 1872, BL, IOR,
L/P&J/5/15.
[38] NAI, Home, Legislative (A), May 1872, Nos. 395–444.   [39] Ibid.

influenced by the colonial context and by prevalent notions about the peculiarities of Indian culture and the idea that such circumstances required special legislation. In the case of evidence, the special circumstance was the perceived problem of Indian mendacity. Unlike the constant debate and dissent that surrounded the codification of criminal procedure, cultural stereotypes about Indian untrustworthiness, deceptiveness, and difference actually helped expedite the codification of evidence.

Prior to the passage of the Indian Evidence Act, the law of evidence in India functioned according to the dual system of justice, which found one set of laws and courts in the Presidencies and another in the *mofussil*. Whereas the Presidency courts administered English rules of evidence, the *mofussil* courts administered what Whitley Stokes described as "a vague customary law of evidence, partly drawn from the *Hedaya* [a guide to Islamic law used by colonial officials] and the Muhammedan law officers, partly drawn from English text books and the arguments of the English barristers who occasionally appeared in the provincial Courts; partly from the lectures on law delivered since 1855 in the Presidency towns."[40] Where one law of evidence ended and another began, no one could say for sure.

With neither statute books nor official law reporters, most of the untrained judicial officers in the *mofussil* were guided by textbooks written by colonial legal scholars. The most widely used text was John Bruce Norton's *The Law of Evidence Applicable to the Courts of the East India Company* (1858), which consisted of a series of law lectures given by Norton at Madras Presidency College. Also important was C. D. Field's *The Law of Evidence in British India* (1867), which advised the judicial officer dealing with evidence that, in the absence of positive rules, "natural sagacity and experience" were the best guides.[41]

In its report on evidence (1868), the third Indian Law Commission linked its legislative suggestions to the peculiar difficulties facing judicial investigations in India. First among these was the absence of a jury system. Because judges in India generally decided cases without the assistance of a jury, the Commissioners recommended a widening of admissible evidence by reasoning that it was "better to afford every facility for the admission of truth although with some risk that falsehood or error may be mixed with it, than to narrow, with a view to the exclusion of falsehood, the channels by which truth is admitted."[42] The move to expand

---

[40] W. Stokes, *The Anglo-Indian Codes: Adjective Law* (Oxford, 1888), p. 812.
[41] Field, *The Law of Evidence in British India* (1867), section 26.
[42] BL, IOR, *Fifth Report of Her Majesty's Commissioners Appointed to Prepare a Body of Substantive Law for India, &c.* (1868).

admissible evidence in India contrasted sharply with contemporary efforts in England to restrict admissible evidence by establishing exclusionary rules.

In 1754, Sir Geoffrey Gilbert published one of the most influential eighteenth-century English evidence treatises, *The Law of Evidence*, which prioritized admissible evidence according to John Locke's "best-evidence rule."[43] Gilbert carefully ordered forms of evidence into a hierarchy of trustworthiness that placed written evidence over unwritten evidence, reasoning that oral testimony was subject to failures of memory and partiality and was therefore inferior.[44] In the early nineteenth century, English legal theorists began to loosen Gilbert's mechanical system by advocating a more balanced appraisal of written and oral evidence.[45] Jeremy Bentham proposed a complete rejection of Gilbert's best-evidence rule, as well as all other exclusionary rules of evidence, emphasizing the capacity of individuals to form judgments about the truth of oral statements: "Evidence is the basis of justice: to exclude evidence is to exclude justice."[46] Consistent with his effort to establish a legal system that was easily accessible and intelligible to all, Bentham proposed a "Natural System" defined by simplicity and common sense, a system devoid of artificial rules and technicalities.

The development of English theories of evidence is associated with a variety of historical factors, the most important being the evolution of the jury system, with its emphasis on live testimony. Exclusionary rules of evidence were developed to assist an unprofessional tribunal (the jury) to sift through and interrogate a variety of evidentiary material.[47] Other significant developments affecting shifts in evidence theory include the increased involvement of trial lawyers,[48] the expansion of law reporting, and the rise of an adversarial court system.[49]

The reform of Indian evidence law occurred in tandem with English reforms, even though none of the historical factors relevant to the English

---

[43] T. P. Gallanis, "The Rise of Modern Evidence Law," *Iowa Law Review*, 84, 3 (March 1999), 499–560.

[44] Quoted in Landsman, "From Gilbert to Bentham," 1153.

[45] Gallanis, "The Rise of Modern Evidence Law."

[46] Quoted in Landsman, "From Gilbert to Bentham," 1177.

[47] J. B. Thayer, *A Preliminary Treatise on Evidence at the Common Law* (Boston, 1898); and J. H. Wigmore, *Wigmore on Evidence: A Treatise on the Anglo-American System of Evidence in Trials at Common Law* (Boston: Little Brown, 1904).

[48] J. H. Langbein, "The Criminal Trial before the Lawyers," *University of Chicago Law Review*, 45, 2 (1978), 263–316.

[49] S. Landsman, "The Rise of the Contentious Spirit: Adversary Procedure in Eighteenth-Century England," *Cornell Law Review*, 75, 3 (1990), 497–609.

experience held in the colony. In India, there was no widespread adversarial system, no general jury system, only a small professional bar, and no formal system of law reporting. Judges in India frequently played the roles of judge, jury, and counsel. In light of these and other differences, the Indian Law Commissioners decided in 1868 that the rules of evidence molded in England were unsuited to the state of society in India. They proposed a draft Evidence Bill that was extremely short, comprised of only thirty-nine short sections filling seven pages.[50]

The Law Commission's Bill met with the near-unanimous disapproval of all of the local authorities in India, who were taken aback by the proposal to place broad discretionary power in the hands of the inexperienced judicial officers who had long been the targets of criticism and embarrassment. What could an untrained judiciary, unfamiliar with the English rules of evidence, do with such a vague, incomplete, and abbreviated Bill?[51] Would they, John Bruce Norton wondered, be able to "sift the wheat from the chaff"? Norton argued that departing from the English law would lead to great expense, delay, and uncertainty, and urged the government to enact an evidence law with positive rules, "framed on the aim to show not what is not but what *is* evidence."[52]

Three years later, James Fitzjames Stephen proposed a codified law of evidence that aimed to "furnish the Judge with solid tests of truth" by stating in a positive form what sorts of facts were relevant.[53] Stephen's Bill was diametrically opposed to the negative and exclusionary system governing the admissibility of testimony in contemporary England. This was because, as Stephen put it, India's "peculiar circumstances" required special legislation.[54] In contrast to the maelstrom of controversy that for decades had surrounded the Code of Criminal Procedure, Stephen's Bill met with hardly any controversy whatsoever. As Stephen noted, this was due to an overwhelming consensus about the need for a new "engine of truth" to assist the untrained judicial officer in discriminating between fact and falsehood. Special circumstances demanded a clear, codified law that was different from the law administered in England. With almost no opposition, the Indian Evidence Act was passed on March 12, 1872.

[50] BL, IOR, *Fifth Report of Her Majesty's Commissioners Appointed to Prepare a Body of Substantive Law for India, &c.* (1868).
[51] NAI, Home, Legislative (A), May 1872, Nos. 6–130.
[52] Norton to the Chief Secretary to Government, Fort Saint George, February 19, 1868, NAI, Home, Legislative (A), May 1872, Nos. 6–130, Appendix E.
[53] Stephen's speech of March 31, 1871, NAI, *Gazette of India*, April 4, 1871.
[54] "Introduction to the Evidence Act," *The Indian Evidence Act.*

Making criminal investigation a science

Expert medical testimony, important in every country, is especially so in the East, where it is often the only trustworthy evidence on which hangs the liberty or life of a human being.

Isidore Lyon[55]

Over the course of the nineteenth century, judicial investigations in England and India aimed to be like scientific investigations, generating certain, factual knowledge under objective conditions. The goal of making criminal investigation a science afforded scientists, scientific techniques, and scientific evidence privileged status in judicial inquiries and trials. Scientific facts were brought to bear in colonial courtrooms not only in new forms of physical evidence, such as fingerprinting and photography, but also in the figure of the medico-legal expert. The legal standing and practice of experts were formally defined by the Code of Criminal Procedure (1861) and the Indian Evidence Act (1872). The former prescribed the methods for performing medico-legal work while the latter attached special value to expert evidence and testimony. Although expert testimony is found in colonial trials prior to the Indian Evidence Act, it had no unique or special legal standing.

The evolution of the expert accompanied the modernization of the judicial system and an evolving confidence in an objective reality knowable by proper observation and analysis.[56] In nineteenth-century England, as physicians became more interested in post-mortem dissections, morbid anatomy, and the physiology of death, forensic medicine took on growing significance as a method of using science to ensure reliable legal decisions.[57] The notion that scientific facts were "infinitely more trustworthy"[58] than oral evidence made the application of science to law in India especially meaningful, as it allowed investigators to locate truth in and on the body, thereby solving the perceived problem of oral testimony.

---

[55] I. B. Lyon, *Lyon's Medical Jurisprudence for India with Illustrative Cases* (10th edn, Calcutta: Thacker, Spink, 1953).

[56] See T. Golan, "The History of Scientific Expert Testimony in the English Courtroom," *Science in Context*, 12, 1 (1999), 7–32; A. Kenny, "The Expert in Court," *Law Quarterly Review*, 99 (1983), 197–216; and S. Landsman, "Of Witches, Madmen, and Products Liability: An Historical Survey of the Use of Expert Testimony," *Behavioral Science and the Law*, 13, 2 (1995), 131–158.

[57] C. Crawford, "The Emergence of English Forensic Medicine: Medical Evidence in Common-Law Courts, 1730–1830," unpublished D.Phil. thesis, University of Oxford (1987).

[58] J. Woodroffe and A. Ali, *Law of Evidence Applicable to British India* (Calcutta, 1898), p. 26.

The use of medicine in the administration of law dates back to diverse global regions, including ancient India.[59] The *Lex Salica* (486–511), one of the oldest of the Barbarian Codes, permitted medical testimony in cases of poison, injury, and rape. From the fifth to the tenth centuries, medical experts in continental Europe were commonly used by the courts to determine the severity of wounds and to aid in the assessment of monetary compensation for victims of crimes and their families. During the medieval period, continental medical doctors came to play important roles in cases involving poison, abortion, pregnancy, impotence, legitimacy, witchcraft, and wounding.[60] The criminal code of the Holy Roman Empire made medical testimony obligatory by requiring post-mortem examinations and medical opinion in cases of violent death, determination of insanity, and a variety of other criminal charges. In continental Europe, medical jurisprudence grew in accord with formal legislation and institutional opportunities, such as pay for medico-legal inquiries and formal government appointments. Paolo Zacchia, the "father of legal medicine," published his nine-volume work, *Quaestiones Medico-legales*, between 1621 and 1666. By the mid-seventeenth century, there was a steady production of medico-legal literature coming out of Italy, Germany, and France.[61]

By contrast, medical jurisprudence in England – as a field of study and practice – advanced more slowly. Although medical evidence appeared in English courtrooms as early as the fourteenth century, medical testimony was not required by law until much later, and English treatises on medical jurisprudence are scant prior to the nineteenth century.[62] One of the earlier English publications, William Hunter's "On the Uncertainty of the Signs of Murder in the Case of Bastard Children" (1783), appeared 200 years later than similar literature on the European continent. Medico-legal practice also developed more slowly in England. Autopsies, for example, were being done in Italy and Germany 500 years before medical evidence was received at the coroner's inquest in England.

Scholars attribute the divergent developmental paths of medical jurisprudence in England and the European continent to broad differences in

---

[59] J. Nemec, *Highlights in Medicolegal Relations* (Washington, DC: US Government Printing Office, 1976); and V. S. Reddy, "Side Lights on the Medicolegal Problems of the Mouryan Era," *Indian Medical Record*, 64 (1944), 97–101.

[60] T. R. Forbes, *Surgeons at the Bailey: English Forensic Medicine to 1878* (New Haven, CT: Yale University Press, 1985).

[61] J. D. J. Havard, *The Detection of Secret Homicide: A Study of the Medico-Legal System of Investigation of Sudden and Unexplained Deaths* (London: Macmillan, 1960).

[62] C. Crawford, "Legalizing Medicine: Early Modern Legal Systems and the Growth of Medico-Legal Knowledge," in M. Clark and C. Crawford (eds.), *Legal Medicine in History* (Cambridge: Cambridge University Press, 1994).

their legal systems. In early medieval Europe (including England), trials were decided by ordeal, oath, and duel. The innocence or guilt of the accused in a trial by ordeal was established by procedures that included submersion in cold water and branding with a hot iron: in the former, the innocent would be "received" by the water and would sink; in the latter, the wounds of the innocent would heal with supernatural speed. Trial by ordeal was premised on the conviction that God would intervene to visually demonstrate the truth or falsity of a charge.[63] God's judgment was deemed to be perfect and unerring, and such trials provided no opportunities for appeal. In 1215, priestly participation in trial by ordeal was banned, and new methods of proof and procedure were charged with the ambitious task of replacing the certainty of divine judgment with equally reliable human methods.

In continental Europe, trial by ordeal was succeeded by an inquisitorial method of investigation and fact-finding that featured a professional judge without a jury. The continental system emphasized the judge's capacity to decide a case based on facts and according to formalized and rational methods of proof. The emphasis on written evidence encouraged the introduction of technical treatises into the courtroom and thereby enabled the development of medico-legal literature. By contrast, the adversarial system of trial by jury in England was slow to adopt complex and scientific forms of evidence. Although medical evidence did feature in English trials prior to the widespread appearance of English textbooks, manuals, and other prescriptive rules, without a strict evidentiary distinction between facts and opinions, medical testimony was not necessarily provided by trained doctors, nor was it received as a privileged source of evidence in English courts.[64]

Medico-legal legislation in early colonial Bengal

The development of medico-legal science in India accompanied the expansion of colonial authority. In the 1790s, as the East India Company became more involved in the administration of criminal justice, medico-legal work was adopted in local police practice. Evidence for this is found in the early Bengal Regulations and in the Nizamut Adalat's Circular Orders and case law. There is also evidence of early medico-legal work in the Madras and Bombay Presidencies, although Bombay generally

---

[63] P. R. Hyams, "Trial by Ordeal: The Key to Proof in the Early Common Law," in M. S. Arnold, T. A. Green, S. A. Scully, and S. D. White (eds.), *On the Laws and Customs of England* (Chapel Hill, NC: University of North Carolina Press, 1981).

[64] Crawford, *The Emergence of English Forensic Medicine*; and Forbes, *Surgeons at the Bailey.*

adopted the medico-legal practices directed by the Bengal Nizamut Adalat.[65] These sources demonstrate that, as in England, medical evidence in India emerged as a system of practice rather than by legal requirement.[66] Medico-legal examinations were done at the summons of the magistrate or the court and were never a required part of a civil surgeon's public duties.[67]

The use of medical evidence became more clearly defined in practice over the course of the late eighteenth and early nineteenth centuries. The Charter Act 1793 empowered the Governors-General of the Presidencies to appoint coroners with the same powers held by coroners in England.[68] Bengal Regulation IV of 1797, which replaced the Islamic law of homicide, formed a kind of police code that specified methods for performing inquests upon the bodies of murdered persons. In a Circular Order issued to the lower courts in 1798, the Nizamut Adalat emphasized the inquest's "material use both in ascertaining the fact and in weighing the credibility of witnesses."[69] Around this same time, the Nizamut Adalat also began to stress the importance of medical evidence in insanity cases, requiring circuit court judges to subject prisoners showing "signs of derangement" to examination by the surgeon of the station in order to form an opinion about the prisoner's state of mind.[70]

Bengal Regulation XX of 1817 formalized the legal procedures for all police investigations requiring a civil surgeon. In cases of unnatural or suspicious deaths, the *darogah* (village constable) was instructed to examine the body of the wounded or dead person to ascertain the number, size, and location of wounds and injuries, and to note what weapons had been used.[71] After making this initial inquiry, the body was to be handed over to the deceased's relatives,

[65] See A. J. Arbuthnot, *Select Reports of Criminal Cases Determined in the Court of Foujdaree Udalut of Madras, 1826 to 1850* (Madras, 1851); C. R. Baynes, *The Criminal Law of the Madras Presidency, As Contained in the Existing Regulations and Acts with Statement of Crimes and Punishments and also Circular Orders of the Foujdaree Udalut 1805–1848* (Madras, 1848); *The Circular Orders of the Court of Foujdaree Udalut, from 1805 up to the end of 1841* (Madras, 1842); *The Circular Orders Issued by Government in the Police Branch of the Judicial Department (1852–53)* (Bombay, 1853); and *Cases Disposed of by the Sudder Foujdaree Adaulut of Bombay, 1854–1857* (Bombay, 1857).

[66] J. C. Marshman, *The Darogah's Manual* (Serampore, 1850), section XIII.

[67] D. G. Crawford, *A History of the Indian Medical Service 1600–1913* (London: W. Thacker, 1914), vol. II, p. 354. Also, *Tabu Sing v. The Empress* (1879), *Punjab Record (Criminal Judgments)*, vol. VIII, p. 16.

[68] 33 Geo. III. cap. 52, section 157. *The Statutes of the United Kingdom.*

[69] Circular Order No. 17, April 19, 1798, in Carrau, *Circular Orders.*

[70] Circular Order No. 137, August 3, 1814, in ibid.

[71] Marshman, *The Darogah's Manual*, section XIII.

except in cases of murder by poison, or on occasions where the injury sustained by the deceased may be of a doubtful nature, requiring the inspection and report of a surgeon, in which case the *Darogah* shall, if the state of the weather and the distance from the Magistrate's court will admit of the body to be transported without the risk of putrefaction on the road, forward the corpse covered with a cloth, in the most decent and expeditious manner practicable, to the Magistrate's place of residence.[72]

Although by 1840, it was general practice in cases of murder and mortal wounding to have a body inspected by the local civil surgeon, local judges were unsure how to handle medical evidence or what status to accord to it. As the Patna Circuit Judge noted in a case from 1822: "With respect to taking the examination of the Surgeon on oath as to his opinion regarding the appearance of bodies supposed to have died a violent death, I have only to observe, that during the course of six years that I have officiated in the Court of Circuit, I have never received any instructions on the subject."[73] A proper "death investigation machinery"[74] and the status of expert testimony were not formalized until the passage of the Coroner's Act in 1871 and the Indian Evidence Act in 1872. In the absence of prescriptive legislation, questions about the status and nature of medical evidence were adjudicated in court.

Medical evidence in the Nizamut Adalat

The Nizamut Adalat case law (1805–1859) demonstrates that medical evidence played an ambiguous and uncertain role in colonial criminal trials in the first half of the nineteenth century. Medical evidence was not necessarily received as a superior brand of evidence, nor was it always presented by a medical officer. The Nizamut administered the Islamic criminal law (until 1861) and the Islamic law of evidence (until 1855), which emphasized direct proof (such as confessions and eye-witness testimony) and evidence of intention. Within the Islamic evidentiary system, physical evidence was not in and of itself sufficient to convict, and no special status was accorded to the opinions of experts.[75] In fact, murder convictions could be established in the Nizamut without the discovery of a corpse, which speaks to the relative unimportance of

---

[72] Regulation XX of 1817, section 14, clause 12.
[73] *Ramdial Bukkal against Musst. Ludroun* (1822), *Nizamut Adalat Reports*, vol. I, pp. 213–216.
[74] The phrase is A. S. Taylor's, *The Principles and Practice of Medical Jurisprudence* (London, 1865).
[75] *Manika against Begaroo* (1830), *Nizamut Adalat Reports*, vol. III, pp. 329–331; and *Government against Ryan* (1832), *Nizamut Adalat Reports*, vol. IV, pp. 140–142.

physical proof under the Islamic law.[76] Medical evidence appeared most frequently in cases of poisoning, rape, murder, and insanity. In all of these crimes (except insanity trials, which will not be examined here), its status was unstable and for the most part not critical to legal decision-making.

Poisoning did not much interest colonial administrators until the late 1840s, when the crime of *thagi* (collective murder and robbery) was expanded to include professional poisoners.[77] While medico-legal work would later become centrally focused on the crime of poisoning, in the first half of the nineteenth century, poisoning was not a very common charge. Official concern with poisoning in India coincided with the growing fascination with and fear of this "secret crime" in Victorian England.[78]

The significance and judicial value of medical evidence in early colonial poisoning cases varied greatly. By and large, medical evidence tended to be received on equal terms with non-expert testimony and did not play a predictable role in determining trial outcomes. In some instances it definitively established the guilt or innocence of the accused and in others it was disregarded completely. In *Vakeel of Government against Mussummaut Hooleea and Bhidea* (1815), the court relied entirely on medical evidence in acquitting Mussummaut Hooleea, who had confessed to poisoning her husband. Although no inquest was done on the body, when a "suspicious yellow substance" discovered on her clothing was found by the Medical Board to be sulfur, which is not a poison, Hooleea was acquitted.[79] At the opposite end of the spectrum is *Vakeel of Government against Mussummaut Sookhoo* (1810), where the medical testimony was totally dismissed. Mussummaut Sookhoo was charged with poisoning her boyfriend's father with *dhuttora* (a powdered form of thornapple, a medicinal plant). At trial, a native doctor named Syed Sulamut Aly who analyzed the potency of *dhuttora* found that it would not cause death. The law officers disregarded Aly's testimony and that of the British civil surgeon in finding that *dhuttora* was a potentially lethal drug and sentencing Sookhoo to life in prison.[80]

---

[76] *Government against Fukeerchund Mundul* (1832), *Nizamut Adalat Reports*, vol. IV, pp. 148–150; *Bungsee Maloo against Ruggoo Pal* (1832), *Nizamut Adalat Reports*, vol. IV, pp. 164–166; *Suttroo Mullick against Musst. Kunchunnee* (1834), *Nizamut Adalat Reports*, vol. IV, pp. 327–328; *Anund Mundul* v. *Thakoor Doss Chuckerbuttee, Cartick Khan, and Gunesh Mundul* (1839), *Nizamut Adalat Reports*, vol. V, pp. 147–150; and *Sadee* v. *Bajeed Sheikh* (1840), *Nizamut Adalat Reports*, vol. V, pp. 172–173.

[77] R. Singha, "Providential Circumstances: The Thuggee Campaign of the 1830s and Legal Innovation," *Modern Asian Studies*, 27, 1 (1993), 83–146.

[78] I. Burney, *Bodies of Evidence: Medicine and the Politics of the English Inquest, 1826–1930* (Baltimore: Johns Hopkins University Press, 2000); and I. Burney, *Poison, Detection and the Victorian Imagination* (Manchester: Manchester University Press, 2007).

[79] *Nizamut Adalat Reports*, vol. I, pp. 307–308.   [80] Ibid., pp. 216–218.

In rape cases, medical evidence also played an ambiguous role, particularly in the early period. By the 1850s, the search for physical facts had become more consequential to trial outcomes, and if a doctor found no bodily evidence of assault, a victim's testimony could be dismissed altogether. In *Government* v. *Azeez-oo-Rahaman* (1851), a family of three attended defendant Azeez-oo-Rahaman's house for dinner. During the course of the evening, the mother of the invited family found her daughter crying on a bed in the inner verandah of the house. When they returned home, the girl claimed that Azeez-oo-Rahaman had raped her. Finding blood on her child, the girl's mother immediately filed a charge at the *thana*. The following day, the girl was taken to the sub-assistant surgeon for examination who testified during the trial that the girl had been "recently violated." The judges described the medical testimony as being of the "utmost importance" and convicted the defendant.[81]

By constrast, in *Phelanee Bewah* v. *Fuqueerah Nusha* (1852), a 7-year-old girl charged that her neighbor had raped her. Eleven days later, when a medical officer examined her, he found no marks of violence, no rupture of her hymen, and no swelling. Citing the absence of affirmative medical evidence, the court acquitted the defendant.[82] That same year, in *Government* v. *Azim Kaneegur, Moniroodin Sheikh, and Doogoo Sheikh* (1852), a 14-year-old girl alleged that she had been gang-raped by the three defendants. As no physical examination was performed, and because the only direct proof was the girl's testimony, the judges concluded that the evidence to convict was presumptive, and the defendants were acquitted.[83]

The increasing emphasis on medical evidence in rape trials grew out of an English legal tradition that was skeptical of rape victims, as well as out of a profound colonial distrust of native female testimony. However, the emphasis on "the body evidencing the crime" failed to consider the structural and cultural obstacles that stood in the way of an Indian rape victim's ability and willingness to submit to a medical examination. As I have demonstrated elsewhere, this resulted in a decreasing rate of criminal conviction over the course of the nineteenth century.[84]

Murder is by far the most common criminal charge reported in the Nizamut Adalat's records. Even when compelling, medical evidence in murder trials played an unpredictable role in determining trial outcomes. At times, it was the lynchpin around which guilt or innocence in a case revolved. At other times, it was entirely inconsequential to the court's verdict. It would be a stretch to refer to scientific testimony about the

[81] *Nizamut Adalat Reports*, vol. I.   [82] *Nizamut Adalat Reports*, vol. II.
[83] *Nizamut Adalat Reports*, vol. II.   [84] Kolsky, "'The Body Evidencing the Crime.'"

appearance of corpses, wounds, and external marks of violence as "expert" testimony, as it was commonly provided by both laypersons and trained medical personnel.

Under Islamic evidentiary rules, a causal link had to be proven between death, the instrument of death, and intent to kill. Medical evidence appeared in Nizamut murder cases in the form of depositions, live testimony, and inquest reports. Inquests in cases of murder were requested by the Nizamut Adalat beginning in 1798, though there are surprisingly few recorded mentions of inquests being held on dead bodies, especially in the first quarter of the nineteenth century. When the inquest report was received in evidence, it primarily served to attest to marks of violence upon the body rather than to confirm causal links between those marks and the death of a victim. In *Vakeel of Government against Sonaram* (1805), the prisoner was charged with murdering his wife by hitting her on the head with the handle of a hatchet. The inquest report, which stated that "she had received a severe contusion and wound on the back of the head," was received by the court as an ordinary piece of evidence and was not accorded any special status.[85]

In *Anoop against Muthoo* (1805), the court specifically found that an inquest was "not full legal proof." Muthoo was charged with murdering his mother-in-law, Anopa. Muthoo admitted to striking Anopa twice with his sword, and witnesses in the street also gave direct testimony about the beating, from which Anopa died two days later. An inquest performed on Anopa's body certified the appearance of two wounds. However, the law officers refused to view the inquest as documentation of anything more than the presence of wounds, denying any causal link between the wounds and the fact of her death. Although it was determined that Anopa died of her wounds, the eye-witness testimony and the inquest were disregarded. Muthoo was acquitted.[86]

In the 1830s, there was a distinct shift in the way medical testimony was received in murder trials. During this time, medical doctors and police personnel began to be more detailed and exacting in their depositions and descriptions of wounds, corpses, crime scenes, and weapons. This shift correlates to the declining status of the Islamic criminal law and the status of the Islamic law officers. As the law officers played a less important role in sifting through and assigning value to evidence, medical testimony grew in importance.

Take, for example, *Musst. Sheeta against Shumsooddeen* (1838). The deceased in the case, Beeshye (Sheeta's husband) returned from his

[85] *Nizamut Adalat Reports*, vol. I, pp. 5–6.   [86] Ibid., pp. 46–47.

paddy with wounds on his head and neck. After a report was made at the *thana*, Beeshye went to the hospital. He died shortly thereafter. Dr. Sealy, the civil surgeon, testified that Beeshye had severe and dangerous wounds, one of which was 1 foot long and extended from his right cheekbone to the vertebrae of his neck, dividing the ear. Sealy concluded that Beeshye died of fever caused by the wounds, which were inflicted by a sharp, cutting instrument like a *dao* (sword). Citing the medical testimony, the defendant was sentenced to death.[87] The physical evidence was similarly decisive in *Omed Ally* v. *Ashoory Akhoond* (1840), where the defendant was tried for the murder of his father-in-law and stepmother (Nooree). The wounds on the stepmother's body were described in great detail by the police inquest:

One wound on the right arm, 9 fingers in length, 2 ½ in breadth, and 1 ½ in depth, and to have been cut to the bone; another wound above it, 6 fingers long, 1 broad and deep; a wound on the neck under the left ear, 3 fingers long, ½ broad, and about the depth of a grain of corn; a wound under the left shoulder, 2 ½ fingers long, ½ finger broad and deep; one wound extending from the back of the neck across the left shoulder blade, one span long, about 3 fingers in breadth towards the middle, and about 2 fingers at each end cut to the bone; and the fingers of both hands slightly cut in several places.

In its decision, the court paid especially close attention to these details and to the testimony of the assistant surgeon, who concluded that Nooree unquestionably died from her wounds. Ashoory Akhoond was convicted and sentenced to death.[88]

By the 1840s, medical testimony and post-mortem examinations appeared in almost all murder and wounding cases in the Nizamut Adalat. The general practice was to hold an inquest at the local level and then to send the body for examination and report to the civil surgeon. In *Musst. Sookree* v. *Boodhun Bhooya* (1849), an inquest and a post-mortem examination were presented in the trial of a man who had butchered his wife (Jhonia). The civil assistant surgeon described the horrific nature of Jhonie's mortal wounds: "the vertebrae were entirely severed, including the spinal marrow; and the knife, which was still in the body when it reached the hospital, had penetrated so deeply into her side that it was with difficulty he could extract it." Relying on the surgeon's deposition, the court sentenced Boodhun Bhooya to death.[89]

There are two general conclusions that can be drawn from this brief analysis of select criminal cases in the Nizamut Adalat (1805–1859). First, it is clear that medical experts were involved in the administration of

---

[87] *Nizamut Adalat Reports*, vol. V, pp. 98–99.   [88] Ibid. pp. 197–205.
[89] *Nizamut Adalat Reports*, vol. VI, pp. 163–165.

criminal justice in India prior to the appearance of instructive treatises or prescriptive statutes defining their practice and legal status. As in England, colonial doctors and magistrates in India were *doing* medico-legal work before the rules and regulations organizing the practice were formally established. Second, medical testimony played an uncertain role in determining trial outcomes and was mainly relevant to the extent that it fulfilled the Islamic requirement of direct proof. As the role of the Islamic law officers declined, the emphasis on physical facts increased, and medical evidence became more important at trial. Around this same time, didactic manuals and textbooks on "Indian medical jurisprudence" began to provide physicians with practical guidance on how to gather medical evidence so it could be legally submitted in a court of law.

"Indian medical jurisprudence": a new form of colonial knowledge

The first and most important published work on medical jurisprudence in India was Dr. Norman Chevers' pioneering article, "Report on Medical Jurisprudence in the Bengal Presidency," which appeared in the *Indian Annals of Medical Science* in 1854.[90] Two years later, a revised version of the article was published as a book, *A Manual of Medical Jurisprudence for Bengal and the North-Western Provinces*.[91] The book became an instant classic. Within ten years, Chevers' text was in its third edition and was deemed by the editors of the *Indian Medical Gazette* to be "essential" for all civil surgeons.[92]

Chevers framed his book as a supplement to the work of Dr. Alfred Swaine Taylor, whose *Elements of Medical Jurisprudence* (1836) and *Principles and Practice of Medical Jurisprudence* (1865) were the contemporary English standards. Viewed side by side, the texts of Taylor and Chevers demonstrate the bending of universal concepts around the specificities of cultural otherness. Whereas Taylor's book opens with an overview of the general history of medial jurisprudence, Chevers begins with introductory remarks on the "Criminal Characteristics of the People of India." While Taylor's book is cast in neutral terms as "a practical guide for the Medical

---

[90] N. Chevers, "Report on Medical Jurisprudence in the Bengal Presidency," *Indian Annals of Medical Science*, 3 (October, 1854), 243–426.

[91] N. Chevers, *A Manual of Medical Jurisprudence for Bengal and the North-Western Provinces* (Calcutta, 1856).

[92] "New Edition of Dr. Chevers' Medical Jurisprudence for India," *The Indian Medical Gazette*, 3 (1868), p. 157. The third edition of Chevers' work is titled *A Manual of Medical Jurisprudence for India, Including an Outline of a History of Crime against the Person in India* (Calcutta, 1870).

Jurist," Chevers' is squarely located within the domain of Indian culture, advising the medical practitioner to "possess an intimate acquaintance with the dispositions, customs, prejudices, and crimes of the people among whom his investigations are to be pursued." Taylor's book is not illustrated; Chevers' cover page displays a drawing of "Sacrificial Instruments used in the murder of a child in a temple at Jessore."[93] In fact, Chevers explicitly locates Taylor's text as the universal pivot point against which Indian peculiarity and dissimilarity are measured in his own work (see Figure 3.1).[94]

By wrapping the field of Indian medical jurisprudence around the concept of Indian difference, Chevers established legal medicine in India as a form of colonial knowledge. What made Chevers' "Indian medical jurisprudence" distinct from Taylor's "medical jurisprudence" was that Indian medical jurisprudence was constituted as a way of "thoroughly knowing the people." Chevers proposed that medico-legal knowledge could provide an "insight into the deeper and darker recesses of the Bengalee and Hindustanee nature" and promised that "by fixing the mind sedulously upon the records of their crimes, an European can learn how strange a combination of sensuality, jealousy, wild and ineradicable superstition, absolute untruthfulness, and ruthless disregard of the value of human life lie below the placid, civil, timid, forbearing exterior of the native of India."[95] Chevers tied his work to the imperial project of "advancing the progress of civilization" by offering a means of "enabling us to detect and grapple with those deeply-rooted errors in the native character which now, in eluding our notice, most effectually baffle our best laid scheme for improvement."[96] Reading Chevers' 861-page text, one gets an acute sense of the desperate desire of colonial authorities to know and control their wily and irascible Indian subjects.

For Chevers, the medico-legal investigation was a cultural event. His text abounds in ethnographic observations about "these ingenious, calm-tempered, indolently pertinacious sensualists," the "Criminal Characteristics of the People of India," the "Uncertainty of General Evidence in India," the untrustworthiness of the Indian police, the tendency towards "fraudulent impersonation," and customary modes of killing. As Chevers writes: "The Hindustanee usually strikes with the sword (*tulwar*) or iron-bound cudgel (*lohar ki latthee*)." The Bengali's "readiest weapons," he notes, are "the *dhao* (bill-hook) and the bamboo (*bans ki latthee*)."[97] "Sexual jealousy is the most frequent cause of homicide among the

---

[93] Chevers, *Manual of Medical Jurisprudence for India*.   [94] Chevers, "Report," p. 243.
[95] Chevers, *Manual of Medical Jurisprudence for India*, p. 8.
[96] Ibid., p. 13.   [97] Ibid., p. 8.

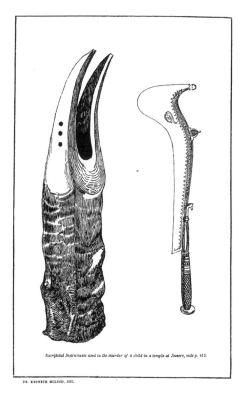

Figure 3.1 **Sacrificial instruments used in the murder of a child in a temple at Jessore**

This illustration appears on the cover page of Norman Chevers' *A Manual of Medical Jurisprudence for Bengal and the North-Western Provinces* (Calcutta, 1856) and signals the ethnographic origins of medico-legal work in colonial India. Colonial administrators consistently expressed their concern about the untrustworthiness of Indian witnesses. Medical evidence in the Indian context was meant to circumvent this crisis of oral testimony by providing the courts with a rational and objective form of proof. However, the search for a new way of getting to the truth about India produced yet another form of colonial knowledge steeped in the subjective preoccupations of its foreign practitioners.

Mussulmauns; Criminal Abortion and Child Murder are rifest among the unhappy class of Hindu widows."[98] Needless to say, none of these observations are scientific.

[98] Chevers, "Report," p. 250.

The marriage of ethnology and technology in the administration of criminal justice was not unique to the developing field of medical juris-prudence. In the 1860s and 1870s, colonial administrators experimented with photography as a technology of criminal identification. Photographs of life- or long-term convicts were accompanied by measurements and notes recording their caste, tribe, and place of birth. These were regarded by the government as "valuable from an ethnological point of view."[99] In 1876, when it was determined that convict photographs did little to assist the authorities in recapturing escaped prisoners, the Government of India opted to leave the system in place for another year, reasoning that "the photographs will have great ethnological value anyway."[100] The colonial jails themselves were viewed as ethnological research sites. As Donald Lambert observed in his practical manual, *The Medico-Legal Post-Mortem in India* (1937): "The local jail can usually provide living examples of the principal tribes round about, and a study of these can supplement the study of books."[101]

Late nineteenth-century European imperialists prided themselves on their scientific superiority and achievements, using science as the "meas-ure of men" to condemn the superstition and barbarity of colonized people.[102] As David Arnold argues, however, despite their claims to objectivity, "European medical attitudes often remained highly subjec-tive, embodying the social and cultural prejudices of the age."[103] It is not surprising that Norman Chevers' scientific observations were unscientific or that Indian medical jurisprudence developed in the ethnographic mode, as this was the lens through which nineteenth-century British scientists looked at India. Cultural assumptions about Indian mendacity were what made medical jurisprudence so appealing to colonial admin-istrators to begin with. As the editors of the *Madras Quarterly Journal of Medicine* observed in 1862:

In a country situated as India is, where all the cunning of a native mind is but too often directed to the criminal destruction of life; where violation of young girls, and murder by subtle poisons or by open violence are matters of daily

[99] Government of India to the Government of Madras, NAI, Home, Port Blair, February 1876, Nos. 5–13. Also see C. Anderson, *Legible Bodies: Race, Criminality and Colonialism in South Asia* (Oxford, New York: Berg, 2004).

[100] Inspector General of Jails Bowie, Lower Provinces, to the Government of Bengal (Judicial), April 29, 1876, NAI, Home, Port Blair, July 1876, Nos. 20–25.

[101] D. Lambert, *The Medico-Legal Post-Mortem in India* (London: J. & A. Churchill, 1937), p. 27

[102] M. Adas, *Machines as the Measure of Men: Science, Technology, and Ideologies of Western Dominance* (Ithaca: Cornell University Press, 1989).

[103] D. Arnold, *Imperial Medicine and Indigenous Societies* (Manchester: Manchester University Press, 1989), p. 7.

investigation; it is essentially necessary that we should be made aware of the most scientific method of investigating the medical and general evidence of a crime.[104]

The medico-legal literature that followed Chevers' work reflected these same subjective prejudices and cultural assumptions. In 1876, Robert Harvey published his *Report on the Medico-Legal Returns*, which aimed to provide "broad and general indications of the topography of Indian crime" and encouraged civil surgeons to record the tribe, class, and occupation of bodies, "as well as the bare division into Hindoos and Mussalmans."[105] In a book review of J. D. B. Gribble's *Outlines of Medical Jurisprudence for India* (1885), the *Indian Medical Gazette* called its "most useful feature...the information which it contains regarding criminal practices and criminal trials in India."[106]

In 1888, a new text supplanted Chevers' as the standard medico-legal authority in India. Described by its author as a concise manual "specially adapted for use in India," Isidore B. Lyon's *Medical Jurisprudence for India with Illustrative Cases* (1888) became the standby of civil surgeons in the *mofussil*. In twenty-five years, the book went through six editions. The *Indian Medical Gazette* judged the book's utility by testing for references to peculiar subjects unique to India, such as "infanticide, cattle poisoning, thuggee, burial alive, imputed wounds, snake-bite, rape of infants, mechanical abortion, &c., &c."[107] As in Chevers, ethnographic musings on the peculiarities of Indian society are copious in Lyon's text. Insisting that differences in race, class, sex, and religion could be determined scientifically, Lyon writes at great length about "the data supplied by the body" – "A comparatively fair-skinned body of an Indian is that of a Northerner; one of very dark complexion may be a Southern Indian"; "Indians, as a rule, are dark-eyed"; "It is possible to differentiate Oriental from European skeletons by means of peculiarities in the vertebral column, pelvis, and lower extremities, the result of changes in the bones brought about by the different modes of sitting. The European uses a chair; the majority of Orientals squat either cross-legged or on their heels."[108]

Lyon expounds upon the cultural and physical obstacles obstructing the medical jurist's pursuit of truth. These include the hot climate, which caused corpses to rapidly decompose, and the wild terrain, which provided

---

[104] *Madras Quarterly Journal of Medicine*, 5 (1862), 157.
[105] R. Harvey, *Report on the Medico-Legal Returns, Received from the Civil Surgeons in the Bengal Presidency during the Years 1870, 1871, and 1872* (Calcutta, 1876), pp. 4–5.
[106] Book review of J. D. B. Gribble, *Outlines of Medical Jurisprudence for Indian Criminal Courts* (Madras, 1885), *Indian Medical Gazette*, 26 (1891), 123.
[107] *Indian Medical Gazette*, April 1889, 128.
[108] Lyon, *Lyon's Medical Jurisprudence*, pp. 91–92.

opportunities for the concealment of dead bodies. He also addresses the long-standing colonial concern with sifting truth from falsehood:

Evidence in India is known to be very untrustworthy. In nearly every case in law, more or less false evidence is given, whether it be from fear, stupidity, apathy, malice, or deceit. It is referred to by the Privy Council as "the lamentable disregard for truth prevailing amongst the natives of India." As regards Bengal, an Inspector-General of Police once stated that this "is a country where perjury is the rule and not the exception, where no man will tell the whole truth or the simple truth... where false witnesses can be bought for a few annas." The constant difficulty, therefore, is to sift the truth from the falsehood.[109]

Prior to the passage of the Indian Evidence Act (1872), the colonial courts did not formally accord special status to the evidence of experts. In 1869, the Calcutta High Court decided that "The evidence of a medical man, or other skilled witness, however eminent...is ordinarily a mere matter of opinion."[110] Three years later, however, an expert clause was included in the Indian Evidence Act. Section 45 provided that: "When the Court has to form an opinion upon a point of foreign law or of science or art, or as to identity of handwriting, the opinions upon that point of persons specially skilled in such foreign law, science or art are relevant facts. Such persons are called experts." Whereas ordinary witnesses were strictly permitted to testify to facts personally seen or perceived, an expert witness could testify to both facts personally observed and opinions deduced on the basis of expert knowledge.[111] The law accorded the testimony of the expert with privileged truth-value even though it did not clearly delimit the scope of expertise. Thus whether an expert testified to the width of a wound or the untrustworthiness of native evidence, both opinions were received in court as expert opinions.

By the 1890s, medico-legal work was a constant, though not specially remunerated, component of the civil surgeon's duties in India.[112] In addition to textbooks of medical jurisprudence, serialized articles began to appear in the *Indian Medical Gazette*, allowing for local civil surgeons to share the results of their practical experience with others in the profession. As the *Indian Medical Gazette* pointed out, the working conditions were still woefully inadequate, "the so-called mortuary usually consists of an ordinary hut with mud-walls and mud floor containing generally a dilapidated wooden table and no other appliances." Bodies were often sent to headquarter stations for post-mortems from up to 100 miles away, and

---

[109] Ibid., pp. 24–25.
[110] *Queen v. Ahmad Ally and others*, *Sutherland's Weekly Reporter*, vol. III, p. 25.
[111] *The Indian Evidence Act*, sections 45–51.
[112] "The Coroner in the Mofassal," *Indian Medical Gazette*, October 1899, 362–364.

doctors frequently complained that the bodies did not arrive "fresh," making for "disgusting work," if not "the most loathsome duty that falls to a European in this country."[113]

White violence, medical experts, and the vulnerable Indian body

Asiatics are subject to internal disease which often renders fatal to life even a slight external shock.

Viceroy Lytton[114]

Operating at the crossroads of medicine and anthropology, "Indian medical jurisprudence" was framed by a scientific method and an ethnographic imagination. By "making a mute piece of physical evidence reveal additional facts,"[115] medical experts offered the colonial state a more reliable brand of testimony, relieving its investigative machinery from dependence on the oral testimony of a people perceived to be morally defective and pathologically untrustworthy. With the enactment of the Indian Evidence Act (1872), colonial ideas about the peculiarities of Indian people, bodies, and culture could be expressed in a scientific discourse that was accorded a privileged truth-value in court.

A survey of the ethnographic classifications served up by colonial manuals of Indian medical jurisprudence is of little value in and of itself. On their own, these texts do little more than show that colonial medicine reflected contemporary social and cultural prejudices and practices. It is important, therefore, to demonstrate how the ethnographic lens through which medical experts observed India had an impact on case law. Indian medical jurisprudence not only served the colonial state's interest in circumventing oral testimony, it also came to play a central role in mitigating European criminal culpability in murder trials.

One Sunday morning in 1875, an English barrister in Agra named Fuller was preparing to drive to church with his family. Fuller summoned his groom, Katwaree, for assistance. When the groom failed to appear immediately, Fuller slapped him across the head and face and pulled him by the hair, causing Katwaree to fall to the ground. When Fuller returned from church, Katwaree was dead. The European medical officer who conducted the post-mortem later testified in court that Katwaree died from rupture of the spleen, "which very slight violence, either from a blow

---

[113] "Medico-Legal Work of Civil Surgeons," ibid., November 1895, 433–435.
[114] Lord Lytton's "Fuller Minute," in R. G. Sanyal, *History of Celebrated Criminal Cases and Resolutions* (Calcutta, 1888), p. 18.
[115] A. C. Bose, *A Handbook of Criminology* (Calcutta: Sri Gouranga Press, 1960).

or a fall would be sufficient to cause." As a result, Fuller was convicted of voluntarily causing wounding and fined 30 rupees by a magistrate named Leeds. When the Allahabad High Court declined to review the decision, Viceroy Lytton publicly condemned the case as "injurious to the honour of British rule and damaging to the reputation of British Justice in this country."[116] A storm of public controversy erupted, and in non-official circles a catchy little ditty circulated about the incident that expressed contempt for the Viceroy's interference: "Robert Lord Lytton / Had little to sit on, / Being slender of body and limb, / Till he heard of the deeds / Of the lenient Leeds, / And proceeded to sit upon him."[117]

In the late nineteenth century, British criminals like Fuller were routinely relieved of the capital consequences of a murder charge by a diminished-responsibility defense that made death an accident or attributed the cause of death to internal, rather than external, causes. In trials of Britons who killed Indians by striking them with sticks, bricks, whips, and kicks, medical evidence was often presented by colonial doctors to support the claim that Indians had weak insides and were therefore more susceptible to such blows. In a notorious case from Mysore, a coffee planter named De Winton gave his cook a "box in the ear" and a few kicks, after which he was "unable to pass water naturally."[118] The cook, who the defense alleged was already "suffering from a malady," died several weeks later. Although De Winton was charged with culpable homicide not amounting to murder, the court convicted De Winton of the even lesser crime of simple hurt and sentenced him to one month's imprisonment.[119] The De Winton verdict infuriated the editors of the pro-planter *Madras Mail*, who reminded their readers that the frail and childlike constitutions of Indian bodies required paternalistic restraint from European managers:

Englishmen ought to refrain from striking natives much on the same principle that would restrain them from aiming a blow at a cripple. Added to this the knowledge that the average constitution of natives does not fit them for rough treatment, which among English boys at school, and even among adults in certain classes, is taken as a matter of course, should make Europeans scrupulous beyond measure in their treatment of natives.[120]

The "diseased spleen" was an especially popular defense that effectively exonerated Britons from legal responsibility by asserting that a man could not be held liable for the death of another whose body, unbeknownst to

---

[116] Sanyal, *History of Celebrated Criminal Cases*, p. 17.
[117] D. Kincaid, *British Social Life in India, 1608–1937* (London: George Routledge and Sons, 1938), p. 212.
[118] BL, IOR, L/PJ/6/74, File 803.   [119] *Madras Mail*, February 14, 1882.   [120] Ibid.

him, was in an internally (and therefore hidden) state of disease and decay. In 1882, Mr. Fox was charged with striking and killing his *punkhawallah*. The medical evidence concluded that the *punkhawallah* had an enlarged spleen, and that he would not have died had he been healthy. Fox was charged with one month's rigorous imprisonment and a fine of 200 rupees.[121] Three years later, Mr. Glover was charged with killing his coolie in Dacca. The European doctor who examined the corpse testified that the coolie's death was caused by the rupture of his spleen following a heavy fall. Several eye-witnesses testified that the dead man fell on a piece of iron only after Glover repeatedly kicked him in the back. Glover was acquitted of murder and fined 200 rupees in connection with the man's death. Commenting on the case, *Navavibhakar*, a native newspaper, suggested that European juries should be instructed: "(1) that the spleen is not so fragile as it is supposed to be by Englishmen; (2) that the spleen and arteries are ruptured because the blows of Englishmen fall upon them with the force of thunder."[122]

In 1893, Private John Rigby was tried in connection with the death of a *punkhawallah*. The *punkhawallah* apparently fell asleep at his post, which infuriated Rigby and caused him to jump out of bed and "give him one or more blows on the body." The medical evidence presented in court "showed that the cause of death was rupture of the spleen, which was in such a state that the slightest blow might have broken it, and there were no external marks of violence." Rigby was convicted of voluntarily causing hurt and sentenced to pay a 100-rupee fine, which was awarded as compensation to the relative of the deceased. The weakness of the body – not the strength of the attack – was determined to be the cause of the man's sudden death (see Figure 3.2).[123]

Viceroy Curzon described the spleen defense as "an Indian classic." Commenting on a case where a British official was fined 100 rupees for kicking a coolie who later died, Viceroy Curzon sarcastically remarked, "Of course he had a big liver or a big spleen; and equally of course the kick was represented as a 'push with the foot' – the phrase is now an Indian classic."[124] The vulnerable Indian spleen could even rupture owing to violence directed at other body parts. In 1903, a Briton named Corbett was sentenced to fourteen days in jail for killing his servant. Corbett's defense was that the servant's spleen had ruptured after he slapped him in the face.[125]

---

[121] Ibid.   [122] *Navavibhakar, February 23, 1885*, BL, IOR, L/R/5/11.
[123] BL, IOR, L/PJ/6/360, File 2170.
[124] Curzon to Hamilton, November 5, 1902, BL, IOR, Mss Eur/F111/162.
[125] *Bengalee*, February 27, 1903; *Ananda Bazar Patrika*, February 27, 1903; *Basumati*, March 7, 1903; *Bangavasi*, March 7, 1903; *Samay*, March 13, 1903, BL, IOR, L/R/5/29.

Figure 3.2 **British doctor in India indicating the size of a
young child's spleen enlarged by malaria, c. 1929**
The "diseased-spleen defense" was a common and successful plea made in
the late nineteenth century by Europeans accused of murdering Indians.
The general argument went that a European who beat an Indian could not
be held liable for his death if the man's body was in an unknown state of
disease and decay (in this case, suffering from an enlarged spleen). An
enlarged spleen is, in fact, a medical condition that can result from malaria.
This photograph of a British doctor in India examining the body of a child
with an enlarged spleen makes the spleen defense even more ludicrous. As
unlikely as it is that so many Indians died from rupture of the spleen after
being flogged by Europeans, given what is shown in this image, it is hard to
believe that one could not notice the diseased state of the body.

In a particularly infamous case from 1903, Mr. Bain, the Assistant
Manager of the Kumbirgram Tea Estate in Assam, was tried in connection with the death of a tea worker.[126] The dead man, Lalsu, along
with his wife and niece, were contract laborers who had been caught
"absconding," as it was called, from the tea plantation. When the three
were returned to Kumbirgram, Bain tied up Lalsu and beat him with a
stirrup leather until he fell unconscious and soon died. Charged with

---

[126] NAI, Home/Public (A)/April 1903/261–271; NAI, Home/Public (A)/July 1903/51–65;
BL, IOR, L/PJ/6/630, File 603; and BL, IOR, L/PJ/6/630, File 609.

culpable homicide and causing grievous hurt, Bain was tried before a jury of fellow planters at the Silchar Sessions Court. Despite the extensive eye-witness testimony of the many tea workers who saw Lalsu's beating and subsequent death, it was the medical evidence of Dr. Candler, a social acquaintance of Bain's, that proved pivotal to the verdict. Dr. Candler testified that the marks discovered the following morning all over Lalsu's back, shoulders, buttocks, heels, and legs were caused by cadaverous lividity and that although Lalsu appeared well outwardly, prior to his death he was in "weak health" and suffered from heart and lung disease. The jury concluded that Bain could not be held criminally liable for Lalsu's death, as he did not know about his poor health. Bain was acquitted of the more serious charge of homicide and convicted of simple hurt, for which he was sentenced to six months of simple imprisonment.

The Bain case caused a huge public uproar in Calcutta that reverberated across India. The Indian press was outraged by the verdict, symbolic as it was of the general trend of acquittals in cases involving violent European offenders. The editors of the *Bengalee* observed: "If the white man has his 'burden' so has he his privileges. One of the latter is that when he is found guilty of causing the death of a poor Indian, he is either let off scot-free or is sentenced to simple imprisonment."[127] The *People and Prativasi* bitterly remarked, "The result of cases like that of Mr. Bain must make us abandon hope. The justice of our Law Courts is not the sort of justice that people look for."[128] Another paper, *Surodaya Prakasika*, noted that the same punishment had recently been inflicted on an Indian clerk whose only offense was that a deficit of 1 rupee had been discovered found in the accounts.[129]

The European planters and their supporters in Calcutta were incensed by the Government of India's subsequent effort to have Bain's punishment enhanced and established the "Bain Fund" to contribute to his defense. J. Arthur Bain sent a letter condemning the harshness of his brother's sentence for a simple assault on a coolie "who looked strong but was in reality in extremely weak condition."[130] When the Calcutta High Court refused to retry the case, the Secretary of State lamented in a private letter to Lord Curzon: "It is these things that make me so pessimistic about India's future. We cannot ultimately hold the country with the assent of the better class of Natives if these miscarriages of justice are to be associated with our rule. Popular we can never be, but if we lose our reputation for justice, the foundation of our prestige is gone."[131]

---

[127] *Bengalee*, February 28, 1903, BL, IOR, L/R/5/29.
[128] *People and Prativasi*, September 3, 1903, ibid.
[129] *Surodaya Prakasika*, March 11, 1901, BL, IOR, L/R/5/111.
[130] BL, IOR, L/PJ/6/630, File 609.   [131] BL, IOR, Mss Eur/F111/162.

In the late nineteenth and twentieth centuries, the problem of white violence and the miscarriages of justice associated with trials of Europeans accused of brutalizing natives were increasingly reported on by a host of vernacular and English-language newspapers. Prejudicial medico-legal evidence, and the diseased-spleen defense in particular, were frequently singled out by critics for tilting the scales of justice in the white man's favor. In 1903, one journalist sardonically offered

an infallible remedy for spleen disease…(1) Shoe powder, 5 *tolas*. The shoe must be the shoe of the left foot and must belong only to someone among the British Privates who, while out on a shooting excursion, mistake human beings for bears, wild boars, young birds or birds' eggs or insects. (2) Ashes derived from burning the blows dealt with the muskets held high in the rights hands of those Privates, 5 *tolas*.[132]

One of the first Indian cartoons to make a major political impact appeared in *Sulabh Samachar* in 1870.[133] The cartoon depicted a European doctor conducting a perfunctory post-mortem examination on the body of a dead laborer. In the background, the accused European stands nonchalantly smoking a cigar. This cartoon expressed the pervasive Indian frustration about the many criminal cases where medical evidence was presented to support the specious European defense that Indians had "weak insides" or "enlarged spleens" and were therefore more susceptible to blows, beatings, and "accidental shootings." As "A Lover of Justice" wrote in *Panjabi Akhbar*: "It often happens that whenever a Native is killed by a European, the Civil Surgeons, after examining the remains, are of opinion that the deceased was in such a weak state of health that he might have died at any time without violence. We are always suspicious when this is the result of an examination."[134]

Conclusion

The codification of the law of evidence in India was part of the process of legal modernization. The attempt to rationalize the Indian law and make the criminal investigation like a science, however, butted up against prevalent colonial notions about the problem of Indian mendacity and other peculiarities of Indian culture. In contrast to the codification of criminal procedure, these "special conditions" expedited rather than thwarted the codification of evidence. Nonetheless, the end result was

---

[132] *Ratnagar*, November 28, 1903, BL, IOR, L/R/5/29.
[133] P. Mitter, "Cartoons of the Raj," *History Today*, 47, 9 (1997), 16.
[134] *Panjabi Akhbar*, January 7, 1871, NAI, *Selections from the Vernacular Newspapers Published in the Punjab, North-Western Provinces, Oudh, and Central Provinces* (1871).

largely the same. In both instances, the particular circumstances of the colony were deemed to demand special legislation that departed from contemporary legal rules and practices in England. Anxiety about the unreliability of native knowledge and the need for scientific engines for eliciting truth produced a medico-legal machinery that was grounded in a distinctly subjective ethnographic approach. Indian medical jurisprudence and medical experts played a critical function in mitigating European criminal culpability in cases of violence and murder by emphasizing the vulnerabilities of the Indian body and hidden causes of death.

4 "One scale of justice for the planter and another for the coolie": law and violence on the Assam tea plantations

At around 11 p.m. on April 11, 1893, a European planter named Cockburn heard his two mastiffs barking loudly outside his bungalow at the Baladhan Tea Garden in the Cachar district of Assam. Cockburn stepped out onto the verandah to investigate the commotion. There he spotted the dead body of his *chowkidar* lying on the ground surrounded by a group of men. Cockburn attempted to retreat back into his bedroom but fell over the threshold of the door where, as his Indian paramour (for lack of a better word) Sadi described it, he was "hacked to death while he lay prone on the ground on his face." (Sadi was the wife of a former Baladhan tea worker. The previous year, after her husband had been expelled from the plantation, she began to cohabit with Cockburn, though the conditions under which this happened – coercive or consensual – are unclear.)

The next morning, Cockburn's butler discovered his corpse strewn across the entranceway to the bedroom in a pool of blood. The *chowkidar*'s body lay several feet away, covered rather more respectfully with a blanket. Sadi was later found alive but seriously wounded and naked in the woods near the bungalow. Despite her suggestive physical state, no charges of sexual violence were ever lodged or investigated.[1]

Although physical attacks by Indian laborers against their European employers were not terribly rare, murder was certainly unusual. Given the powerful influence that the European planters exerted over the colonial state, such cases were always attended to with great vigilance. After Cockburn's death, as often happened following incidents of extreme violence on a plantation, all of the laborers fled, leaving few witnesses behind for the police to question. The only eye-witness to the murder was Sadi, who lay pregnant and mortally wounded in the hospital. Three days after the assault, in a condition described by her Bengali doctor as *pagal kariya amar boda pailana* (translated by the police as "not delirious"), Sadi

---

[1] Files related to the case at BL, IOR include: L/PJ/6/365, File 44; L/PJ/6/366, Files 143, 169; L/PJ/6/369, Files 459, 467, 468; L/PJ/6/374, Files 961, 962, 963; L/PJ/6/376, Files 1132, 1133, 1134; and L/PJ/6/377, 1287.

made a formal statement to two European officials, Assistant Commissioner Howell and District Police Superintendent Shuttleworth. In her statement, Sadi claimed that she, Cockburn, and the *chowkidar* were attacked in the bungalow by a band of men whom she had never seen before, identifying them as several Cacharis and a Kabuli. She insisted that there were no Manipuris, Kukis, Nagas, or any other people from the garden at the bungalow on that fateful night when she saw Cockburn get "cut down." On April 17, after delivering a still-born baby, Sadi died.

Under pressure from the local European planting community, the police scrambled to crack the case. They hired a spy named Labai Cachari to make inquiries among the local villagers before summoning Bengali Police Inspector Jay Chandra Bhadra from the neighboring district of Sylhet. Inspector Chandra was referred to as "an experienced and trustworthy officer" prepared to deal with what the Government of India later called the "special" difficulties on the "remote and irascible" frontier. When Inspector Chandra arrived on the scene, he indiscriminately began to arrest men, women, and children, confining, tutoring, and torturing them to procure confessions.[2] Several witnesses later claimed that Chandra and his men had threatened many of the local women and their daughters with "dishonor" if they refused to turn over Cockburn's murderers. On August 8, upon the uncorroborated statements of two approvers (men who turned state's evidence), seven people (six Manipuris and one Gurkha) were charged with murder committed in the course of committing *dacoity* (armed robbery) – the killers had escaped with 778 rupees in cash and a few stolen articles, including a double-barreled gun and some clothing.

The men were initially tried at the Cachar Sessions Court by Judge John Clark and a panel of three Indian assessors. Assessors were non-binding advisors who assisted colonial judges in determining issues of fact. Unlike a jury, which delivers a joint and usually binding opinion, the opinions of the assessors were given individually in open court, and the judge had the discretion to ignore their opinions if he wished. The case for the prosecution rested entirely on the evidence of the two approvers, Mohan and Mukhta Singh, who testified that the murders were premeditated. Mukhta Singh stated:

He [Cockburn] troubled us much; he made his coolies break down work we had done, and made us do it over again two or three times, and said that he would not pay us until we did it. Most of us left Manipur because we had no food, and we could not get food for our work here. Therefore we are all very angry with the

---

[2] Chief Commissioner to the Government of India, May 4, 1894, *PP*, 1894, vol. LVIII, p. 325.

Sahib. Some of us said we would like to bury our teeth in his throat...We had come to fight; those whose fate it was to die would have died.

The prosecutor argued that the seven defendants were former employees of Cockburn's who came to the bungalow that night to kill him out of revenge for the money they were owed in back pay. Cockburn was depicted as a notoriously abusive planter who had a volatile relationship with his own employees and with the locals in the surrounding area. The barking mastiffs were important symbols of Cockburn's brutality, as he set them on villagers who attempted to pass through the garden on their way to the local marketplace. Like many plantations in Assam, the Baladhan Tea Garden was built on land that previously had provided local access routes.[3]

During the trial, Judge Clark excluded Sadi's dying deposition from the admissible evidence on procedural grounds, determining that it had not been taken under oath or in the presence of the accused. He also referred to her narrative as a jumble of imaginary facts. (John Woodroffe, the High Court counsel for the defense, would later argue that Sadi's deposition was consistent, rational, and sufficiently clear, given her morbid condition.) Without this key piece of evidence, the defense rested on the consistent claims of police torture and forced confessions to make an argument about the illegality of the police investigation. Sagal Samba Sajow, the alleged ringleader of the group, testified that he was arrested, tortured, and pressured into making a confession by the police who "beat me very much and ill-used me in other ways." Sajow claimed that he only agreed to confess before Assistant Magistrate Lees in exchange for his release. After he confessed, however, Sajow was thrown into *hazat* (solitary confinement), where he was denied all human contact, including access to a lawyer. The six other defendants offered disturbingly similar accounts of police torture and harsh confinement.

At the conclusion of the trial, the three Indian assessors acquitted all seven men because they believed that the two approvers had been tutored and tampered with "in view of the large reward offered [2,500 rupees] for bringing home the guilt to anybody." Judge Clark dismissed their acquittal, accepting the prosecution's claim that the prisoners came to the bungalow that night to murder Cockburn in revenge for the money they were owed. Clark sentenced four of the men to death and three to transportation for life. According to standard procedure in capital crimes, the

---

[3] S. Baruah, *India against Itself: Assam and the Politics of Modernity* (Delhi: Oxford University Press, 1999), pp. 48–49.

case was referred to the Calcutta High Court for confirmation of the death sentences.

On December 11, 1893, Calcutta High Court Judges Ameer Ali and H. T. Prinsep acquitted all of the prisoners on account of the many "irregularities" and "illegalities" committed during the police investigation and trial, as well as the lack of corroborating evidence. The English and the Indian press immediately erupted in outrage. The *Englishman and Military Chronicle*, a pro-planter publication, bemoaned the vulnerability of the lonely planter on the lawless Assam frontier and condemned the government's failure to "safeguard the lives and property of the men who have made the wealth and prosperity of Assam." The editors opined:

The conditions obtaining in remote and lonely tea districts, where solitary Englishmen are practically at the mercy of the predatory hordes of the frontier should make a more imperative demand for protection from Government than any other circumstances under which our fellow countrymen live and work in India. Instead of granting it a *laissez faire* policy as has been largely adopted, and the planter has been left to the protection, visibly growing weaker, of his own prestige as an Englishman.[4]

Although the Indian press was pleased by the rare but important vindication of justice, the controversy evoked commentary about what the *Amrita Bazar Patrika* called the "atrocious manner in which criminal justice is often administered in this country…We do not know how to begin with this case, what comments to offer upon it, and how to end it."[5] The *Hindoo Patriot* thundered: "There was absolutely not a scintilla of evidence against any of the accused men, but when a European is murdered, British prestige and British revenge require the shedding of some blood – sometimes even of innocent men. 'Life for life' is the procedure usually observed in such cases, and sometimes for one European murdered, two, three, or four natives are hanged."[6]

Under parliamentary pressure, the Government of India initiated an inquiry into the widespread allegations of judicial misconduct in the handling of the case. Most of the Assam officials (including the Chief Commissioner) maintained that the police had arrested the right men and behaved precisely as they must in the "wilder parts of the country,"[7] where the people were "notorious for their clannish habits, and their indisposition to assist the authorities in making enquiries among them."[8] The

---

[4] "The Tragedy of Baladhan," *The Englishman and Military Chronicle*, December 13, 1893.
[5] *Amrita Bazar Patrika*, December 13, 1893.   [6] *Hindoo Patriot*, December 14, 1893.
[7] Government of India to the Secretary of State, June 5, 1894, BL, IOR, L/PJ/6/376, Files 1132, 1133.
[8] Police Department Proceedings, June 4, 1894, BL, IOR, L/PJ/6/376, Files 1132, 1133.

boundaries

Deputy Commissioner of Cachar went so far as to claim that the forced confessions confirmed what local officials *already knew* about the "treacherous and unscrupulous" Manipuris:

> They were Manipuris and the Sahib had insulted them so they resolved the Sahib should die. "When they attack a fort, they kill the sentry and then put everyone therein to death." This was the gist of a conversation with Mr. Carnac [Cachar District Superintendent of Police]. This agrees with what we know of the treacherous and unscrupulous conduct of these hill Manipuris. They lived under no law till lately, except that of their village custom. Their conduct in the Manipur rebellion in 1891 brought into the strongest light their savage disposition and their lawless conduct in this district has necessitated the quartering of a small punitive police upon their villages near Baladhan and in the South Cachar, where Sagal Samba [the ringleader] was hidden away for many weeks.[9]

According to this logic of frontier lawlessness and the exceptional measures it demanded, the Government of India determined that nothing untoward, illegal, or irregular had occurred in Baladhan. In fact, rather than constituting signs of police torture, the forced confessions were interpreted as evidence of perjury and proof of the corrupt nature of the Manipuris. The final report to London concluded, "There is no reason for regarding this case as anything very special."[10]

The Baladhan murder case raises a number of significant questions about the administration of criminal justice in colonial India and the politics of violence on the Assam tea plantations. It was highly unusual that a European was murdered and no one was punished for it. Given the violence and oppression that accompanied the enforcement of labor on the Assam tea plantations, it was rather rare for a European to be murdered at all. It stands to reason that Cockburn's killers were not simply motivated by localized sentiments of personal revenge, and his unsolved murder can only be understood within the broader context of violence that defined everyday life on the tea plantations.

The region of Assam sat on the geo-political edge of empire and possibly beyond the pale of justice (see Map 4.1). Within an imperial framework that distinguished the metropolitan center from the colonial periphery, a frontier zone such as Assam occupied a marginal space that one English writer called "a wild – almost unknown – tract of jungle."[11] I have chosen to focus on Assam in this chapter because the widespread, systematic, and controversial problem of white violence on the tea plantations offers a vivid example of how violence simultaneously menaced

[9] Herald's Report, February 28, 1894, ibid.
[10] Government of India to the Secretary of State, June 5, 1894, ibid.
[11] *Indian Planters' Gazette and Sporting News*, July 7, 1885.

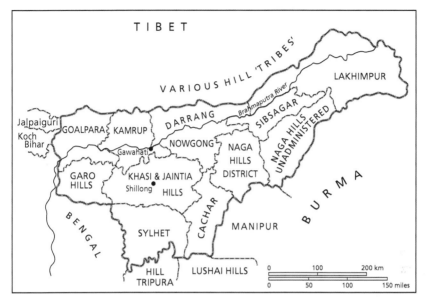

Map 4.1   Assam under the jurisdiction of the Chief Commissioner, 1875

and maintained the empire. The brutal European tea planter was indispensable to the expansion of the profitable tea industry even as he was a source of embarrassment to the better class of Englishman in India and a ready target of anti-colonial nationalists. By the late nineteenth century, the scourge of planter violence and the failure of the state to convict in several highly publicized cases had become symbolic of the injustice of empire itself.

Colonial Assam was dominated by the British tea planters and a system of indentured servitude and labor recruitment that provided penal powers to employers to enforce labor contracts.[12] Viewed through the prism of the colonial tea plantation, the political foundations, cultural conditions, and legitimizing functions that structured law and legal practice in British India appear in bold relief. Although colonial law was described by officials as a guarantor of liberty and agent of civilizational progress, in letter and in practice the law of the tea plantations was designed to secure capitalist control over labor. This placed the planter above the law and justice beyond the reach of the laborer's grasp.

Most historical scholarship on colonial Assam takes the presence of European violence for granted as part of a larger coercive labor system.

[12] Inland Emigration Act I of 1882.

This chapter does not. Here we take the Baladhan case as a jumping-off point to explore how different social actors in colonial Assam – the planters, the tea workers, the press, the state, the missionaries – sought to resolve the tension between the theoretical promise of colonial justice and the material practice of colonial command. The lack of impartiality associated with *safed insaaf* (white justice) made law both an instrument of oppression and, sometimes, a tool of resistance for those who experienced colonial power in its rawest form. Although the rule of law provided the political and ideological framework for imperial domination, it also offered real and rhetorical spaces to make claims upon the state.

Law, labor, and the "opening-out" of Assam

In 1826, when the East India Company annexed the region of Assam, a handful of European planters had already begun to experiment with the cultivation of tea.[13] Europeans saw themselves as the only force capable of reforming and modernizing the Assam Valley and harnessing its resources. However, the Company did not possess the manpower to harness the potential riches of what Jayeeta Sharma calls this "new El Dorado of imperial agrarian enterprise."[14] To assist in the "opening-out" of Assam, the Government of India offered favorable land-holding conditions to attract foreign capitalists and planters. By 1901, European planters held more than a quarter of the total settled area in the Assam Valley, 85 percent on privileged terms that greatly disadvantaged indigenous entrepreneurship.[15] Colonial expansion and state formation in Assam were utterly dependent upon the planters, making the notion of "Planter-raj" a literal appraisal of their power and position.[16]

Early European efforts to expand the tea industry were hindered by labor shortages and the high cost of local workers. By 1859, the tea planters and their lobbyists in Calcutta were pressing the colonial government for a law to secure the recruitment, transportation, and employment of tea workers from outside the region. Within a few years, they had achieved their goal with the passage of a law (Act VI of 1865) specifically designed to recruit laborers from outside Assam. Act VI established an indenture system that bound laborers to the plantations through the

---

[13] H. Antrobus, *A History of the Assam Company, 1839–1953* (Edinburgh: T. and A. Constable, 1957).

[14] J. Sharma, "An European Tea 'Garden' and an Indian 'Frontier': The Discovery of Assam," *Centre of South Asian Studies Occasional Paper*, 6 (2002), 11–12.

[15] Ibid., 15.

[16] A. Guha, *Planter-Raj to Swaraj: Freedom Struggle and Electoral Politics in Assam, 1826–1947* (New Delhi: Indian Council of Historical Research, 1977).

implementation of a penal contract that gave employers the power to arrest anyone in the district who was alleged to have fled from a plantation and to prosecute those workers who breached their contracts. The law empowered employers to arrest and punish "absconding" laborers and those who failed to work with fines, forfeiture of wages, and imprisonment. (In Assam, deserting the plantation was referred to as "absconding.") A new law passed in 1882 further strengthened the hand of the planters by authorizing them to arrest deserters without a warrant or the assistance of the police if the deserters were found within 5 miles of their plantations.[17]

The penal contract system – so called because of its criminal rather than civil penalties for breach of contract – was first introduced into India by Governor-General William Bentinck under Regulation V of 1830, which gave the indigo planters of lower Bengal the power to hold summary trials and to imprison laborers who broke their contracts. Bentinck's Regulation was subsequently struck down by the Court of Directors. However, after 1857, the indigo planters were again invested with the powers of honorary magistrates. In 1903, at the behest of European tea and coffee planters in Madras who complained about "the necessity of criminally punishing breaches of contract where the master is more or less at the mercy of his servant," the government also introduced a penal contract system in Madras.[18] The criminal authority conferred on the tea, coffee, and indigo planters stood in sharp contrast to the extensive exemptions granted to Europeans from being tried in criminal cases in the *mofussil*. Likewise, the idyllic connotations of the term "tea garden" bore no relation to the brutal reality of the lives of the laborers who worked on them.[19]

The use of the indenture system in Assam mirrored its application elsewhere in the British empire. After the abolition of slavery in 1833, Indian indentured laborers sustained Britain's plantation economy in its various colonies. Dubbed by Hugh Tinker "a new system of slavery," the lives of Indian laborers in this system of overseas indenture were scarcely better than the lives of the African slaves whose places they took.[20] It is within this global context that European planters in India successfully pressured the Indian Government to institute a system of inland emigration and indenture in Assam.[21]

The state's rationale for the "exceptional" labor legislation in Assam was that in return for secure pay and working conditions, and to protect

[17] Inland Emigration Act (I of 1882).
[18] "Petition from the Wynaad Planters' Association," BL, IOR, L/PJ/6/635, File 978.
[19] Sharma, "An European Tea 'Garden.'"   [20] Tinker, *A New System of Slavery.*
[21] Behal and Mohapatra, "'Tea and Money versus Human Life.'"

Figure 4.1 **Tea-making in Chaubattia, 1880s**
G. W. Lawrie's carefully staged photograph offers a nice visual representation of Commissioner Elliott's description of the pristine and orderly tea plantation. The reality on the ground was rather different, as laborers worked long hours under extremely harsh and brutally inhumane conditions. See Figures 4.2a and 4.2b for a different and more accurate portrayal of work and life on the tea garden.

the planter's economic investment, the laborer should be bound to the plantation (see Figure 4.1). In defense of the penal contract, Assam Chief Commissioner C. A. Elliott observed in 1885:

As to the tea-coolie, the protection he gets, the excellent cottage he lives in, the good water-supply, the fairly cheap food, and the fairly reasonable wage he gets are a *quid pro quo* granted in return for the penal clauses which compel him to carry out his part of the contract. He would not get the one without the other and he certainly would be worse off if he had to part with both. The alternative would be a migratory class of labourers, whom no one would go to too much expense in hutting and providing for because he could not be sure of retaining their labour; who would be constantly shifting from one place to another under the influence of enticement and bribery; who would have to build their own houses; and would build them of poor materials on unhealthy spots; who would be entitled to no medical care when ill and would have no opportunity of making complaints or getting grievances addressed such as they have now, when the Inspector's official visit takes place. Such a state of things would be good neither for their morale nor for their bodily welfare, but such a state of things would necessarily arise as long as population is scarce and the labourer of great value to the planter, if no law did intervene to give permanence and solidity to the mutual relations of planter and labourer.[22]

The pleasant picture painted by Commissioner Elliott did not square up with the reality of daily life on the plantations, nor did it acknowledge the underlying economic logic of the penal contract.[23] Whereas labor contracts are normally adjudicated by civil means (lawsuits), the colonial state recognized that one could not sue a person with no property. Rather than confronting the root causes of Indian poverty and landlessness, workers were bound to the tea plantations by a law that made it a crime to leave.

Eugene Genovese argues that in the era of American slavery, the manager's and the magistrate's powers constituted a "system of complementary plantation law" in which the state's public protection of the worker under law was subordinated to the planter's private power over labor.[24] This paradigm also applies to colonial Assam, where the planter was defined as an authority figure who required special disciplinary powers: "discipline must be maintained upon tea gardens and for its maintenance we must depend upon the authority of the Manager, not upon that of the Magistrate."[25]

While the exceptional legislation did increase the labor supply – by 1883, 95 percent of the labor force on the tea plantations came from outside Assam – it certainly did not protect the workers or guarantee decent living conditions.[26] If anything, the new labor laws were directly linked to widespread criminal fraud, abduction, and abuse of workers. Though the penal contract promised some protection in the form of state inspections, these inspections were ineffective and occurred at most once a year. Planters were generally given advance notice to prepare for the visits, and the social relations between planters and public officials foreclosed the possibility of honest reporting. Dwarkanath Ganguli, a

---

[22] Elliott's note of July 15, 1885 in "Conditions of Tea Laborers on the Tea Plantations in Assam," BL, IOR, L/PJ/6/233, File 1431.

[23] R. P. Behal, *Wage Structure and Labor: Assam Valley Tea Plantations, 1900–1947* (Noida: V. V. Giri Labour Institute, 2003).

[24] E. Genovese, *Roll, Jordan, Roll: The World the Slaves Made* (New York: Pantheon, 1974).

[25] Letter from the Chief Commissioner of Assam, February 13, 1903, BL, IOR, L/PJ/6/767, File 1982.

[26] Das, *Plantation Labor in India*, p. 27.

journalist who published a series of influential articles on the mistreatment of tea workers in Assam, noted that:

> The Inspectors when they visit the gardens generally dine and peg with the planters, play and exchange with them the social amenities of life...The coolies are often not mustered before him and if mustered they are made to stand in rows, those who have been won over by the promise of Sardarship [a low-level native management position] or any other reward being allowed to occupy the front row and to answer for the whole lot any questions which may be asked.[27]

The destitution of bonded laborers in colonial Assam should also be considered within pre-colonial structures of economic and social oppression.[28] In fact, colonial administrators often deflected criticism of the indenture system by pointing out that life under Indian *zamindars* was no better than life under the European planters. It is certainly true that the plantation system could not have functioned without the assistance of a variety of Indian intermediaries, including the managers, recruiters, railway menials, and other "coolie-catchers" who performed many of the planters' recruiting and disciplinary functions. Exploring the links and the gaps between colonial and pre-colonial labor practices would be interesting, but the focus here is on the implications of a new system of law that promised abstract equality and uniform justice, but practiced something quite different.

Contemporary critics compared the indenture system and the penal contract to slavery and consistently used conditions on the slave plantations in the American South and the specious arguments of Southern slave-holders as scurrilous points of comparison. Ganguli observed that "the position of the laborers in many tea-gardens is almost as bad, if it is not worse, than the condition of the American Negro slaves before their emancipation."[29] Kristodas Pal denounced the 1882 law that gave planters authority to arrest absconding laborers without warrant or police assistance as "a veritable Slave Act."[30] In response to the planters' demand for more "freedom" to define and defend their industry, the Reverend Charles Dowding, a longtime chaplain and social activist in Dibrugarh, wrote: "The 'fight for freedom' is a noble thing: but it is a whimsical suggestion in this connection, and somehow reminds one of the Confederate States of America, who fought for freedom to hold slaves and liberty to 'whop their niggers.'"[31]

---

[27] D. Ganguli, *Slavery in British Dominion* (Calcutta, 1872), p. 33.

[28] On the push-and-pull factors that caused laborers to migrate to Assam, see J. C. Jha, *Aspects of Indentured Inland Emigration to North-East India, 1859–1918* (New Delhi: Indus Publishing, 1996).

[29] Ganguli, *Slavery*, p. 1.   [30] Pal, *Memories*, p. 446.

[31] C. Dowding, "Assam Coolie Recruiting," in Buckingham, *Tea-Garden Coolies in Assam*.

Dowding compared popular methods of "coolie-catching" – including advertisements in local newspapers that offered rewards for the return of absconding laborers – to efforts made to capture runaway slaves in the American South.[32] Indian activists also used the practices of Southern slave-owners to condemn the tea planters. A popular book among the Bengal intelligentsia at the time was *Uncle Tom's Cabin*, which was translated into Bengali by Babu Chandi Charan Sen. As Bipin Chandra Pal recalled, "We had read of the inhumanities of the American planters perpetrated on the helpless Negro slaves...We readily compared the condition of tea garden labourers in Assam to that of Negro labour in America before the Emancipation."[33]

Planters, by contrast, also used the same language of race and slavery, but in an uncritical fashion. Veronica Westmacott, daughter of Calcutta barrister Richard Westmacott and his wife Veronica, was born in India but educated in England. She returned to India as a planter's wife and stayed until 1945, when she was forced to leave due to a severe bout of malaria. She describes her memoir, *We Were Survivors*, as a depiction of "a way of life with the British Raj from about 1830 to 1945." The memoir includes photographs of European domestic life in Calcutta, river scenes in Bengal, and views from the tea plantation, including an aerial shot titled, "Hunting down a negro deserter."[34]

The Government of Assam spent significant administrative energy monitoring labor recruitment, employment practices, and social relations on the tea plantations. The annual "Reports on Labour Immigration into Assam" provide extensive documentation about life and living conditions, including data on: immigration and fraudulent recruitment; age and gender composition of the labor force; contracts and wages; desertions and other criminal offenses; birth and mortality rates; health, disease, and sanitary conditions; relations between employers and laborers; and the working of the general system. These reports not only provide a chilling insight into life on and around the plantations, they also indicate the state's intimate awareness of the brutal conditions under which the system functioned (see Figures 4.2a and 4.2b).

The government openly recognized that the widespread problem of desertions, which constituted the bulk of Indian criminal offenses, was directly connected to increased mortality, as laborers tended to flee when deadly diseases spread.[35] On the tea plantations thousands of men, women, and children worked under harsh and crowded conditions for

---

[32] BL, IOR, L/PJ/6/832, File 3639.   [33] Pal, *Memories*, p. 446.
[34] BL, IOR, Mss Eur C394.
[35] "Report on Labour Immigration into Assam for the year 1878," BL, IOR, V/24/1222.

Figure 4.2a **Sorting tea, date unknown**

Figure 4.2b **Tea pickers in the Himalayas, c. 1890**

In contrast to the image of order and civility presented by G. W. Lawrie's "Tea-making in Chaubattia," these photographs of tea sorters and tea pickers offer a more realistic reflection of the grueling work performed by indentured tea workers, many of whom were women and children. Health and sanitary conditions on the colonial tea plantations were abysmal. The spread of deadly diseases such as cholera and typhoid and the poor nutrition of workers made the mortality rate on certain gardens as high as 30 percent.

low wages where food was scarce and deadly diseases such as cholera and typhoid spread like wildfire. Between 1863 and 1866, 32,000 of the 84,000 laborers brought to Assam died.[36] As one official observed, "they have to choose between the risk of death if they stay or imprisonment if they desert."[37] Nonetheless, little was ever done to seriously improve health and sanitary conditions even on the notoriously "unhealthy" plantations, where mortality rates could be as high as 30 percent. Two Rajput laborers who attempted to flee the Mesaijang Tea Garden sardonically expressed their awareness of this die-if-you-stay and die-if-you-go predicament when, in response to their manager's warning that he would shoot them if they refused to return, the men replied, "Shoot away."[38] Of course, there were other causes for desertion, including resistance to compulsory labor, homesickness, indebtedness, personal issues, enticement, and the pursuit of better economic opportunities.

Despite the appalling conditions documented by the annual immigration reports, the tea planters, and the government officials who legislated in their favor, repeatedly asserted that "the coolie is better off in Assam than he would be probably anywhere else."[39] The pro-planter position held that the labor laws worked to the laborers' benefit by providing secure living and working conditions, establishing a minimum wage above the market rate or "free wage" in neighboring territories, and securing for the worker the protection of law. In January 1893, the *Indian Planters' Gazette and Sporting News* held that critics of the tea plantations had no clue how good the workers had it and "absolutely no conception of the immense change for the better which life in the tea districts effects upon the imported coolie, simply by filling his stomach and covering his bones with flesh and raiment...the transformation from an ill-fed, supine, dirty creature almost bestial in its stupidity, to a smart well set-up fellow."[40] Two months later, the same paper noted that "residence in Assam smartens natives up wonderfully," by providing better food, pay, and housing than they would get anywhere else (see Figure 4.3).[41]

The planters and their supporters also argued that labor recruitment and the special contract designed to enforce it were necessary to deal with the "jungly races" who were otherwise unresponsive to free market forces. As the special correspondent to *The Times* in Calcutta remarked, "These classes are not mobilized for competition. The obscure forces of custom

---

[36] Jha, *Aspects*, p. 145.
[37] Karimgunj Subdivisional Officer Porteus, in Ganguli, *Slavery*, p. 8.   [38] Ibid., p. 39.
[39] "Report on Labour Immigration into Assam for the year 1877," BL, IOR, V/24/1222.
[40] *Indian Planters' Gazette and Sporting News*, January 21, 1893.   [41] Ibid., March 18, 1893.

Figure 4.3 **Tea party in Calcutta, c. 1890**
The portrait of calm civility captured in this photograph of an afternoon
tea party in Calcutta obscures the inhumane conditions under which the
tea itself was produced in the nearby hills. The pleasures of high tea
offered imperial Britons a civil and orderly ritual for the consumption of
sweet delights and exotic brews from far-away places like Assam and
Darjeeling. The sweet tea, however, came as a bitter pill to the
indentured servants and slaves in the East and West Indies who made
the imperial system of production possible.

and sentiment dominate their lives. Of all the opportunities that lie before
them in the great dawn of India's industrial life, they know nothing at all.
They are blindly rooted to their homes. They will not emigrate for better-
ment; they stay till they starve."[42] The tea plantations, in this view, solved
the problems of the Indian poor:

The labourer has been withdrawn from the fierce battle of the millions, amid the
storm and stress of varying seasons, into the constant shadow of prosperity and
peace. Henceforth, he has nothing to fear. He is protected from famine, from

[42] Special correspondent, "The Assam Labour Question, Recruitment," *The Times*, August
29, 1902.

fraud, from violence, from usury, from all manner of external ills. For him and for his life alone, among the poor of India, the problem of life is solved.[43]

However, as members of the London-based Indian Humanitarian League rhetorically asked, if the conditions on the tea plantations were so desirable, why was working there so unpopular?[44] Did the need for special recruitment laws and a system of compulsory labor not indicate reluctance to working on the plantations? Was the laborers' hesitation to emigrate to Assam explained by their attachment to their backward ways or, as former Chief Commissioner Henry Cotton argued, were low wages and physically abusive planters more likely explanations for the lack of voluntary migration?[45]

Planter violence and the "markets of injustice"

The relations between tea planters and their employees formed what one Assam official called "a source of constant anxiety."[46] The government maintained a watchful, if tolerant, attitude towards the frequency of criminal complaints and the outcome of trials involving planter violence. Although the province of Assam was represented in the colonial imagination as a savage and sparsely populated frontier that could only become civilized under the leadership of European capitalists, officials kept close tabs on relations between the plantations and the surrounding villages as a way to monitor local resistance to dispossession and exploitation.

The colonial state accepted the fact that a certain amount of European violence was necessary to keep the plantations – and the empire – going. The devolution of authority from magistrate to manager reflected the state's willingness to promote the tea industry by allowing it to police itself. Criminal behavior, including physical violence, confinement, and abduction, which would ordinarily have been punishable by the state, was effectively decriminalized and legitimized by the penal contract.[47]

The farming-out of disciplinary powers, however, presented its own problems in terms of social and political control, as the planters' powers were simultaneously authorized by the state and also a-legal, or outside of

---

[43] Special correspondent, "The Assam Labour Question, The Relations Between Employers and Employed," ibid., September 2, 1902.

[44] "The Labour System of Assam," BL, IOR, L/PJ/6/765, File 1731.

[45] Cotton, "Letter to the Editor," *The Times*, September 2, 1902.

[46] "Report on Labour Immigration into Assam for the Year 1899," BL, IOR, V/24/1223.

[47] A. Fede, "Legitimized Violent Slave Abuse in the American South, 1619–1865: A Case Study of Law and Social Change in Six Southern States," *American Journal of Legal History*, 29, 2 (1985), 93–150.

and uncontrolled by law.[48] As the Secretary of State noted in 1903, the tea planters came to expect protection *from* law rather than protection *under* law: "The function of the Viceroy in their judgment is to prevent them from being punished when they whack their niggers; and they have talked themselves into a belief that if he does not so shield them the foundations of British rule are endangered."[49] Having authorized the private use of force, could the state subject the planters to prosecution and punishment under the ordinary criminal law? When the planters took the law into their own hands, which they were expressly permitted to do but which often resulted in "flogging a wretched man to death," were they transgressing or enforcing the colonial order of things?[50] Did the law extend its protection to the body of the laborer? Could the laborer make any claims upon the state? Orlando Patterson describes slavery as a form of social death caused, among other factors, by the power of the master to commit violence against the slave.[51] Indentured servitude was likewise a form of legal death, for just as you could not sue a person with no property, could you unlawfully kill a person with no legal status?[52] Was killing a "coolie" ever murder? If not, what did that say about colonial justice?

One of the primary functions of planter violence was the enforcement of work. Public and private floggings, as well as confinement, cuffing, kicking, and other forms of physical assault, were routine elements of everyday life on the plantation. Violence was used to create a culture of fear designed to enforce the daily labor regime, to prevent workers from deserting, and to inflict exemplary public punishment. Laborers' fear of what could happen for failing to work itself sometimes had mortal consequences, as in a case in Sibsagar, where a young child died of cholera because his mother, who was afraid of being assaulted if she did not turn out for work, left him at home.[53] If workers worked partially owing to fear of the consequences of not working, then not working and desertion may conversely be understood as overt challenges to the planters' labor regime.[54]

The planters routinely downplayed their record of brutality. A satirical portrait in the *Indian Planters' Gazette and Sporting News* noted that "Some

---

[48] Agamben, *State of Exception*.
[49] Letter to Curzon, Curzon's private papers, BL, IOR, Mss Eur/F111/162 (1903).
[50] Secretary of State to Curzon, October 2, 1901, BL, IOR, Mss Eur/F111/160 (1901).
[51] O. Patterson, *Slavery and Social Death: A Comparative Study* (Cambridge, MA: Harvard University Press, 1982).
[52] On the legal treatment of the murder and abuse of American slaves, see T. D. Morris, *Southern Slavery and the Law, 1619–1860* (Chapel Hill, NC: University of North Carolina Press, 1996).
[53] Ganguli, *Slavery*, p. 20.
[54] R. P. Behal, "Forms of Labour Protest in Assam Valley Tea Plantations, 1900–1930," *Economic and Political Weekly*, 20, 4 (1985), PE20.

of them get angry when stupid people annoy them; and swear, and occasionally even hit the stupid people."[55] Another piece proposed that "gentling" the coolies was in the best interests of the garden. An article titled "Gentling a Garden" notes:

the process by which an unruly labour force is best brought under control strongly resembles that by which a refractory horse is "gentled." The coolies must first be thoroughly got the better of, and when fairly mastered, made to see that they are more comfortably off in every way when in a state of obedience to just and firm authority, than when in anarchy on bad pay.[56]

J. Buckingham, chairman of the Assam branch of the Indian Tea Association, argued that "the whole matter of coolie treatment" had to be considered in light of "the enormous difficulties of a planter's position." He compared the planter to the captain of a vessel at sea, stationed far away from the nearest magistrate, controlling a population of unruly men "always ready to hatch disturbances or fan discontent." "What is he to do?" Buckingham asked. "Coolies certainly need a strong hand," Buckingham asserted, so when trouble arose, best:

Go for the ringleader, knock him down, or give him a thrashing, and follow it up with a lecture in round terms to the crowd. They, seeing their leader fall, will declare that he had egged them on and that they are very sorry for their behaviour; go back to their lines, perhaps give him another thrashing on their own account, and turn out the next morning to work as quiet as lambs. No doubt the planter has broken the letter of the law, but he has quelled a disturbance, which might have cost the garden thousands of rupees.[57]

An interesting facet of reported crime in colonial Assam is that as the population of European planters and laborers grew, criminal trials of Europeans declined (see Tables 4.1 and 4.2). Ignoring the social and structural hurdles obstructing the path to justice, the government typically interpreted the annual reports as proof that "coolies are generally well treated and well cared for."[58] Some officials offered a capitalist explanation for the putative decline in planter criminality, arguing that most planters were "just and considerate" and understood it to be in their financial interest to maintain good labor relations.[59] The annual reports of similar types of incident across the region, however, suggest systematic criminal violence rather than the isolated actions of a few bad apples. Others surmised that the negative publicity surrounding notorious cases

[55] *Indian Planters' Gazette and Sporting News*, July 7, 1885.   [56] Ibid., January 21, 1893.
[57] Buckingham, *Tea-Garden Coolies in Assam*.
[58] Deputy Commissioner of Cachar's comments in the "Report on Labour Immigration into Assam for the year 1883," BL, IOR, V/24/1222.
[59] "Report on Labour Immigration into Assam for the Year 1893," BL, IOR, V/24/1222.

Table 4.1 *Growth of labor force on Assam tea plantations, 1877–1920*

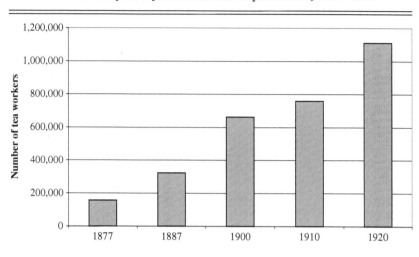

Table 4.2 *Europeans on trial in Assam, 1884–1908*

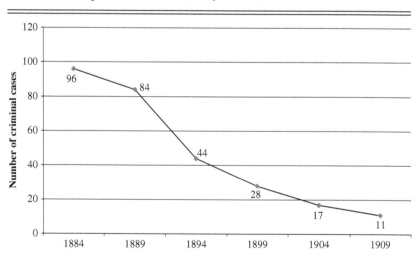

of planter violence contributed to improved treatment of workers over time. In 1900, the Deputy Commissioner of Darrang postulated that "The publicity attaching to cases of systematic ill-treatment, and the consequences entailed, are sufficient in most cases to deter any who may not be alive to the necessity for treating the coolie well."[60] This self-correcting line of reasoning is also not terribly credible. If anything, the increasingly close-knit social and political ties between the non-official and official European populations forged in the face of a growing nationalist movement provide a more likely explanation for the decline in both European criminal trials and the rate of conviction.[61]

The expansion of the tea industry coincided with the rise of anti-colonial Indian nationalism. Indian nationalists used criminal violence in Assam to expose the state's failure to administer justice fairly. The cruel behavior of the planters also provided a vivid platform for a broader critique of the criminality of colonialism itself. Condemnation of the "planters' *zulm*"[62] was loudest in the Bengali-language press. Tyrannical characters like Cockburn were relentlessly condemned by Indian journalists who day after day spoke out against the brutality of the plantation system and the failure of the government to hold the planters accountable. *Samvad Purnachandrodaya* remarked that "planters in the *mofussil* commit heinous offenses and yet go unpunished."[63] *Prabhati* called "The escape of guilty Englishmen with impunity…a disgrace to the British Government."[64] *Surabhi* warned that "These cases have shaken the faith of the people in British justice. If steps are not taken for remedying this evil, Government may be placed in a perilous position."[65] *Sanjivani* declared that "the tea trade should be ruined and Assam should become the abode of wild beasts [rather] than that this fearful custom of selling coolies as slaves should be kept up."[66]

As the nineteenth century drew to a close, members of the Indian public, local Christian missionaries, and parliamentary reformers increasingly called upon the colonial regime to bring offending planters to justice. Many Englishmen in India also had a host of negative stereotypes about the "'brutal planter' – *Messieurs les* 'planters' *du thé – les sauvages*; the wild European tribes on the frontier."[67] As for the planters, they wistfully

---

[60] "Report on Labour Immigration into Assam for the Year 1900," BL, IOR, V/24/1223.
[61] Cotton's private papers, BL, IOR, Mss Eur/D1202/2, 3, and 8.
[62] "The Planter and the Ryot," *Beharee*, September 11, 1912.
[63] *Samvad Purnachandrodaya*, January 2, 1885, NAI, Report on Native Newspapers (Bengal).
[64] *Prabhati*, January 26, 1885, ibid.   [65] *Surabhi*, February 17, 1885, ibid.
[66] B. Chandra, *The Rise and Growth of Economic Nationalism in India* (New Delhi: Anamika, 1966), p. 370.
[67] *Indian Planters' Gazette and Sporting News*, July 7, 1885.

Table 4.3. *Indian tea exports*

Year	Quantity (lbs)	Value (rupees)
1870–71	12,700,000	10,800,000
1880–81	38,400,000	30,700,000
1890–91	110,200,000	55,000,000
1900–01	255,000,000	96,800,000
1910–11	255,000,000	124,600,000
1920–21	285,000,000	121,000,000

Source: K. N. Chaudhuri, "Foreign Trade and Balance of Payments," in D. Kumar *et al.* (eds.), *The Cambridge Economic History of India*, vol. II (Cambridge: Cambridge University Press, 1983), p. 855

longed for the days when "the old rights of servility were exacted by Europeans...[and] the dignity of the sahib [were] maintained no matter at what inconvenience to the native."[68]

The problem of non-official European violence tested the official monopoly over the "privilege of taking life" and highlighted the state's dispensation of a grossly unequal justice.[69] It also put the Government of India in an uncomfortable bind, as the colonial economy depended on the planters to extract wealth from the profitable and growing tea industry (see Table 4.3). Under the indenture system, Indian tea (most of it produced in Assam) quickly supplanted Chinese tea as the dominant force in the global tea market. In 1860, tea produced in China constituted 100 percent of world exports. Forty years later, that number had fallen to 26 percent as Indian tea assumed 41 percent of the total market share. By 1920, over 1 million Indian laborers were producing 285 million pounds of tea for export. Pressure on Assam tea workers to produce continued to grow as per capita consumption of tea in the UK increased from 5.9 pounds in 1900 to 9.6 pounds in 1931.[70]

Although the colonial administration rhetorically expressed its preference for the order of legal process over the disorder of arbitrary violence, the principle of force and the use of exceptional extra-legal measures buttressed British power. The corporal punishments found on the plantations, including caning, flogging, and confinement in subterranean

---

[68] G. Barker, *A Tea Planter's Life in Assam* (Calcutta: Thacker and Spink, 1884), pp. 87–88.
[69] Singha, "The Privilege of Taking Life."
[70] B. Gupta, "The History of the International Tea Market, 1850–1945," http://eh.net/encyclopedia/article/gupta.tea

lock-ups, were all legal practices in colonial prisons, where solitary confinement, treadmills, restricted diets, and other forms of painful physical restraint were regularly meted out to prisoners. How were the manager's floggings qualitatively different from the magistrate's whippings, legalized by the Indian Whipping Act of 1864? How was the cruel behavior of the "wild European tribes on the frontier"[71] qualitatively different from the state's own exercise of "pain-related power"?[72] If, as *The Times* argued, "the coolie who strikes a planter strikes authority and deserves to be punished with the full measure of severity," what made the violent reprisals of the brutal planter any worse than the colonial official's exercise of corporal punishment?[73] An article in the *Amrita Bazar Patrika* titled "Which are the more friendly of the two – the Police or the Planters?" drew attention to this link between official and non-official oppression:

The oppression of the indigo-planter, tea-planter or the *zamindar* will never be removed by the police, the members of which, in several instances, side with the wealthy…The planters are not friendly to us; they do much evil to the country; they oppress the people. But the police also do not seek our welfare. The oppressions of the planters are confined to a part of the country, those of the police extend over the whole. The former oppress with fear, the latter fearlessly.[74]

European tea planters worked on the geographical fringes of the empire, and their brutal violence reflected their virtually unrestrained authority to control the lives and movement of laborers, as well as their acute sense of vulnerability and fear of collective resistance. The planters were always vastly outnumbered by laborers. In 1904, the 143 tea gardens in operation in upper Assam employed 100,849 laborers and only 199 Europeans.[75] Assam tea planter George Barker gestured to this fear in a chapter of his memoir on "Fanaticism," in which he advises newcomers about the dangers in the area:

If well in the jungle or near the Naga territory, it is advisable to sleep with a loaded revolver either under the pillow or near at hand for use against tigers or panthers… Again there is the fear of a vindictive coolie, who perchance may think it a happy deliverance, so far as he is personally interested in your demise to brain you.[76]

The savage white tea planter on the margins of the empire not only saw terror when he looked into the eyes of the coolie, he also held up a

---

[71] *Indian Planters' Gazette and Sporting News*, July 7, 1885.   [72] Paton, *No Bond*, p. 12.
[73] Special correspondent, "The Assam Labor Question, The Relations Between Employers and Employed," *The Times*, September 2, 1902.
[74] *Amrita Bazar Patrika*, December 24, 1874, NAI, Report on Native Newspapers (Bengal).
[75] Jha, *Aspects*, p. 20.   [76] Barker, *A Tea Planter's Life*, pp. 112–113.

looking-glass in which the colonial state saw a dark and monstrous reflection of itself. Official disavowal of the unspeakable actions and excesses of the few bad planters, sailors, and vagrants in India deflected attention from larger questions about the culture of colonial terror and the disquieting violence that inevitably accompanied imperial forms of power. The continuum connecting official (legal) and non-official (illegal) violence was vividly exemplified in the Balladhan murder case, and in a Cockburn the colonial official undoubtedly saw his ugly and frightful double.

"One scale of justice for the planter and another for the coolie"[77]

On April 28, 1893, shortly after Cockburn's murder, the pro-planter Indian Tea Association met to determine an appropriate course of action. "We must appeal unto Caesar," they decided, "the sooner it is done the better...Think of the number of Europeans in Cachar who consider, and rightly consider, their lives and the lives of their families to be in jeopardy." In response to this familiar invocation of black peril, the Reverend Charles Dowding replied, "Does an appeal unto Caesar only lie when Europeans – or [if] natives, at least wealthy ones – are concerned?" In a series of critical articles, Dowding contrasted the stir caused by the Baladhan murder case – which focused only on the death of Cockburn and not on the death of his *chowkidar* or of Sadi – with "the indifference shown as to the death of thousands of coolies." As Dowding ironically noted, one European manager condemned Cockburn's death even though the mortality rate on his own estate was 30 percent![78]

Like many missionaries in late colonial India, the Reverend Dowding was tireless in his efforts to expose British tyranny and oppression.[79] He was a constant critic of the physical, economic, and social abuses on the tea plantations and the irresponsible behavior of the government towards the industry.[80] He met regularly with individual tea workers and documented their abuse at the hands of their employers. In Dowding's view, if the tea plantations could not function in a morally responsible fashion, they should not be permitted to function at all:

If you cannot open out Assam without this frightful waste of life, you had better leave it unopened. It is not to be borne that the defence-less coolie is to be pushed hither and thither in the interest of the idle capital of England with absolute

---

[77] Curzon to the Secretary of State, Letter No. 62, September 11, 1901, Curzon's private papers, BL, IOR, Mss Eur/F111/160.
[78] Buckingham, *Tea-Garden Coolies in Assam.*   [79] BL, IOR, L/PJ/6/417, File 575.
[80] C. Dowding, "Coolie Notes," BL, IOR, L/PJ/6/832, File 3639.

indifference (coolies being cheap) whether he lives or dies. A coolie is not a pawn but a living man with wife and children depending on him. He is not to be classed with livestock.[81]

Dowding's dissident voice was drowned out by the much louder chorus of European planters who exerted tremendous influence over the local colonial bureaucracy. The legal and political privileges of the planters are the keys to understanding the administration of justice in Assam. Unlike the tea workers, who were poor, disenfranchised, and internally divided along lines of region and language, the planter class was extremely powerful, organized, stable, and well connected. Most of the local political organs and committees in Assam were dominated by the planters, and all municipalities in Assam had ex-officio European chairmen until 1912.[82] The planters also worked through lobbying groups, including the Indian Tea Association, to exert formal and informal pressure on the governments in London and Calcutta.[83]

Official partiality in favor of the planters defined legal and police practice, and all records regarding the criminal activities of the planters must be read with this relationship in mind. As the Reverend Dowding observed, "in spite of enactments meant to protect the coolie, local officers of the highest rank consider themselves entitled to put them aside or soften their action if they seem likely to embarrass those who are engaged in 'opening up the Province.'"[84] The intimate links between the planters and local officials were sometimes subtle, as when they dined, hunted, or played polo together.[85] At other times, the cozy relationship was more obvious, as demonstrated by a 1903 police circular that instructed local officials to present criminal complaints lodged by laborers against their bosses to the plantation managers for comment and explanation before taking action.[86] The tyrannical architecture of plantation justice was most vividly exemplified by allegations in 1906 that a European magistrate in Backergunge disposed of criminal cases in his private room and occasionally at his domestic bungalow.[87] The social affinities between managers and magistrates translated into differential

---

[81] C. Dowding to the Secretary of State, September 23, 1896, BL, IOR, L/PJ/6/417, File 575.

[82] Guha, *Planter-Raj*.   [83] Renford, *Non-Official British*.

[84] C. Dowding to the Secretary of State, September 23, 1896, BL, IOR, L/PJ/6/417, File 575.

[85] M. Sinha, "Britishness, Clubbability, and the Colonial Public Sphere: The Genealogy of an Imperial Institution in Colonial India," *Journal of British Studies*, 40, 4 (2001), 489–521.

[86] BL, IOR, L/PJ/6/767, File 1982.   [87] BL, IOR, L/PJ/6/766, File 1841.

criminal charges and light punishments that inevitably tilted the scales of justice in the planters' favor.

In 1878, a group of laborers from the Balipara Tea Plantation set out to see the magistrate at the sub-divisional station. The European assistant manager in charge of the garden pursued them and attempted to force the group back to the plantation. During the ensuing confrontation, the manager struck one of the laborers over the head with his heavy walking-staff, causing his death a few days later. The assistant manager was tried in Calcutta, where he was convicted and sentenced to fifteen months of rigorous imprisonment.[88] The Balipara case is a good example of the overt methods used by the planters to subvert justice – physically preventing laborers from lodging criminal complaints – as well as the exceedingly light sentences passed on Europeans convicted of serious crimes. As Viceroy Curzon observed, "the reign of unjust and partial sentences" ensured "light measure for the white manager, cruel measure for the coolie."[89] As Curzon noted, even the light measures incensed the planters, who resented being punished no matter how serious their crimes:

The planters actually allege in public meetings that they can be certain of no justice, though what they mean by this is that they regard it as the greatest of hardships if a planter is fined Rs 100 for an assault that terminates in the death of a coolie while the coolie gets a term of rigorous imprisonment of from 3 to 6 years if he so much as lifts his hand against a European.[90]

The Balipara case also reveals that a prevalent cause of Indian violence was the inability of a laborer with a grievance to leave the estate to lodge a formal complaint.[91]

The cultural capital and legal know-how possessed by all Britons in India put them at a further legal advantage in court. In addition to their powerful lobbying groups and formal and informal social and political privileges, European planters entered the colonial judicial system with knowledge of the English language and awareness of English legal customs and practices. They invariably had legal representation, as well as families in India and England who advocated their causes by sending personal petitions, letters of good character, and other persuasive documents to the colonial authorities. In contrast, most tea workers did not possess even the language skills to communicate their grievances either to

---

[88] "Report on Labour Immigration into Assam for the Year 1878," BL, IOR, V/24/1222.
[89] Curzon to Cotton, July 22, 1901, Cotton's private papers, BL, IOR, Mss Eur/D1202/2.
[90] Curzon to the Secretary of State, Letter No. 55, August 5, 1903, Curzon's private papers, Mss Eur/F111/162 (1903).
[91] "Assam Labour Enquiry and Committee's Report and Amendment of the Labour and Emigration (Assam) Act 1901," BL, IOR, L/PJ/6/753, File 954.

the planters or to the local authorities. They were unfamiliar with the written provisions of the law and usually appeared in court without legal counsel.[92] The Calcutta High Court recognized the impact of these inequalities during the trial of a planter named Gibbons when they held that: "The helplessness and ignorance of the labourers and the superior intelligence and position of the accused aggravates the offence."[93]

One of the underlying obstacles complicating any attempt to make sense of the overall picture of crime and criminal justice in Assam is the fact that the planters themselves acted as judges and juries for their workers.[94] The plantations were generally located far from the nearest magistrate, and tea workers were often prohibited from lodging complaints with the authorities not only owing to the geographical distance but also because of the environment of intimidation that enveloped the plantation (see Figure 4.4). Armed native agents made the European magistrate physically inaccessible to laborers, who could not travel to file a complaint. Indian magistrates were not permitted to try "coolie cases" at all. The fact that leaving the plantation *itself* constituted a crime – the majority of criminal convictions in Assam were for desertion – created the possibility of double jeopardy for a laborer who wanted to initiate criminal proceedings against a planter. It also made avoiding work a weapon of the weak, with consequences that were potentially as serious as open confrontation.[95]

Medical evidence figured centrally in the planter cases, generally mitigating, if not completely absolving, European defendants of criminal culpability. In July 1871, the Commissioner of Assam was simultaneously investigating four cases of violence against a planter named Smith and twenty-two cases against a planter named Reade. The charges against these men included beating laborers across tea boxes and wrongful confinement for anywhere between four and fifteen days (including one case of wrongful confinement for three months). Many of the laborers were found to have hideous, multiple scars from the stripes – their wounds tended to go untreated because the tea gardens had no hospitals or medicines. In one case, a man died, but the examining doctor claimed he was sick before the beating and died owing to his poor health.[96]

---

[92] Emma Williams' letter, March 24, 1906, BL, IOR, L/PJ/6/749, File 632.

[93] Ganguli, *Slavery*, 28.   [94] Barker, *A Tea Planter's Life*, p. 174.

[95] M. Adas, "From Avoidance to Confrontation: Peasant Protest in Precolonial and Colonial Southeast Asia," *Comparative Studies in Society and History*, 23, 2 (1981), 217–247; and J. C. Scott, *Weapons of the Weak: Everyday Forms of Peasant Protest* (New Haven, CT: Yale University Press, 1987).

[96] NAI, Legislative (A), June 1872, Nos. 141–346.

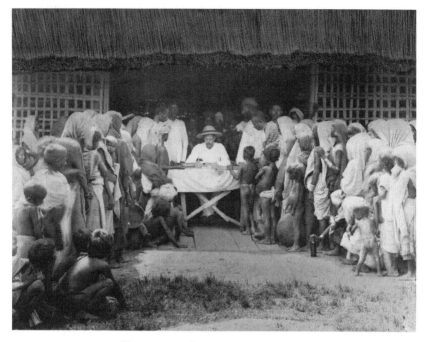

Figure 4.4 **Payment of wages to tea laborers, c. 1900**
This image of a European manager paying his laborers evokes a sense of
the planter's unitary position of power and authority on the tea plantation.

In Namdang, where a laborer died after a severe beating by his manager,
the defendant was acquitted on account of the fact that he was unaware of
the deceased's enlarged spleen and could therefore not be held responsible for the man's death. How could a planter know that a worker who
appeared healthy on the outside was incapable of withstanding "one or
two slight blows"?[97] The manager was convicted of voluntarily causing
hurt and fined 250 rupees.[98] In 1899, the manager of the Rangliting Tea
Estate seriously flogged a boy who died three days later. The civil surgeon
testified that the flogging had nothing to do with the boy's death, and the
manager was given a nominal fine for causing hurt.[99]

The problem of light sentences for the planters was connected to both
the biased nature of medical evidence and to the light charges lodged
against them. As Curzon frankly noted, "What is called 'grievous hurt' in

[97] *Madras Mail*, February 14, 1882.
[98] "Report on Labour Immigration into Assam for the Year 1904–05," BL, IOR, V/24/1223.
[99] "Report on Labour Immigration into Assam for the Year 1899," ibid.

India [often] bears the more uncompromising title of 'murder' at home."[100] In 1890, the European manager of a plantation in North Lakhimpur was tried for voluntarily causing grievous hurt to a laborer who later died. The examining doctor testified that "the body of deceased was in many parts a pulp. There were four medical men present and none had ever before come across such a case." Not only did the initial charge of grievous hurt not square up to the fact of the man's death, but the defendant was ultimately convicted of simple assault, for which he was fined 50 rupees.[101] As Hypatia Bradlaugh Bonner of the Indian Humanitarian League acidly observed, justice worked "differently" in the colony: "In England, we should speak of these things as murder or manslaughter, in India they manage these things differently."[102]

Compounding the linked problems of light charges, light sentences, and prejudicial medical evidence was what Assam Chief Commissioner Henry Cotton called "the difficulty, if not impossibility, of bringing an offending planter to justice."[103] Due to the geographical distance separating most plantations from police stations, the social ties that bound the planter class to the colonial bureaucracy, the legal restrictions placed on the laborers' physical movement, and the planters' rights of disciplinary authority, the cases that did make it to court undoubtedly represent a small fraction of the actual incidents of European violence. The editor of *Bengalee* said as much when he rhetorically asked:

Can anyone deny that it is only the most aggravated cases which are brought before British Magistrates and find a place in the official reports and that in the great majority of cases, no complaint is preferred nor any report made? We therefore submit that the number of cases reported conveys but a most inadequate idea of the actual amount of oppression practised by some planters.[104]

Official responses to Indian violence contrasted starkly with the leniency shown towards European planters. As *Hindu Hitoishini* noted, "Crimes for which natives are severely punished, are overlooked when committed by Englishmen."[105] In 1900, the Deputy Commissioner of Darrang reported an incident involving a European manager named Wilcox who had struck a laborer with a cane. In response to the public beating, thirty of the laborer's co-workers threatened to assault Wilcox with their hoes. Wilcox reported the

---

[100] Curzon to the Secretary of State, Letter No. 59, August 28, 1901, BL, IOR, Mss Eur/ F111/160 (1901).
[101] "Report on Labour Immigration into Assam for the Year 1890," BL, IOR, V/24/1222.
[102] Indian Humanitarian League, "The Labour System of Assam," BL, IOR, L/PJ/6/765, File 1731.
[103] BL, IOR, Mss Eur/D1202/3.   [104] *Bengalee*, September 25, 1902.
[105] *Hindu Hitoishini*, June 12, 1875, BL, IOR, RNNB L/R/5/1.

threat to the police, and six of the laborers were sentenced to six months of rigorous imprisonment. Commenting on the case, Deputy Commissioner Melitus remarked: "As between man and man, I should consider this sentence excessive, but as between the Manager of a garden and his coolies, I am not prepared to say it is excessive."[106] In relation to his manager, that is, the coolie was something less than a man.

In some cases, the organs of justice were influenced by the pro-planter lobbying groups and newspapers that colluded to produce an unrelenting environment of hysteria in cases where their countrymen were assaulted or murdered. In 1907, in regard to the murder of an English planter named Bloomfield, the editors of the *Englishman* urged the government in no uncertain terms to take "the promptest of action...Once the impression is allowed to get out that a European may be assaulted and even murdered without any risk there will be an end to the British prestige in India."[107] In the Bloomfield case, the entire village seems to have participated in the attack. In 1883, at the Baramchal Tea Garden in Sylhet, a group of laborers attacked the manager and his assistant at pay-time. Fourteen of them were sentenced to long terms of imprisonment according to the official reasoning that "Examples have to be made in cases of this description on tea-gardens, as insubordination is contagious."[108]

European planters who killed their laborers were generally punished with minimal monetary fines, whereas Indians were seriously punished and sometimes executed for the same and lesser crimes. In 1908, the manager at a garden in Darrang ordered a coolie to turn out for work. The coolie shot and killed him with an arrow, and was hanged for the offense. By contrast, the European manager of a tea garden in North Lakhimpur was fined 50 rupees for simple assault after attacking a laborer who later died. To give an even closer comparison from the same year and district, in 1900, the European manager of the Eraligul Tea Estate was fined 150 rupees for wrongfully confining and severely assaulting the wife and daughter of his *chowkidar*. That same year, a group of laborers at the Alinagar Tea Estate who attacked an assistant manager for trying to "take their *izzat* [honor]" were sentenced to between three months and five years of rigorous imprisonment.[109]

The tension between state power and planter prerogative came to a head when, in response to the growing agitation in the Indian press and at

---

[106] "Report on Labour Emigration into the Province of Assam for the Year 1900," BL, IOR, V/24/1223.
[107] *Englishman*, July 21, 1907, and BL, IOR, L/PJ/6/802, File 846.
[108] "Report on Labour Immigration into Assam for the Year 1883," BL, IOR, V/24/1222.
[109] "Report on Labour Immigration into Assam for the Year 1900," BL, IOR, V/24/1223.

the direct request of Viceroy Curzon, Assam Chief Commissioner Henry Cotton pressed his district officers to dwell at greater length and detail on what were benignly called "collisions between employers and laborers." In the stinging 1899 labor report that emerged from these inquiries, Cotton concluded that "It is impossible to read the accounts of the cases of which an abstract has been given above without feeling that justice has not been always well and duly administered between man and man."[110] In a long and intense private correspondence conducted over the course of several months, both men expressed their deep concern and ambivalence about what to do with the planters. Cotton, "distressed beyond measure," bemoaned the "tale of misery and wrong" revealed by his district officers. Describing it as his "duty not to conceal the truth," Cotton highlighted the low wages, high mortality rates, widespread violence, and persistent failure of the courts to administer justice in cases involving laborers and planters.

Initially, Curzon shared Cotton's concern about the unjust and unequal sentences meted out to the planters. The two agreed that impartial justice encouraged white violence and destabilized a key imperial pier, "which is to secure justice between man and man."[111] During the summer of 1901, Curzon repeatedly urged Cotton to "let it be known that there is much dissatisfaction at headquarters" and promised that the Government of India "will most certainly intervene and some of your magistrates will find themselves in a position which it is most desirable for their own careers that they should avoid."[112] However, the government's support began to wane when the planting community erupted in outrage at Cotton's attempt to monitor and control them.

The planters viewed Cotton's report as a "declaration of war," and they raised a ruckus in Calcutta. *The Times* sent a special correspondent from London to Calcutta to vindicate the planters,[113] and the Indian Tea Association condemned Cotton's "spirit of antagonism towards the planters, which is without justification and regrettable from every point of view."[114] Some noted that not since the Ilbert Bill had such excitement been caused in non-official commercial circles in Calcutta.[115] The *Englishman* printed a cartoon titled "Two Views of the Planter" that

[110] "Report on Labour Immigration into Assam for 1900," ibid.
[111] Cotton to Curzon, September 17, 1901, Curzon's private papers, BL, IOR, Mss Eur/ D1202/2.
[112] Curzon to Cotton, July 22, 1901, ibid.
[113] Special correspondent, "The Assam Labour Question," *The Times*, April 4, 1902.
[114] Memorial from the Indian Tea Association to the Government of India, September 27, 1901, L/PJ/6/595, Files 403, 422, 424.
[115] *Indian Daily News*, March 9, 1901.

contrasted "The brutal planter as seen by Mr. Cotton" to "The brutal planter as he is."[116] In the first image, the brutal planter is seated in a chair, his legs crossed cavalierly, a bottle of beer in his pocket and a whip in his hands. In front of him two emaciated, diminutive laborers lay prostrate on the ground. In the second image, "The brutal planter as he is," the planter stands between a rock and a hard place, so to speak. In front of him is a strong, muscled native ready "to brain him with a club." In back of him, another laborer prods the planter forward with a stick. The planter, his umbrella drawn open, opines, "If I poke him with my umbrella, I get quod [imprisoned], and if I allow him to brain me, I am a dead man!!!!!!!"

Cotton was undeterred by the planters' vicious attacks. "Animated by a principle of justice," he refused to apologize for the "tale of misery and wrong" revealed by his district officers.[117] As he wrote in a "Letter to the Editor" in *The Times*:

No one can recognize more emphatically than I do that most gardens are well managed. But in a large number of gardens abuses are prevalent. I know of cases where contracts of sickly and unfit labourers have been cancelled for the purpose of keeping down the rate of mortality of Act labourers and of others where deaths have been treated as desertions for the same reason. I know of cases where it was the practice to expel sickly coolies who had become unfit for labour. I have seen with my own eyes a Government hospital full of sickly and dying contract coolies who had just been eliminated from his garden by one of the oldest and most respected tea-planters in the province. I know of cases in which coolies in the fourth year of their agreement were not paid the higher rates of salary to which they were entitled. In other cases, rice has not been provided at the statutory rate, and the subsistence allowance prescribed by law has not been paid to sick coolies or pregnant women...A case occurred lately in which a coolie woman who had escaped from a garden was recaptured and flogged and another in which a coolie who was suspected of helping others to abscond was flogged. Still more lately a case came to my notice in which coolies were confined for days in what was described as a "prison-house" on the garden and were mercilessly beaten. I must add that these bad cases have not occurred on bad gardens only. Some of the worst were reported from gardens which field a good dividend and are under the control of most respectable boards of management.[118]

As the public storm escalated, Curzon pulled back, urging Cotton in private to "go slow" and exercise "a little caution and restraint." Once unequivocally supportive of his man in Assam, Curzon now began to equivocate: "I am very much troubled at all this feeling that has been stirred up for if it be fomented and magnified, I cannot see where it will

[116] *Englishman*, September 4, 1901.
[117] Cotton, "Letter to the Editor," *The Times*, September 5, 1902.
[118] Cotton, "Letter to the Editor," *The Times*, September 11, 1902.

stop."[119] The rug was completely pulled out from under Cotton's feet when Curzon capitulated to the planters in a sympathetic letter sent to the Indian Tea Association:

The Governor-General in Council is glad to acknowledge that the relations between the great majority of planters and their coolies are of a kindly nature, that the planter takes a humane interest in the well-being of the families amongst whom he lives and with whom he is in almost daily contact, and that the coolies look to their employer with the regard which is ordinarily felt by Indian servants for their masters. Instances of oppression are unhappily not altogether rare, and the Governor-General in Council entirely sympathizes with the Chief Commissioner in the desire that they should be severely dealt with. But he sees no reason to find in them a stigma which should apply to the planting community as a whole.[120]

In private correspondence with the Secretary of State, however, Curzon continued to speak disparagingly about the planters: "These managers are drawn from a most inferior class of Englishmen and Scotchmen; they do not know the language; they have a profound contempt for the Native and they are sometimes guilty of serious acts of lust and oppression."[121] Cotton was astonished by Curzon's "double-faced manner: writing confidently from one standpoint and acting publicly from exactly the opposite." Nonetheless, Cotton was forced to take the fall, returning home after a long and fruitful career in India.[122]

As the controversy with Cotton demonstrated, the relationship between the planting community and the colonial state was complex and contentious. The ambiguous and strained nature of this relationship was neatly captured at the time by the Secretary of State who, in reference to the "mean whites," wrote: "They have their merits, and in emergencies many of them could be relied on, but their intelligence is narrow, their standard low, and their prejudices invincible." In the Secretary of State's view, the planters could be relied on in a political pinch, but their uncontrolled behavior at the vulnerable margins of state control threatened to "ultimately upset our rule in India."[123]

---

[119] Curzon to Cotton, September 10, 1901, Cotton's private papers, BL, IOR, Mss Eur/D1202/2.

[120] Government of India to the Indian Tea Association, February 5, 1902, Cotton's private papers, BL, IOR, Mss Eur/D1202/3.

[121] Curzon to the Secretary of State, August 5, 1903, Curzon's private papers, BL, IOR, Mss Eur/F111/162 (1903).

[122] Cotton's private papers, BL, IOR, Mss Eur/D1202/3.

[123] Letter No. 68, September 30, 1903, Curzon's private papers, BL, IOR, Mss Eur/F111/162 (1903).

European critics of planter violence, including Cotton, continued to implore the colonial government to hold the tea planters to account, if only to protect the empire from a growing political threat:

The tea industry and tea planters as a body have become so intolerant of Government control and interference that they regard a derogatory word as an insult and the official who utters it as an enemy...it will become a very serious element in the political situation if the non-official European community should from one cause or another find reason for encouraging itself to believe that officials who are confronted with facts damaging to an industry in which European interests are involved, may be induced to keep silence for fear of being overwhelmed by a storm of invective.[124]

Indian critics of the tea industry were less concerned with the question of colonial stability than with the physical consequences and legal meaning of the state's failure to administer fair and equal justice. The Indian press ultimately interpreted Cotton's departure as proof that "The primary object of British rule in India is to benefit the European capitalist and merchant, even, if necessary, at the sacrifice of justice and humanity."[125]

Crime, conflict, and the politics of peasant resistance

If the violence of the planter was born simultaneously from his sense of power and powerlessness – "One against a thousand hostile to him"[126] – the violence of the laborer had equally complex roots. Official reports on labor immigration, the administration of criminal justice, and policing in Assam present a statistical portrait of plantation violence that offers hints towards understanding strategies of everyday peasant resistance and insights into the coercive nature of colonial justice. Due to the limited availability of sources, I rely here on the official record and the private papers of planters, which I read "upside down"[127] or "against the grain,"[128] to offer a glimpse of how tea workers resisted their oppressors.

The annual reports on collisions between employers and laborers document both laborers' complaints about their employers' criminal behavior and management's complaints about rioting, assaults, and acts of intimidation by workers. The government openly recognized the connection between the two, because attacks by coolies on management were often understood as reactions to the injustices committed against them. As the

---

[124] Cotton's Minute of October 8, 1901, BL, IOR, L/PJ/6/595, File 424.
[125] *Bengalee*, March, 10, 1901.   [126] *Englishman*, August 18, 1874.
[127] A. L. Stoler, *Capitalism and Confrontation in Sumatra's Plantation Belt, 1870–1979* (New Haven, CT: Yale University Press, 1985).
[128] R. Guha, "The Prose of Counter-Insurgency," in R. Guha and G. C. Spivak (eds.), *Selected Subaltern Studies* (New York: Columbia University Press, 1988), pp. 45–88.

labor report of 1902–03 noted, even as labor riots had to be controlled, so did the root causes of peasant unruliness require government oversight: "Discipline must be maintained on tea gardens, and unruliness which may lead to rioting must be strictly checked. But the occurrence of cases of this description throws upon the State some responsibility for preventing any such injustice as would give the coolies a substantial grievance."[129] Read in this way, each reported incident of Indian crime has dual implications – evidencing both a European attack and an act of Indian retaliation. As the government itself noted in the labor report of 1890, "a disturbance or rising on the part of the coolies generally indicates mismanagement or a want of touch between employers and laborers."[130]

The terms of the penal contract and the highly controlled nature of life on the plantation made it almost impossible for workers to lodge their complaints with the authorities.[131] The inability of peasants with grievances to leave the estate also led to violent acts of peasant reprisal. Tea workers resisted the compulsory labor regime through violent and nonviolent means, using overt actions (refusing to work, labor strikes, violent confrontations) and other weapons of the weak (indolence or avoidance, threats, destruction of property). In 1886, twenty-seven laborers assaulted the manager, engineer, and native doctor on a garden in Kamrup because they said they were given too much work.[132] Although multiple incidents of Indian resistance are found in every annual labor report, the political basis of these acts was generally denied until the early twentieth century, when local peasant movements were drawn by Gandhi and the Congress into the larger nationalist movement.[133]

Whereas European violence was viewed as a rational and necessary mode of labor control, peasant attacks were generally described as acts of insubordination, fanaticism, or insanity rather than motivated and determined actions with rational objectives. George Barker tells the story of a European planter in Assam who awoke to find a "fanatical" employee standing over him with a knife in his hand:

He [the worker] had a dream, wherein, at the peril of offending his deities, he was ordered to kill the sahib...When asked in court to give some explanation for his dastardly behavior, and whether the sahib was cruel, he candidly confessed that the sahib was an exceptionally good master, treated all the coolies well, and they had

[129] "Report on Labour Immigration into Assam for the years 1902–03," BL, IOR, V/24/1223.
[130] "Report on Labour Immigration into Assam for the Year 1890," ibid.
[131] Ganguli, *Slavery*, p. 39.
[132] "Report on Labour Immigration into Assam for the Year 1886," BL, IOR, V/24/1222.
[133] J. Pouchepadass, *Champaran and Gandhi: Planters, Peasants and Gandhian Politics* (New York: Oxford University Press, 1999).

no grounds for complaint in any way. This and many other stories of the fanatical vagaries of the coolies are in circulation throughout the country and are at the outset rather terrifying to newcomers.[134]

Contrary to Barker's description of the irrational, terrifying, and semi-conscious coolie, accounts of peasant violence in Assam clearly reflect premeditation, organization, and rational inspiration. Attacks on European planters usually involved one of four elements: a manager with an abusive reputation; refusal to work (often on a Sunday, a holiday, or after the expiration of a labor contract); retaliation for having been struck first or having seen a fellow worker struck; and physical and sexual assaults on women workers.

Laborers tended to act collectively, using their work tools – knives, hoes, and pickaxes – as weapons to threaten and attack their superiors. The tendency, in Cotton's words, "to resent a blow by striking a blow in return" could turn the oppressive plantation environment on its head, as the laborers had the advantage in terms of their numbers and formidable instruments.[135] As planter J. H. Williams recalled in his memoir, *Tea Estates and Their Management*, "It is quite startling to be surrounded by a gang of 100-odd pruners armed with their pruning knives."[136] George Barker also observed that the pruner's 8-inch-long blade "in the hands of an irate coolie forms a very awkward weapon."[137]

The bungalow itself was often a symbolic target of attack, and it was not uncommon for workers to either burn the planter's home – an act referred to in official reports as "mischief by fire"[138] – or to use it to imprison its owner (see Figure 4.5). In 1884, the European manager of the Bowalia Tea Garden was seriously assaulted and confined in his home for several hours after he publicly caned a boy in the presence of assembled laborers. Twelve tea workers were sentenced to rigorous imprisonment for terms ranging from three days to one year; the manager was fined 50 rupees.[139]

Collective attacks on European planters were always coordinated efforts that required planning. Indeed, the potential consequences of resistance were so high that insurgencies on the plantation occurred only after prolonged oppression and careful consideration. On February 6, 1892, the manager of the Barhalla Tea Estate ordered his laborers to

[134] Barker, *A Tea Planter's Life*, pp. 112–113.
[135] "Report on Labour Emigration into the Province of Assam for the Year 1899," BL, IOR, V/24/1223.
[136] BL, IOR, Mss Eur 235/1.   [137] Barker, *A Tea Planter's Life*, p. 130.
[138] "Report on Labour Immigration into Assam for the Year 1888," BL, IOR, V/24/1222.
[139] "Report on Labour Emigration into the Province of Assam for the Year 1890," BL, IOR, V/24/1223; and "Report on Labour Emigration into the Province of Assam for the Year 1884," BL, IOR, V/24/1222.

Figure 4.5   **Tea planter's bungalow, Khorhaut Tea Estate, Assam, India, 1935**

Tea workers resisted their employers in a variety of ways, frequently through acts of collective violence. The tea planter's bungalow was often a symbolic target attacked by angry laborers. This particular bungalow in Khorhaut, occupied by Edward Goodall in 1934 and sketched the following year, was not attacked in this fashion. However, Edward Goodall's son, Richard, notes that his father used to recall hearing the cobras sliding over the thatched roof at night.

remove a man named Harilas who was causing a disturbance while pay was being distributed. Harilas called out to his others co-workers to "seize Mr. Smith," and a large group threw broken bricks and dry clay at Smith and his assistant.[140] In 1883, at the Baramchal Tea Garden, a large group of workers attacked the manager and his assistant on payday and fled with the cash. After resisting arrest, fourteen of the ringleaders were tried and sentenced to long terms of rigorous imprisonment.[141] In March 1903, seven laborers were convicted of rioting and one of attempting to cause hurt with an instrument in connection with an attack on Mr. A. Lea-Juckes, manager at the Sephanjuri Tea Estate. One of the defendants, Basu, had stopped the manager "in a threatening way" by holding up a *lathi* (wooden club) and asking for leave. Lea-Juckes told him to come

[140] "Report on Labour Immigration into Assam for the Year 1892," BL, IOR, V/24/1223.
[141] "Report on Labour Immigration into Assam for the Year 1883," BL, IOR, V/24/1222.

along to the bungalow. When Basu refused, Lea-Juckes took him by the neck and pushed him saying, "Go along." Basu immediately shouted something in Oriya, and fifty to sixty Oriyas came rushing out armed with *lathis*. One of them knocked Lea-Juckes' hat off with his hand, and another lifted a *dao* (sword) to strike him before others interfered to stop him. In his decision, Judge B. B. Neubould noted: "The attack on the Manager appears to have been pre-organized and it seems highly likely that Basu behaved as he did with the deliberate intention of provoking the Manager to assault him and then give the other coolies who were waiting about armed with *lathis* an apparent justification for their action." Basu was sentenced to nine months of rigorous imprisonment.[142]

Refusal to work was another common tactic of collective resistance that often led to violent confrontation. In 1891, ten workers from the Borjuli Tea Garden refused to turn out for work. According to the manager, Mr Creagh, they had been up the night before celebrating. The following morning, some were "sulky and obstinate and refused to speak" to him as he made his way through the lines. At one point Creagh turned on his heel and found a worker with his stick raised above his head poised to strike him. Creagh knocked the man down and was attacked by the others on the line who chased him as he ran towards his bungalow.[143] The following year on the Tiphuk Tea Estate, thirty laborers struck work and left the plantation. The guard who was sent after the group was beat up, and the armed workers returned to attack the European manager.[144] On *Kali pujah* day (a Hindu holiday) in 1900, James Begg, the manager of the Halungari Tea Estate, tried to force his laborers to work. In response, they threw anything they could at him and surrounded him with sticks in their hands; Begg escaped without injury.[145]

In Assam, planters and officials were keenly aware of the incendiary use of women as signs by which positions of power and powerlessness were communicated between men. European managers often flaunted their despotic authority by laying their hands on Indian women workers. Due to cross-culturally held notions about women as property, and specifically South Asian ideas about male honor, European sexual advances and physical assaults on Indian women invariably provoked violent reprisals. Recognizing this, in 1893, the Chief Commissioner of Assam directed all magistrates to imprison for a substantial term any employer who flogged a woman or caused her to be flogged.[146] This order did little to stop the gender violence.

---

[142] BL, IOR, L/PJ/6/527, No. 27.
[143] "Report on Labour Immigration into Assam for the Year 1891," BL, IOR, V/24/1223.
[144] Ibid.   [145] Ibid.   [146] Ibid.

In 1890, at the Silghat Tea Garden, the manager, H. L. Smith, was "set upon and somewhat severely handled by about forty coolies, who at the trial alleged that the manager had assaulted a coolie woman for disobedience to orders and that this led to their attack upon him." Fourteen men were sentenced to nine months of rigorous imprisonment.[147] Eight years later, the manager and assistant manager of the Kellyden Tea Estate tried to force their tea workers to return to work after a three-day *Holi* holiday (a Hindu holiday). When the laborers refused to obey, the assistant manager took a woman by the hand to force her to work, at which point "A number of coolies attacked him and the manager with sticks, while one made a dangerous assault on the manager with a hoe. The labour force was in a dangerously excited state for two or three days, the police, who were called up, being at first not strong enough to restore order." The ringleaders in the incident were sentenced to up to two years of rigorous imprisonment.[148]

When the violence directed at women was of a sexual nature, the reactions from tea workers were even more explosive. In 1899, Mr. Bellwood, the manager of the Nadua Tea Estate, was seriously assaulted with sticks by six of his workers, who were enraged by charges that Bellwood had raped a girl on the garden. Bellwood remained in a critical condition for many weeks, and the men who attacked him were each sentenced to two years of rigorous imprisonment.[149] In another case that was relayed to the annual session of the Indian National Congress in 1896, a large group of laborers from the Mesaijan Tea Garden claimed that the clothes of three fellow women workers had been lifted to their waists, and that after the women had been tied to the porch of the manager's house, they were beaten on the buttocks with a stirrup leather under the orders of the assistant manager.[150]

The sexual violence of the planters existed within the context of their virtually absolute power on the plantation. In a case involving both sexual assault and wrongful confinement, C. O. Walling, manager of the Maduri Tea Estate, summoned a 15-year-old girl to come into his bedroom and fan him. Walling had previously made "indecent overtures" to the girl, and when she refused to enter the bedroom, he hit her over the shoulders with a cane and detained her for the rest of the day in the bathroom. When the girl and her mother made a complaint at the *thana*, they (rather than Walling) were held in custody. Three months later, Walling began to harass the girl again by grabbing her arm in the garden and trying to

---

[147] "Report on Labour Immigration into Assam for the Year 1890," BL, IOR, V/24/1222.
[148] "Report on Labour Immigration into Assam for the Year 1893," BL, IOR, V/24/1223.
[149] Ibid.
[150] "Report on Labour Immigration into Assam for the Year 1888," BL, IOR, V/24/1222.

force her back to the bungalow. Walling was ultimately convicted of wrongful restraint and sentenced to one week of rigorous imprisonment.

In a notorious rape case involving a planter's agent named Charles Webb, a woman named Sukurmani was abducted from a flat that held a "batch of coolies" en route to the Hoolongari Tea Garden. Before abducting her, Webb's henchmen had asked the laborers to "give one of our women to the Sahib." When the men refused to "forfeit our honour," Webb beat Sukurmani's husband with a leather belt and demanded that the remaining laborers "have connection with [their] wives before him."[151] Webb confined and raped Sukurmani repeatedly in his cabin overnight, ultimately causing her death. The post-mortem report dubiously concluded that Sukurmani had died of natural causes, and Webb was convicted only of wrongful confinement, for which he was fined 100 rupees and released.

Tea workers did not always resist plantation violence with violence. In spite of the odds stacked against them, they sometimes used the law in strategic ways that did not simply reinforce the power of the colonial legal system. Often, this involved bringing the power of numbers before the law. In 1896, during the trial of eleven laborers who had attacked the manager of the Bojran Tea Estate, 300 workers from the plantation sat outside the court on strike.[152] Six years later, the Deputy Commissioner of Sibsagar noted a "special device" used by workers from several gardens in the Sadr subdivision: "It is that of coming into the headquarters in a body to the number of one hundred to two hundred on the pretext of making some complaint."[153] Mass strikes during criminal trials of co-workers simultaneously demonstrated the demand for justice and public accountability, as well as a formal transgression of law.

Sometimes tea workers violently transgressed the law by attacking the figures and symbols of authority, while at other times collective action was used to intimate the possible use of force. In 1910, after attacking the manager of the Kurma Tea Estate, the laborers gave a "formidable show of resistance to the Subdivisional Officer and the police which necessitated the despatch of armed police to the garden."[154] These types of action remind us that although the legal system clearly favored the planters, the law did not always and unambiguously act on oppressed peoples. For the most part, tea workers knew that they had no legal redress. But there is

[151] "Papers Relating to the Webb Case," Ganguli, *Slavery*, p. 72.
[152] "Report on Labour Immigration into Assam for the Year 1896," BL, IOR, V/24/1223.
[153] Ibid.
[154] "Report on Immigrant Labour in the Assam Districts of Eastern Bengal and Assam for the Year ending June 30, 1911," BL, IOR, V/24/1224.

also evidence that they understood, engaged with, and sometimes found ways to appropriate the mechanisms of justice to their own ends.

Planter violence and Indian nationalism

Everyday resistance on the Assam tea plantations preceded organized intervention by the Indian nationalist leadership. Broad public awareness about the oppressive tea industry grew in the late nineteenth century due to the efforts of journalists, reformers, and activists, especially in Bengal.[155] In the 1870s, Ram Kumar Vidyaratna, who was assigned to do missionary work in Assam by the Sadharan Brahmo Samaj, printed trials of brutal planters in the Bengali newspaper *Sanjibani* and ultimately published a highly critical work based on interviews with tea workers titled *Kulikahini* (1888). The book was an instant success.[156] Having read Vidyaratna's work, the Indian Association dispatched Dwarkanath Ganguli to Assam to investigate. Ganguli also published a series of critical articles about life on the tea plantations in *Bengalee* and *Sanjibani*, and later printed these pieces in book form as *Slavery in British Dominion*.

Vidyaratna, Ganguli, and the organizations they represented made important interventions into the lives of the tea workers. Although their method of polite, written redress was quite different from the non-cooperative and violent forms of struggle embraced by the laborers themselves, these Bengali activists painstakingly scoured the official record and tirelessly called upon the "Christian Government" to fulfill its promises to protect the poor and to enforce its own laws. The "lamentable poverty and abject degradation" which they wrote about but did not experience firsthand not only catapulted their political critique of British rule forward, it was a crucial contribution to the Indian labor movement.[157]

The labor question played a complex role in the growth of Indian nationalism owing to the impact of colonialism on India's largely poor and working population and because the labor question frequently put the class interests of India's nationalist leaders at odds with the mass struggle for freedom. Nationalist reactions to labor issues in the nineteenth century tended to be pro-employer and resistant to legislation designed

---

[155] N. Varma, "Coolie Strikes Back: Collective Protest and Action in the Colonial British Indian Tea Plantations of Assam, 1880–1920," *Indian Historical Review*, 33 (2006), 259–287.

[156] J. C. Bagal, *History of the Indian Association, 1876–1951* (Calcutta: Indian Association, 1953), p. 102.

[157] Ganguli, *Slavery*, p. 18.

to protect Indian workers. The British Indian Association, a proto-nationalist organization founded by Bengali *zamindars* in 1851, went as far as to ally themselves with the ultra-conservative and virulently racist European and Anglo-Indian Defence Association in order to oppose the pro-peasant Bengal Tenancy Act of 1885. As Bipan Chandra notes, most of the leading nationalist newspapers of the period "remained either silent or adopted an attitude of hostility towards labour."[158] The issue of plantation labor and white violence, which pitted British planters against Indian workers, offered an exception to this nationalist moment of silence on labor, as the abuses of the white planters could be attacked without fracturing the fragile bonds that held India's rich and poor together in anti-colonial unity.

Nationalist leaders and the Indian press drew frequent attention to the morbidity, mortality, abysmal living arrangements, and slave-like working conditions on the tea gardens. Although many of those who were incensed by the situation in Assam probably lorded over their own domestic servants and tenants in a way that was immoral, if not illegal, the Indian national leadership turned the "coolie question" into a scandalous and chilling national issue that captivated and motivated public opinion.

The Indian National Congress was at first reluctant to adopt the cause of the tea workers, which was at that stage seen as a provincial rather than a national issue. Although four Assam delegates attended the Congress session at Calcutta in 1886, the Congress did not pass a formal resolution condemning the inhumanity of the indenture system until 1896.[159] In 1898, the Indian Association sent a long memorial to the Government of India detailing the grave abuses that were prevalent in Assam and requesting the appointment of an independent commission of enquiry. While the tone of their petition was disturbingly paternalistic – the Association framed the problem in language that assumed their duty to protect "the ignorance of the laborers and their utter helplessness and inability to protect their interests" – the emphasis on the "interest of justice" placed the Indian Association's concerns within the context of larger questions about European violence and "the firm and impartial administration of justice" in India.[160] The Congress eventually turned the "coolie question" into a matter that mobilized the Indian masses. The abolition of Assam's indenture system was in no small part due to their interventions and activism.

---

[158] Chandra, *Rise and Growth*, p. 357.   [159] Guha, *Planter-Raj*, pp. 64–67.
[160] Bagal, *History*, Appendix E.

Conclusion

In both letter and practice, law in colonial Assam bore down brutally on the bodies of tea laborers. The letter of the law accorded the tea planters private powers of punishment, which effectively sanctioned acts of criminal violence. As *The Times'* special correspondent noted, a region like Assam required an exceptional law to sustain the manager's dominance over the working masses:

> In a country like Assam, where the planter rises every morning with the consciousness that his own safety and that of his wife and children depend very largely upon his moral influence and authority over several hundreds of ignorant and excitable natives…a frankly egalitarian doctrine…in practice is likely to result not merely in the weakening of the authority of the managers of tea gardens [but is also] exceedingly injurious to the position of Englishmen in India as a whole.[161]

In practice, the strength of racial solidarity in the region produced startlingly biased judgments and punishments. This was aided in large part by medical evidence about the weak coolie constitution that effectively exonerated Europeans from criminal liability and punishment, and made a flogged man responsible for his own death. As George Trevelyan vividly remarked: "The physical conformation of these men is so frail, that a blow on the body is liable to cause instant death. It is commonly believed that this proceeds from the large size of the spleen."[162]

The racially differential treatment of British and Indian defendants in Assam reflected the hierarchical and unequal order of the empire and the racial basis of its laws. The relationship between the planters and the colonial state, managers and magistrates, was both co-dependent and contentious. Control of Assam was simply not possible without the planters' participation, and for this the planters were accorded special legal powers. At the same time, their uncontrolled behavior at the empire's fragile margins sometimes unsettled the imperial conscience and threatened to upset state stability. Although officials like Cotton and Curzon believed that the extreme and enduring plantation violence was an exception to the colonial order rather than an intrinsic feature of it, many in India and at home argued that the criminal behavior of the "brutal planters" offered a graphic example of the centrality of violence to empire.

The workers' daily acts of disobedience, dissent, and violence on the tea gardens mark the tension between law and labor. It was, after all, the law that bound the worker to the oppressive plantation environment, and it is

[161] "Letter to the Editor," *The Times*, September 9, 1902.
[162] Trevelyan, *Competition Wallah*, p. 62.

therefore not surprising that labor confrontations frequently involved violent assaults rather than formal legal claims. At the same time, laborers also devised clever strategies to use the law in ways that did not simply reinforce the power of the legal system. For the bonded laborers of Assam, and for the Indian activists who made their mistreatment and oppression a nationalist issue, the colonial promise of justice sometimes offered a language and method of resistance.

Don't really convincingly demonstrate that cooties used the law to evade justice.

5 "A judicial scandal": the imperial conscience and the race against empire

What does it matter if a Native dies? His life has no value. If a Native kills a European, nay, even if he does a slight injury to him, heaven and earth will be moved by them to crush him. What is the moral to be drawn from this deplorable state of things? What does it point to? It is nothing else than this: that Europeans may take, with impunity, the lives of Natives. They may shoot them; they may beat them; they may do anything with them they please. They have to fear nobody. The law is powerless to bring them within its clutches. The Magistrates, who are their brethren, will connive with them as much as possible. They can raise every possible defence and it will be most favourably entertained. They may safely urge that the native was suffering from enlarged spleen; that they mistook him for an animal; that they acted in self-defence; that they were not in their senses; that they were intoxicated. In short, whatever defence they raise will be sufficient to save them. This is how the law lies. The question is how long is this deplorable state of things to continue?

Native Opinion, December 28, 1893[1]

The English may be in danger of losing their command of India, because they have not learned how to command themselves.

Viceroy Curzon, July 26, 1902[2]

In the late nineteenth century, newspapers across India were reporting daily on the menace of white violence and the scandalous acquittals of Britons accused of brutalizing natives. In August 1895, *Bengalee* (Bengal) expressed the "firm conviction that no justice is to be had in our courts where Europeans are charged with acts of violence done to the natives of India. It is not a baseless conviction. A long series of cases support it."[3] In February 1903, *Hindu Punch* (Bombay) commented that "Scarcely a week passes by without our hearing a report of some European having either killed, assaulted or insulted a native of this

[1] BL, IOR, L/R/5/148.
[2] Curzon to the Commander-in-Chief, July 26, 1902, BL, IOR, Mss Eur/F111/402.
[3] Sanyal, *Record of Criminal Cases*, pp. 159–160.

country."[4] In March 1903, a European soldier who stoned a native police constable to death at the Delhi Darbar was sentenced to nine weeks of simple imprisonment. When his already too light sentence was quashed on appeal, *Surodaya Prakasika* (Bangalore) acidly remarked: "Really it seems to be no crime to kill a Hindu."[5]

This chapter brings the contests over white violence and the rule of law squarely into the field of anti-colonial politics. Despite the Government of India's rhetorical stance of equality before the law, the political and legal framework for tolerating or rationalizing racial violence actually grew over time. In the 1880s and 1890s, Indian nationalists and anti-imperialists abroad brought constant attention to the perverse verdicts delivered by European judges and juries in so-called racial cases. The mounting legal and political claims that were instigated by various well-publicized trials culminated in the appointment of the Racial Distinctions Committee (1921), which sought not only to eliminate race-based privileges in the Indian law, but also to redress "the color of the law" in the wider imperial system.[6]

Colonial racism and "accidental" death

As I have argued throughout this book, white violence was not exceptional but an everyday part of British rule in the subcontinent. Individual acts of violence must be understood in the institutional context of colonialism and a legal system that enabled it. The colonial promise of uniform legal equality was blatantly undermined by the institutionalization of race-based legal privileges and by the discriminatory practices of police, judges, and juries that consistently tipped the scales of justice. Britons accused of assaulting and murdering Indians were booked on lesser, if any, criminal charges that invariably resulted in little to no punishment. As *Faridpur Hitaishini* bitingly noted in 1903, the colonial law was even inferior to the Hindu law when it came to delivering justice:

> According to the Hindu *Shastras* [treatises], when a man kills a cat, he must, by way of expiation for his sin, make a gift of salt to the Brahmin priest equal in weight to the animal killed. When a cow is killed, the *Shastras* require the sinner to give away many *kahans* [silver coins] of cowries. But when a black nigger is murdered by a European, the murderer is in most cases either let off or fined a few rupees.[7]

Although white violence was institutionalized in the policies and practices of the colonial government, there was a constant strand of official

---

[4] *Hindu Punch*, February 25, 1903, BL, IOR, L/R/5/158.
[5] *Surodaya Prakasika*, March 18, 1903, BL, IOR, L/R/5/111.   [6] O'Brien, *Color of the Law*.
[7] *Faridpur Hitaishini*, November 1, 1903, BL, IOR, L/R/5/29.

opinion that expressed horror at its excesses and attempted to restrict the problem to the lower classes of British society. In 1876, Viceroy Lytton observed that:

> Our greatest danger in India is from the whites, who with far less justification for it, have all the arrogance of the Jamaica Planters, or American Southerners, and, claiming absolute liberty to outrage in every way the feelings of a vast alien population, resent the slightest control on the part either of the Government at home or the Government in India.[8]

Lytton's successor, Lord Ripon, argued that the increasing number of Europeans in India was one of the chief difficulties facing the government owing to their deep sense of racial superiority and their "'damned nigger' style of conversation."[9]

Despite the state's disavowal and condemnation of the physical excesses of "the lower classes of Europeans," who, as George Trevelyan bluntly noted, "are a little too apt to be free with their fists," British criminal violence was a consistent feature of colonial life, as were the laws that enabled it.[10] By 1898, the Code of Criminal Procedure provided legal privileges to European British subjects defined as:

> (i) any subject of Her Majesty born, naturalized or domiciled in the United Kingdom of Great Britain and Ireland or in any of the European, American, or Australian Colonies or possessions of Her Majesty, or in the Colony of New Zealand, or in the Colony of the Cape of Good Hope or Natal; (ii) any child or grand-child of any such person by legitimate descent.[11]

No magistrate, unless he was a justice of the peace and a magistrate of the first class and a European British subject (or a district or Presidency magistrate), had jurisdiction to inquire into or try any charge against a European British subject. European British subjects could also claim a trial by jury with no less than half European or American jurors in every case before a District magistrate, Sessions Court, and High Court, which exceeded their right to claim trial by jury in England. All capital charges against European British subjects had to be tried before the High Courts; Sessions Courts could not sentence European British subjects to more than one year in prison; European British subjects had an unrestrained right of appeal to the High or Sessions Court and wider remedies in *habeas*

---

[8] Lytton to John Morley, September 24, 1876, Lytton's private papers, BL, IOR, Mss Eur/218/522/15.
[9] S. R. Mehrotra, *The Emergence of the Indian National Congress* (Delhi: Vikas Publications, 1971), p. 379.
[10] Trevelyan, *Competition Wallah*, p. 63.
[11] Code of Criminal Procedure (1898), ch. 1, section 4.

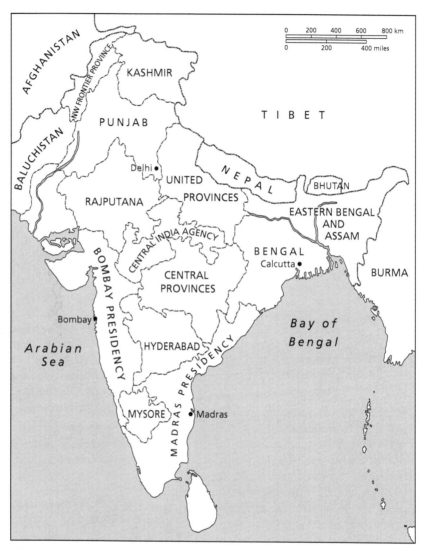

Map 5.1   India in 1909.

corpus.[12] The special privileges provided to European British subjects, combined with their close social ties to European judicial officers, ensured that they received especially light charges and punishments in cases where they brutalized natives (see Map 5.1).

[12] Code of Criminal Procedure (1898), ch. 33, "Criminal Proceedings against Europeans and Americans."

The best available source on British violence in the nineteenth century is the wide variety of Indian newspapers that vigilantly brought public notice to *safed insaaf* (white justice), *jati-bairata* (racial animosity), and the racial discrimination perpetrated daily in colonial courtrooms. In the eyes of the Indian press, the courts failed miserably when it came to white-on-black crime. As the editor of *Kesari* vividly observed, "The goddess of British Justice, though blind, is able to distinguish unmistakably black from white."[13] What began in the 1860s in the Bengal-based press as a condemnation of the oppressive indigo system erupted into a constant stream of reporting in the English language and vernacular papers on the "perverse verdicts" delivered by white juries in trials of Britons charged with murder, assault, wrongful confinement, and other violent crimes against Indians. "In our country," *Rangalay* remarked in 1903, "there are only two killers – the Almighty and the Englishman; otherwise men in this country would not die."[14] That same year, *Basumati* blasted the "race-animosity" of Englishmen who "turn up their noses at the name of the Indians, call the Indians niggers, and break their spleens and livers at their sweet will and pleasure."[15]

In the late eighteenth century, violent whites had generally escaped justice because the law had little power to apprehend, try, or punish them at the local level. It was one thing to get no justice where there was no law, but as law's empire expanded, European British subjects remained largely immune from prosecution and punishment. In the late nineteenth century, Britons who mortally assaulted and murdered Indians routinely had the charges against them reduced from murder (killing with malice aforethought) to manslaughter (unlawful killing without malice or premeditation), to grievous hurt, to sometimes nothing at all. Reduced charges meant mitigated punishment and little to no culpability, which, as *People and Prativasi* pointed out, contradicted imperial pledges of racial equality: "If it had not been proclaimed by the late Empress of India that she would observe perfect equality between her British and Indian subjects, we would have looked on partiality in administration of justice in silence and known that the ruling race possesses an undisputed right to kill the natives of this country."[16]

In contrast to colonial modernity's promise of progress, a promise that included formal legal equality and impartial justice, the Indian public perception was that colonial justice became *less* just over time in cases

---

[13] *Kesari*, November 12, 1907, BL, IOR, L/PJ/6/848, File 453.
[14] *Rangalay*, November 22, 1903, BL, IOR, L/R/5/29.
[15] *Basumati*, October 24, 1903, BL, IOR, L/R/5/29.
[16] *People and Prativasi*, September 16, 1903, ibid.

where Britons were charged with violence against Indians. In 1893, *Pratod* noted that:

> Justice was impartially administered by Englishmen when they first came to India...Now-a-days an Englishman fires at a Native woman from a distance of 30 feet taking her to be a bear, the woman dies, her husband is pacified by being paid Rs. 50 and it is asserted by all from His Excellency the Governor to a Police officer that no crime has been committed![17]

This public perception is, in fact, supported by the historical record. The harsh punishments meted out to convicted Europeans in the first chapter of this book – incarceration, deportation, and even execution – stand in marked contrast to the leniency shown to them one hundred years later.

As Richard C. Hula demonstrates in his work on crime in colonial Calcutta, colonial justice did not over time grow more effective or more just. In fact, the conviction rate of Europeans charged with serious crimes in Calcutta declined over the course of the nineteenth century.[18] The cases that appear in the record on "European Misconduct in India 1766–1824" also suggest that the Calcutta Supreme Court was more likely to convict violent Europeans in the early colonial period than the High Courts were later on.

Take, for example, the case of James Halkett. In 1812, Halkett, an assistant ship-builder in Calcutta, was charged with the murder of an Indian carpenter named Soobul. Soobul had summoned Halkett for instructions on how to join a piece of plank to the ship. An annoyed Halkett disdainfully responded, *"Banchod tum"* (you sister-fucker), and struck Soobul three times with his fist. When Soobul repeated his request for assistance, Halkett kicked him in the groin and punched him. Soobul fell down unconscious and died within thirty minutes. The surgeon who opened Soobul's body, Dr. Thomas Larkins, found blood coagulated in his abdomen, an inflamed and enlarged left kidney, an inflamed left lung, an enlarged spleen, and a "very much emaciated" body. Larkins concluded that Soobul died from violent external injury. Halkett was convicted of murder and sentenced to death. His death sentence was subsequently commuted to transportation for life at Botany Bay.[19]

By contrast, in the late nineteenth century, Europeans were routinely acquitted in cases where the evidence against them was more than compelling. In 1885, two British planters in Assam (Hext and Bragg) were

---

[17] *Pratod*, May 29, 1893, BL, IOR, L/R/5/148.
[18] R. C. Hula, "Calcutta: The Politics of Crime and Conflict, 1800 to the 1970s," in T. R. Gurr, P. N. Grabosky, and R. C. Hula (eds.), *The Politics of Crime and Conflict: A Comparative History of Four Cities* (London: Sage Publications, 1977), pt. V.
[19] BL, IOR, O/5/13.

acquitted in the murder of an Indian boy who enraged them by failing to dismount from his horse as their carriage approached. Hext and Bragg horsewhipped and kicked the boy, and then ran him over with their carriage, killing him on the spot. In court, death was determined to be an accident, and Hext and Bragg were released. As *Pataka* remarked, "Beasts are killed for the sport of Englishmen, and natives are killed for the pacification of their anger."[20]

Between 1880 and 1900, there were eighty-one reported "shooting accidents" in which European defendants claimed to have mistaken their Indian victims for animals such as monkeys, birds, and buffalos. *Som Prakash* noted that "Anglo-Indians now hunt natives under the mistaken impression that they are birds or beasts."[21] *Samvad Purnachandrodaya* remarked that "shooting natives has become something like a disease with them. They are tried by their own countrymen, so they are generally acquitted after shooting natives."[22] And *Karnatak Patra* wondered how the courts could let them get away with this:

Has the Government not heard that a Native is made to assume the form of a beast or a bird in order to be murdered with impunity by his European conqueror? Has it not been sufficiently public that blood stains on the clothes and person of a European charged with the murder of a native constitute no evidence to prove his crime?[23]

Indian-killing was likened by critics to other violent colonial sports such as pig-sticking and tiger-hunting (see Figure 5.1). In reference to a case where a European boy shot an Indian dead and was fined 10 rupees, *Sulabh Dainik* remarked: "The English are the ruling race in this country and India is their sporting ground. Englishmen come to India to make money and to make themselves merry. Here shooting of tigers and bears is not sufficient sport; there can be no full sporting without occasional indulgence in native shooting."[24] In 1885, the *Amrita Bazar Patrika* sarcastically compared the plethora of European shooting accidents to the total absence of Indian accidents: "it is strange that natives, many of whom use guns, so rarely shoot at people by accident. The reason doubtless is that, while natives fear the punishment prescribed by law for such offences, Europeans are quite free from such fear."[25]

The "accidental shootings" demonstrated two key points about the relationship between law and violence in colonial India. First, the literal

[20] *Pataka*, February 20, 1885, BL, IOR, L/R/5/11.   [21] *Som Prakash*, April 6, 1885, ibid.
[22] *Samvad Purnachandrodaya*, February 2, 1885, ibid.
[23] *Karnatak Patra*, 30 January, 1893, BL, IOR, L/R/5/148.
[24] *Sulabh Dainik*, July 6, 1893, BL, IOR, L/R/5/148.
[25] *Amrita Bazar Patrika*, February 2, 1885, BL, IOR, L/R/5/11.

Figure 5.1 **Pig-stickers, 1870**
Europeans in India entertained themselves by engaging in a variety of
sports and recreational activities, many of them violent, such as hunting,
shooting, and pig-sticking. Pig-sticking, or hog-hunting, involved the
chasing of wild boar on horseback and was particularly popular among
British soldiers in India. As the *Encyclopedia Britannica* (1911) notes, pig-
sticking was encouraged by the military authorities as a sport that offered
good training, since "a startled or angry wild boar is a fast runner and a
desperate fighter [and thus] the pig-sticker must possess a good eye, a
steady hand, a firm seat, a cool head and a courageous heart."

taking of Indians for animals was a vivid expression of colonial racism.
Those Britons who believed that Indians were subhuman beasts treated
them accordingly. As *Surodaya Prakasika* wrote:

Europeans have no regard for the lives of the Indians. They rank them with the
beasts. Near Jullundher in Bengal a certain European seeing a Muhammadan lad
taking away a bird which he had shot began to beat him with the butt end of his rifle
and when he saw that two other Muhammadans were coming to the lad's rescue he
fired on them, killing one and wounding the other...Though a large number of
such offenses has been committed, in none of them have the delinquents been
punished adequately. It is this that encourages the Europeans to deal with the
Indians as if they were no better than beasts.[26]

[26] *Surodaya Prakasika*, January 7, 1903, BL, IOR, L/R/5/111.

Second, the failure of the courts to secure convictions in racial cases demonstrated that the legal system provided an institutional site that normalized and perhaps emboldened the individual Englishman's perceived right to strike someone. Not only did law fail to deter white violence, it may even have encouraged it. The *Ananda Patrika Bazar* noted that Englishmen in India "take a delight in thus cruelly treating natives. The causes of this are to be found, first, in their natural hatred of, and hostility towards natives, and, secondly, in their immunity from punishment either by the State or by society when committing cruelties on natives."[27] A letter from "A Bengalee" to the *Hindoo Patriot* noted that the statutory law and the sympathies of white judges and juries together ensured that Britons were not to be held liable for violence committed upon Indians:

The fact is too notorious to need any demonstration that it is difficult to procure the conviction of a British-born subject in the Supreme Court, more especially when the witnesses are to be brought from a great distance in the *Mofussil*, subjected to the cross-examination of a Peterson or a Doyne, overawed and brow-beaten by the Judge, and appalled by the imposing appearance of the Court and its formidable array of barristers, constables, jurors, clerks and attorneys – a sight so novel and terrific to the rustic peasant of this country – the witnesses who are generally of this class, get confused and forget the facts they come to disclose. There is again the sympathy of the Judge and Jurors enlisted in favour of the offender. Besides, there are many legal fictions and technical absurdities which often help the escape of a criminal in the labyrinth of English law.[28]

European judges and juries in late nineteenth-century colonial courtrooms collaborated across hierarchies of class to buttress the racial basis of British dominance. At times, this collaboration was shockingly brazen. In 1903, Mr. Martin, owner of the Sangramgarh coal mine, was tried in the Burdwan Sessions Court for the murder of Vishnu Bauri. Martin successfully argued that his revolver had unintentionally gone off and killed the man accidentally; he was acquitted. A journalist who attended the trial reported that Martin sat in court surrounded by his wife and friends, "and the whole thing looked as if Mr. Martin was going to be married."[29] This story resembles an incident recounted by Henry Cotton when he was the Magistrate of Chittagong. During the trial of a planter charged with simple assault, Cotton recalled, the accused "calmly came and seated himself on the Bench by my side, and was much surprised when I ordered him to stand down and take his place in court."[30]

---

[27] *Ananda Patrika Bazar*, July 13, 1885, BL, IOR, L/R/5/11.
[28] *Hindoo Patriot*, August 22, 1860.
[29] *Sri Sri Vishnu Priya-o-Ananda Bazar Patrika*, April 8, 1903, BL, IOR, L/R/5/29.
[30] H. Cotton, *Indian and Home Memories* (London: T. Fisher Unwin, 1911), p. 157.

European defendants sometimes even feigned madness to mitigate criminal culpability. In March 1903, *Surodaya Prakasika* reported the case of a European official who shot a *palanquin* bearer for not going faster. To escape prosecution, the official pleaded insanity and was ordered home to England. In Bombay, all signs of madness were gone, and he was moving about freely with friends. On arrival in England, he spent two days in an asylum and then moved to Switzerland, where he wrote to the Secretary of State complaining about the injustice done to him by the Government of India and requesting monetary compensation.[31]

And yet, even as the gap between the promise of colonial justice and the practice of something different produced startlingly biased legal decisions, it also exposed the government to a growing sphere of anti-colonial criticism in India and abroad. From an empirical perspective it is difficult to determine whether acts of European violence increased in the late nineteenth century or whether Indian newspaper editors, anti-colonial nationalists, and imperial critics, whose ability to communicate was improved by the expansion of print media and the invention of the electric telegraph, were simply more willing and able to publicize them. In any event, it is safe to assume that the cases discussed in the public sphere represent a small proportion of the actual incidents of violence, the charges lodged, and the trials heard. As one commentator rather dramatically put it: "Who can say how many such cases occur in the *Mofussil*, but do not see the light of publicity, because it is the habit of the natives to cry with the doors shut."[32]

In the late nineteenth century, various efforts were made to collect and print in book form the wide array of press reports on white violence. In July 1876, Kristodas Pal published a summary of forty-eight European criminal cases in the *Hindoo Patriot* "illustrative of the manner in which justice is meted out to the European and the Native by English Courts in this country."[33] In 1893, in response to an appeal made at the first annual meeting of the Indian National Congress, Ram Gopal Sanyal published *The Record of Criminal Cases as Between Europeans and Natives for the Last Sixty Years*.[34] Having pored over "cart-loads of newspaper writing" in conducting the research for what he anticipated would be a ten-volume series on the subject, the first edition of Sanyal's book contained forty-seven cases. For want of funds, the enlarged second edition contained only 120 selectively culled cases. And yet, as Viceroy Curzon observed,

---

[31] *Surodaya Prakasika*, March 28, 1903, BL, IOR, L/R/5/111.
[32] Sanyal, *Reports of Criminal Cases* (1896), p. 57.   [33] *Hindoo Patriot*, July 31, 1876.
[34] R. G. Sanyal, *Record of Criminal Cases as Between Europeans and Natives for the Last Sixty Years* (Calcutta, 1893).

the "cart-loads" of writing which Sanyal consulted represented only a fraction of the actual incidents and trials. In a private letter to the Secretary of State, Curzon nervously noted, "If the native press got a hold of all these cases, published them verbatim as they occurred, and made the obvious comments, they could render our position in a few years almost untenable in this country."[35]

Anti-imperialists and reformers in London also took issue with the abysmal record of the colonial courts in racial cases. Henry Cotton called the trials of Britons accused of murdering Indians "a judicial scandal":

There were innumerable cases in which men charged with most brutal murders for which no other punishment than hanging was suitable had escaped through the failure to administer justice fairly and fully...In the first place, these offenders were tried by a jury of their own countrymen. It was, of course, a very sound principle in law that a man should be tried by his peers and equals, but it was hardly necessary for him to point out that in a country like India where Englishmen were widely scattered and where any one of them, say, a tea planter was charged with causing the death of an unfortunate coolie, and was arraigned before other tea planters in the same position as himself, it was natural and even inevitable that the jury should be biased and should find the accused guilty of the smallest cognizable offence under the law.[36]

In April 1890, Charles Bradlaugh MP requested a return showing trial outcomes in cases where Indians had been murdered by Europeans over the previous five years.[37] Four years later, William Caine MP told the House of Commons that "the Administration of Criminal Justice in India is such as to bring it into contempt and render it a terror to Law-abiding people."[38] In 1913, Sir Walter William Strickland published a tract titled *British Justice and Honesty: Addressed to the People of England and India* (1913) that opened by stating: "The English in India and elsewhere boast of their even-handed justice...[M]y personal experience is that this boast has no foundation whatever." Strickland cited several cases of European assaults including:

an Irish private soldier [who] murdered a beautiful Burmese girl whom he was "in love" with and her mother, and then raped one or both of the still warm bodies. For this little error of judgment he was awarded such comfortable quarters in Rangoon Gaol that he has no desire whatever to quit them...Very different were the Moslem rulers in their best days, at least in the matter of even-handed justice for they

---

[35] Curzon to Secretary of State George Hamilton, June 17, 1903, BL, IOR, Mss Eur/ F111/162.

[36] Henry Cotton's 1903 speech in London, quoted by Legislative Assembly Member Rangachariar, NAI, Legislative Assembly Debates, September 15, 1921.

[37] BL, IOR, L/PJ/6/275, File 672.   [38] BL, IOR, L/PJ/6/369, Files 459, 467, 468.

condemned their own sons to death rather than deal out one justice for the conqueror and another for the conquered.[39]

Strickland's work was banned by the imperial government.

British soldiers and the imperial dilemma of "nigger-bashing"

The ideologies that justified the empire changed over time, but ultimately, and at all times, Britain's control of India depended on its military dominance. Soldiers always constituted the largest contingent of Britons in India.[40] In 1837, 37,000 of the 41,000 Britons in India were soldiers. By 1906, there were 74,500 British troops in India. The rank-and-file soldiers were literally a class apart from their superior officers and from the elite members of the Indian Civil Service, a small cadre of men who were paid much more generously and were not bound by twenty-five-year enlistment contracts. As Richard Holmes notes: "The British army was – with a few notable exceptions – a body of poor men officered by rather richer ones."[41]

British military culture in India was brutal and aggressive, and the violence of British privates off parade was linked to the violence on parade.[42] Pranks and jokes in the barracks and on marches often amounted to what would have been criminal acts in civilian life. Soldiers lived in cramped, hot, insanitary quarters where they suffered from poor health, disease, and high rates of mortality. The death rate among British soldiers in the barracks in India was 58 per 1,000, over three times higher than it was in Britain.[43] The men passed their free time in both violent and non-violent pursuits, reading, writing, praying, embroidering, drinking, gambling, cock-fighting, fishing, "dogging" (collecting butterflies), pig-sticking, hunting, shooting, "curs[ing] the *punkha-wallahs* for not pulling the *punkahs* strong enough or the *tatty-wallahs* for not throwing sufficient water on the *tatties*,"[44] and "ill-treating the natives and getting killed by them."[45] (*Tatty-wallahs* poured water on mats to cool rooms and people.)

[39] BL, IOR, EPP 37/5.
[40] P. J. Marshall, "British Immigration into India in the Nineteenth Century," *Itinerario*, 14, 1 (1990), 25–41.
[41] Holmes, *Sahib*, p. 221.
[42] D. M. Peers, "Privates off Parade: Regimenting Sexuality in the Nineteenth-Century Indian Empire," *International History Review*, 20, 4 (1998), 844–853.
[43] Holmes, *Sahib*, p. 143.
[44] Frank Richards, *Old Soldier Sahib* (London: Faber and Faber, 1936), p. 239.
[45] Letter from Sergeant Thomas Duckworth to his parents, March 1834, Holmes, *Sahib*, p. 115.

The soldiers were themselves served a brutal brand of justice that included execution by hanging – though elaborate measures were taken so that no Indians ever witnessed European soldiers on the scaffold[46] – as well as imprisonment, penal servitude, and disciplinary floggings, which were regularly meted out in military prisons until 1907. As Private Robert Waterfield observed: "In India, the private soldier is looked upon as the lowest class of animals, and only fit to be ruled with the cat o'nine tails and the provost sergeant."[47]

British soldiers in India were tried in most criminal cases either by military court-martial or by civil courts, except in the five major offenses of murder, manslaughter, rape, treason, and treason-felony, where they had to be tried by the civil authorities (unless there was no civil court within 100 miles).[48] In the early colonial period, justice for an errant soldier could be swift and harsh. A 1678 order from Madras directed that "if any English soldier strikes a Native, he shall stand sentinel in arms or, being made fast to the breach of a gun, shall receive so many stripes as his officer shall think fit, or shall ride the horse (wooden) so many hours."[49] In 1813, the Court of Directors ordered that British officers found ill-treating natives were to be suspended from service and sent home.[50] However, in the later nineteenth century, both the murderous conduct of British soldiers and their acquittals in court were on the rise. In trials by court-martial from 1861 to 1875, British officers tried for assaulting other Britons were convicted in 100 percent of cases, whereas British officers tried for assaulting natives were convicted in only 50 percent of cases.[51] As the number of racial attacks and acquittals increased, administrators, including Curzon and Secretary of State George Hamilton, came to lose faith in the objectivity of the military tribunals. As Hamilton observed:

Wherever we go, to Ireland or to India, we carry with us a system of justice based on the notion that our fellow citizens generally are interested in the repression of crime and the safeguarding of life and property. But a court-martial in India has no more idea of right and wrong than a jury of Irish farmers trying a case of agrarian outrage, and I am afraid that nothing short of a radical change of system, which Parliament would not allow, would effect a cure.[52]

---

[46] "Execution of a Death Sentence," W. Hough, *A Case Book of European and Native General Courts-Martial Held from the Years 1801 to 1821* (Calcutta, 1821), pp. 736–738.
[47] Holmes, *Sahib*, p. 431.
[48] Army Act, section 41. Also see L. M. Peet, *Courts-Martial in India* (Calcutta: Thacker and Spink, 1923) and the royal warrant of April 17, 1761 authorizing the East India Company to hold courts-martial, BL, IOR, L/MIL/5/457.
[49] Quoted in Sanyal, *Record of Criminal Cases*, pp. 154–155.
[50] W. Hough, *The Practice of Courts-Martial* (London, 1825), p. 221.
[51] BL, IOR, L/MIL/5/674.
[52] Hamilton to Curzon, July 11, 1902, BL, IOR, Mss Eur/F111/161 (1902).

On October 4, 1893, thirty to forty women were breaking stones near Guntakul Railway Station in the Madras Presidency when a group of European soldiers from the 2nd Wiltshire Regiment came walking over, "showing or exhibiting rupees, half rupees and quarter rupees."[53] The soldiers began following two of the women, Ellama and Nagamma, who ran frightened towards the gatekeeper Hampanna's shed. Hampanna allowed both women inside and shut the door. Six of the soldiers tried to enter the shed but Hampanna refused them entry. When Hampanna raised a bamboo stick in the air, Lance-Corporal Ernest Ashford fired a pistol at him.

Several people heard the gunshot and ran over to find Hampanna lying on the ground, bleeding from his abdomen, crying out, "Oh, I am dying… come, I am killed." They carried him to the hospital where, later that day, 120 members of the Wiltshire Regiment were paraded before him as he sat mortally wounded in a hospital chair. Hampanna was unable to identify any of the soldiers as his assailants, probably because many of them had, as often happened, shaved prior to the identification parade. In his dying deposition given to the native magistrate in Telegu, Hampanna claimed that the soldiers shot him when he refused them access to the two women in his shed. He died at 3 p.m. the following day.

Although Ashford had immediately admitted to his superior officer that he had shot Hampanna, on February 7, 1894 he entered a plea of self-defense in the Madras High Court in response to two counts of culpable homicide. Ashford claimed that Nagamma had passed by the canteen earlier and "signalled to the soldiers with her hand." When he and five others followed her to the shed, Hampanna let her in and locked the door. One of the soldiers offered him 4 annas, but (Ashford claimed) Hampanna put out his hand and said "Rupee." Private Adam Budd testified that he tried to force his way inside but was pushed back by Hampanna, who grabbed a stick: "Lance-Corporal Ashford put his hand up and the stick struck him on his hand and he told the native, 'if you strike me again I will shoot you.'" "Speaking in English?" the prosecutor asked. "Yes," he replied. Budd continued: "The native tried to make a second clout at him, when he fired. I saw then that Lance-Corporal Ashford fired. I asked him what he fired for and why he fired. He said he fired to defend himself or else the native would have knocked his brains out." Ashford testified:

Hampanna then made a rush at me, my Lord, with his stick. A bamboo stick between four and five feet long. I told him to go back; if not I would fire. The second time he came he had a knife with him. I showed him the pistol and then I

[53] BL, IOR, L/PJ/6/369, Files 459, 467, 468.

turned round to walk away. Someone shouted out that he had a knife, I turned round and thinking he would attack me with the knife, I fired at him.

After a two-day trial before a European-majority jury, Ashford was acquitted of both charges. An article in the *Madras Standard* titled "Gross Miscarriage of Justice" lamented that the Guntakal murder case "adds a fresh instance to the long roll of cases in which Europeans have, with impunity, murdered the natives of India."[54]

The brutality of the soldiers and the failure of the courts to control or punish them were targets of widespread public criticism. In 1903, *Hitavadi* pleaded, "Will no steps be taken to protect the people of this country from these brute-like European soldiers?"[55] That same year, *Naier-I-Asifi* remarked that British soldiers "seem to think that Indians are no better than ants and treat them as they please, believing no one will take any notice of their action."[56] Curzon himself was a harsh critic and constant observer of the terror of Tommy Atkins. Writing to the Secretary of State in 1904, Curzon noted:

You can scarcely imagine what a terror the British soldier has made himself to natives, both in the neighbourhood of cantonments and when on the march, in the main by his drunkenness and lust. Most of the rows take place when a soldier has had too much and four of five have a woman in the background. The result is that, in many places, the inhabitants of a village flee at the approach of British soldiers.[57]

Although rank-and-file soldiers like Ernest Ashford and Adam Budd were a troublesome embarrassment to the empire, their brutality was as nothing compared with that of the thirty soldiers of the West Kent Regiment who gang-raped a Burmese woman in open daylight in Rangoon. On April 2, 1899, Ma Gun, "an elderly woman said to be of weak intellect but of respectable character," was seized by a soldier and dragged up a path to a spot where several other soldiers were waiting. Several eye-witnesses saw Ma Gun screaming and struggling but were afraid to intervene, as the soldiers yelled and threw stones at them. Holding her down, the soldiers raped her one after the other before dragging her into a hollow ditch out of the sight of local onlookers who had gathered upon the road. Soldiers were seen coming and going from the hollow threatening passers-by with daggers and dogs to keep them away. Some of the soldiers were seen with their trousers open.

Four policemen arrived on the spot to find a group of soldiers gathered around Ma Gun. Private Benjamin Edward Horricks was still raping her as she cried out in Burmese, "If you can save me, save me." The police

---

[54] Ibid.   [55] *Hitavadi*, March 6, 1903, BL, IOR, L/R/5/29.
[56] *Naier-I-Asifi*, July 9, 1903, BL, IOR, L/R/5/158.
[57] Curzon to Hamilton, February 17, 1904, BL, IOR, Mss Eur/F111/163.

sent all of the soldiers back to their barracks but arrested Horricks "as he was rising from the woman. The woman was lying on her back, naked, save for a jacket and in an exhausted condition. She was sent to hospital where the nurse gave her a bath. She escaped from hospital almost immediately after."[58] Horricks was taken to the civil police station in a slovenly state with his fly unbuttoned. He was charged with rape and handed over to the military authorities within an hour. The military subsequently held a secret Court of Enquiry but withheld its proceedings from the investigating civil authorities.

On May 8, 1899, Private Horricks was tried at the Recorder of Rangoon. The prosecution called eighteen witnesses, many of whom testified to seeing the soldiers hold Ma Gun's hands down as others raped her. Abdul Karen testified that he saw Private Horricks' erect penis as he was pulled off her. Police Inspector James Hewitt testified that he arrived on the scene to find Horricks covered in dirt, no suspenders on, with his trousers hanging down. About Ma Gun he noted: "The woman was very exhausted and could not stand and could not make any rational statement."

An extensive inquiry into "the history of Ma Gun" turned up a respectable woman of unimpeachable character. At the trial, Ma Gun's brother, Maung Ba Sin, testified that after the rape she had become "deranged and she does not speak rationally...She is now insane and talks nonsense. Her behaviour is not at all what it was. It is quite irrational. She requires someone to wash her as though she were a child." Ma Gun herself testified:

I met a soldier who did nothing. After that I met soldiers. They had sexual intercourse with me. Only one had intercourse with me. I consented. I struggled. I did not wish the soldiers to have connection with me. What can I remember? I have been ill ever since and have no clear recollection of what happened. I am ill now...The man had connection with me for about an hour – about 2 betel-chews...I was then in a very dirty condition and covered with semen. Before getting to the hospital I had a wash in the lake so [I] was clean when I got there.

The Europeans in the courtroom laughed during Ma Gun's jumbled testimony.

The defense called a number of soldiers from Horricks' regiment. Private John Sullivan testified that Ma Gun had come up to the Company's bungalow that morning singing and dancing and pulling her clothes up. He then saw various soldiers go down to the ditch and get on

---

[58] Chief Secretary, Government of Burma to Government of India, June 13, 1899, L/PJ/6/527, File 2354.

top of her: "The woman was motionless during the affair. My impression was that she was dead." Several other soldiers testified that Ma Gun was acting like a prostitute and had beckoned them for a "jig-jig" (sex). Many admitted to having sex with her, but all claimed it was for money and without force. Their superior, Corporal Nurse, testified that he saw Ma Gun filthy, lying in the ditch, "a mass of semen about her private parts. She was lying motionless until she was picked up." He also claimed that Horricks was standing 20 yards away from Ma Gun, clean and properly dressed, and could not have had intercourse with her. Nurse noted that Ma Gun was not crying "and did not appear to be ashamed of her nudity."

Two days later, Private Benjamin Horricks was unanimously acquitted by a jury of nine European men. In subsequent months, under pressure from the Government of India, charges of rape were lodged against other soldiers in the West Kent Regiment. Each of the soldiers was tried separately, and the same witnesses were called to testify at every trial. On September 5, 1899, at the trial of John Thorpe, Ma Gun testified:

I know where I am now. I am here. What place is it? I have been here before. It was last year. I came because there was business. Soldiers' business. It was a case of rape. They raped me. I remember it. It was last year...I know that rape is having connection without consent. They had connection with me without my consent... The man used violence to me. He was going to cut me with a *dao*...

A couple of weeks later, at the trial of William Johnson, Ma Gun's brother testified that her mental condition was worsening:

she is progressing daily. She showed her madness by answering calls of nature in her clothes. She jumped into a big jar filled with water saying she had been told a bundle was to be found in it. She said a man told her gold was to be found at the foot of the mango tree and started digging in broad daylight...I have never been able to get from her an intelligible account of what occurred with the soldiers.

Dr. Robert Pearse testified for the defense that, given her state,

it would not surprise me at all to find that a woman so predisposed should, on the 2nd April, have gone dancing before the barracks in a way to lead men to believe she was a lewd woman...It is common in women predisposed for insanity for the first symptom recognized as such to be an attack of sexual excitement or acts of indecency.

Gang rape, he told the jury, would not produce insanity. John Thorpe, William Johnson, and every other soldier tried for raping Ma Gun was acquitted in the Rangoon Court. Ma Gun died the following year.

Curzon was disgusted by the facts of the Rangoon case and horrified by the failure of the civil and military authorities to secure even one conviction (see Figure 5.2). And yet, he was torn about how to act. In a

Figure 5.2 **Lord Curzon**
Widely reviled among Indians for his unpopular decision to partition the
province of Bengal, Lord Curzon was also despised by members of the
military and by British civilians for his efforts to monitor and control
"collisions" between Britons and Indians across the subcontinent.

confidential letter to the Secretary of State, a distressed Curzon remarked:
"I have throughout felt rather like someone standing on the brink of the
roaring crater of Vesuvius with justice and honour imperiously thrusting
him forward and circumspection and self-interest more cautiously push-
ing him back."[59] The tension between Curzon's imperial conscience and
his concern for imperial stability reflected the thinking of colonial administrators a century prior, such as Governor-General John Shore, who in
1794 condemned the behavior of non-officials and nervously referred to

[59] Curzon to Hamilton, October 18, 1899, BL, IOR, Mss Eur/F111/158.

them as "profligate characters over whom the law has not sufficient control."[60]

With London's approval, Curzon banished the West Kent Regiment to the worst spot he could find within his dominion (Aden), removed Brigadier-General S. E. Rolland from command of the Rangoon District, and requested reports on all cases of what he referred to as "collisions" between European soldiers and Indians since 1880. In these reports, there are three main types of crime: shootings, rape, and what was called "casual violence." We have seen examples of the first two crimes in the cases of Hampanna and Ma Gun. Casual violence, which was probably the most common and the least reported type of criminal violence, tended to be directed at the Indian laborers – syces, cooks, bearers, and punkhawallahs – who served British troops. Indeed, the harsh life of the British soldier in India was partially mitigated by the army of Indian servants at his disposal.[61]

The figure of the punkhawallah was a particularly constant target of verbal and physical abuse in the barracks and in civilian life. Private Frank Richards of the Royal Welsh Fusiliers recalled in his memoir that if during the night "the punkahs ceased to sway for only a second somebody would shout"; the soldiers would immediately threaten violence, "'Cinch [pull], you black bastard, or I'll come out and kick hell out of you.'"[62] In October 1885, the Indian Planters' and Sporting Gazette published a short sketch of "The Punkah-Wallah" in which the writer bluntly stated, "I dislike the punkah-wallah and I don't know why." At the midnight hour, the anonymous author of the piece describes how the hot-tempered sahib's dislike of the punkhawallah mutated into a premeditated attack:

He falls to sleep, his hold of the rope relaxes and all is still. On a sudden, you wake with a start, soaked with perspiration to find that the punkah has stopped, and that the mosquitoes have half devoured your feet. You raise yourself gently and look out in the verandah. There he lies, snoring loudly, all unconscious of the beating in store for him. Hot tempered sahibs generally throw a boot or two at him, or perhaps a brick, which they have placed beneath their bed before they retired to rest for that special purpose.[63]

On November 9, 1893, Alfred Webb MP pressed the Secretary of State to make an inquiry into the case of Private John Rigby, who kicked a punkhawallah to death and was fined 100 rupees. In response, the Secretary of State noted that the dead punkhawallah had fallen asleep at

---

[60] Shore to the Court of Directors, December 31, 1794, in the case of William Duane, BL. IOR, O/5/3.
[61] See the long list of servants required by a married officer, in A. T. Moore, Notes for Officers Proceeding to India (Chatham: Royal Engineers Institute, 1912).
[62] Richards, Old Soldier Sahib, pp. 239–240.
[63] Indian Planters' and Sporting Gazette, October 13, 1885, p. 385.

his post when Private Rigby jumped out of bed and "gave him one or more blows on the body. The medical evidence showed that the cause of death was rupture of the spleen, which was in such a state that the slightest blow might have broken it, and there were no external marks of violence."[64] In reference to another case where a *punkhawallah* had been kicked to death by a soldier, *Banganivasi* sarcastically reported: "The writer has as yet got no information about the size of the coolie's spleen and whether his death was due to a sudden bursting of it. He cannot also say whether in kicking the coolie the soldier hurt himself and whether he is entitled to damages for any injury done to his shoes."[65] About the same case, *Sarasvat Patra* remarked: "Coolies have long been known to possess inordinately large spleens which are at the same time so brittle as to fall into pieces the moment they are touched by a European. And who knows what new theory will not be now started to account for such deaths, namely, that sleep is found to be fatal to a *punkha* coolie?"[66]

While the *punkhawallah* cases undoubtedly represent a small proportion of the daily abuses committed against them, "casual violence" committed by British soldiers against Indian labor was not exclusively directed at the *punkhawallah*. Shortly after arriving in India, Private Richards witnessed an "old soldier" punch a sweeper in the stomach, shouting: "You black soor, when I order you to do a thing I expect it to be done at once." The "old soldier" continued:

My God, it's scandalous the way things are going on in this country. The blasted natives are getting cheekier every day. Not so many years ago I would have half-killed that native, and if he had made a complaint and had marks to show, any decent Commanding Officer would have laughed at him and told him to clear off. Since old Curzon has been Viceroy things are different, you see. An order has been issued, which every soldier in India believes came from him, that Commanding Officers must severely punish men who are brought in front of them for ill-treating natives. We have to be very careful these days. If we punch them in the face they have marks to show, so we have to punch them in the body. Most of the natives on the Plains have enlarged spleens, and a good punch in the body hurts them more than it would us.[67]

The "old soldier's" practice of carefully abusing Indians so as not to leave marks contradicted the warning issued in a 1904 handbook for the Royal Engineers against hitting Indians at all: "Natives should never be struck, as a very large number suffer from enlarged spleens and other complaints, and a blow, or sometimes even a shove, can be fatal."[68]

---

[64] BL, IOR, L/PJ/6/360, File 2170.   [65] *Banganivasi*, June 9, 1893, BL, IOR, L/R/5/19.
[66] *Sarasvat Patra*, August 5, 1893, ibid.   [67] Richards, *Old Soldier Sahib*, pp. 74–75.
[68] Moore, *Notes*, p. 26.

Figure 5.3 **9th Lancers, June 1860**
The 9th Lancers were a highly decorated regiment in India. Although its officers were literally a class apart from the average rank-and-file soldier in India, this did not necessarily mean that they were any less violent. In 1902, when Lord Curzon censured the Lancers for murdering an Indian cook, a crime for which not one of them was tried or punished, he was blasted by the military authorities and by members of European society in Calcutta for his sentimentalism.

Three years after the Rangoon rape case, Curzon had another public confrontation with the colonial military establishment. On April 9, 1902, the highly decorated 9th Lancers arrived in Sialkot in the late afternoon and began drinking (see Figure 5.3). By nightfall, their cook, Atu, had been fatally assaulted by two soldiers and left outside overnight to die. When the local military authorities decided not to take disciplinary action, Curzon intervened and had the entire regiment collectively punished, denying them leave for six months. Curzon called the case "disgraceful to the record of a British regiment and injurious to British rule and reputation in this country."[69]

Curzon's censure of the 9th Lancers was widely reviled across British colonial society. Lieutenant-Colonel George Younghusband recalled that "Lord Curzon was suffering from a severe attack of 'poor black man.' That is, protecting the poor Indian from the assaults of the brutal British soldiery."[70] Private Richards' "old soldier" similarly observed that "Old Curzon is no damned good, this country wants a Viceroy who will keep the bleeding natives down."[71] At the Delhi Durbar, the 9th Lancers rode by to cheering crowds of European civilians. When the regiment passed the Viceroy and the order "Eyes right" was given, "not many men obeyed the order and some even reversed it."[72] As Private Richards noted:

Lord Curzon was very much disliked by the rank and file of the Army, who all agreed that he was giving the natives too much rope. Another thing that added to his unpopularity was that his wife was supposed to have said that the two ugliest things in India were the water-buffalo and the British private soldier. A water-buffalo is larger than an English cow and a very ugly beast indeed. One of our chaps said that he would like to see the whole of the Battalion parade naked in front of Lady Curzon for inspection; with Lord Curzon also naked in the midst of them: for comparison, like a tadpole among gods.[73]

Curzon's confrontation with the military is a well-known chapter of his personal biography.[74] As Curzon saw it, the soldiers resented his interference in their sport of "nigger-bashing": "The thing I believe that the soldiers dislike most of all is that the cases of serious collision between them and the Natives are now reported to the Government of India and taken more notice of than they used to be in former days."[75] Curzon's sense of scandal – the miscarriages of justice, he wrote, "eat into my very soul"[76] – was born of his concern for imperial stability:

The army is in reality the custodian of a more precious charge than even its own honour; since the conduct of a small number of soldiers may sensibly affect the position of all Englishmen, and the attitude of all natives in this country...the natural position of the British soldier should be that of a source of protection, and not of alarm to the people.[77]

---

[69] June 15, 1902, BL, IOR, Mss Eur/F111/402.
[70] Quoted in the Marquess of Anglesey, *A History of the British Cavalry, 1816–1919* (London: Secker and Warburg, 1986), p. 497.
[71] Richards, *Old Soldier Sahib*, p. 109.   [72] Ibid.   [73] Ibid., pp. 76–77.
[74] D. Gilmour, *Curzon: Imperial Statesman* (London: John Murray, 1994).
[75] Curzon to the Secretary of State, March 12, 1903, BL, IOR, Mss Eur/F111/162.
[76] Curzon to Hamilton, June 13, 1900, BL, IOR, Mss Eur/F111/159.
[77] "Minute on the Revision of the Shooting Pass Rules," September 6, 1900, BL, IOR, Mss Eur/F111/402.

In an effort to reduce the number of fatal "collisions" between British soldiers and Indians, Curzon imposed new rules that restricted the ability of soldiers to obtain shooting passes.[78] When the army expressed its disapproval of the new regulations, Curzon observed:

> They cannot see why the poor soldier should not be allowed to go out and shoot and harass at his own sweet will; and if in the course of the excursion a Native is killed, their attitude is that of a very fast bowler at cricket whom I once met and who having killed a man by the ball jumping up and striking him on the temple said to me, "Why did the damned fool get his head in the way?"[79]

Curzon's pressure on the military and his commitment to use executive powers of intervention when the courts failed to deliver justice culminated in the trial of Private Fountain Hedler Emerson. On August 5, 1902, Emerson and two other soldiers from the Lincolnshire Regiment (Lane and Dench) went shooting in the Sholamdevi Forest Reserve in the Madras Presidency. When the forest watchman, Kamaruddin, asked to see their shooting permit, the soldiers produced a regimental shooting pass (which was white) rather than a forest pass (which was green). Kamaruddin told the men that they could not shoot in the forest reserve. One of the soldiers, all of whom had guns, took Kamaruddin's hand and walked along with him "in a friendly manner" for a quarter mile or so. When one soldier raised his gun to shoot a bird, Kamaruddin tried to stop him. Private Lane yelled to his comrades, "Shoot this man, shoot this man." Emerson discharged his weapon from 4 or 5 feet away and shot Kamaruddin in the thigh. After Kamaruddin dropped to the ground, Lane clubbed him repeatedly with the butt of his gun until he fell unconscious.

Forty-five minutes later, Kamaruddin recovered consciousness and was taken to the hospital by a local man named Thekkavalan. Two days later, on August 7, twenty-nine soldiers from the Lincolnshire Regiment were paraded in batches of six before Kamaruddin's hospital bed. Kamaruddin pleaded that he was too weak and dizzy to identify any of them. (There was evidence to suggest that the soldiers in this case had also shaved prior to the identification parade.) On August 25, the soldiers were brought before Kamaruddin again. This time he identified Lane and Emerson as the culprits. Kamaruddin remained incapacitated in the hospital for two months.

---

[78] Government of India Home Department Circular Letter to Provincial Governments, Nos. 248–257, January 31, 1899, ibid.
[79] Curzon to Hamilton, September 17, 1900, BL, IOR, Mss Eur/F111/159.

On October 6, 1902, charges of grievous hurt were lodged against Emerson, Lane, and Dench before Trichinopoly District Magistrate R. H. Shipley. Shipley discharged the men on grounds of insufficient evidence for identification. When Curzon caught wind of the case, he pressured the Madras High Court to revise Shipley's decision. The Madras High Court demanded a retrial of Emerson and Lane, but by then Emerson had taken his discharge and sailed for England. The Madras High Court initiated extradition proceedings, issuing a warrant for his arrest under the Fugitive Offenders Act (1881).[80]

On June 30, 1903, James Stockley, a Metropolitan Police Inspector from Scotland Yard, arrested Emerson at a mill near Norwich. After Stockley read him the warrant for his arrest, Emerson exclaimed, "I know nothing about it! I did not shoot the man. I had never seen the man until I saw him in the hospital. I never went into the forest."[81] Stockley discovered the Madras High Court warrant in Emerson's possession and asked him, "Did you take any action when you received these forms?" Emerson replied, "No, why should I? Don't you think I have had enough of India? Besides I had no money if I had wanted to go there. I wrote to my Commanding Officer and received a reply but I cannot find it. This is all Lord Curzon's doings, he would do anything to please the Natives."

Five weeks later, Stockley and Emerson left for India, arriving in Madras on September 7.[82] The case was widely reported on in the Indian press, for, as *Naier-I-Asifi* noted, "no topic excited so much interest and curiosity as Private Emerson's case."[83] The *Madras Mail* printed a verbatim account of the week-long proceedings in the Madras High Court, which was heard by Justice Benson and a nine-man jury comprised of seven Europeans and two Indians. Emerson was charged with voluntarily causing grievous hurt to Kamaruddin by discharging a loaded gun and wounding him in the left leg. He pleaded not guilty.

The prosecution argued that it was a simple case that rested on identification. The jury heard direct testimony from Kamaruddin and also from Thekkavalan, who testified that he and Kamarrudin had heard a shot fired from afar and that when they confronted the three soldiers, Kamarrudin said something to them in English and Hindustani, neither of which Thekkavalan understood. Thekkavalan claimed that he and Kamarrudin were following the soldiers when he stopped to remove a thorn from his

---

[80] Judicial letter No. 6 to SS, May 7, 1903, NAI, Home/Public (A)/May 1903/406–415.
[81] BL, IOR, L/PJ/6/641, File 1499.   [82] BL, IOR, L/PJ/6/659, File 197.
[83] *Naier-I-Asifi*, October 15, 1903, BL, IOR, L/R/5/111. Also see *The Times*, July 8, 1903; and *Madras Mail*, October 5–10, 1903.

foot. Hearing a shot, Thekkavalan ran ahead to find Kamarrudin lying unconscious on the ground.

Emerson's attorney, Nugent Grant, argued that the entire case rested on Kamarrudin's ability to identify his attacker, which was inconsistent and uncorroborated and did not constitute proof beyond a reasonable doubt. Grant also commented on "the policy of Government which interfered with the action of the Judicial Department and had brought Emerson all the way out from England to undergo a trial when there was not sufficient evidence to establish a conviction. The jury might have lately heard of several flagrant cases of such interference by Government, such as the Bain case and the case of Lieut. Rennick." Condemning the colonial authorities for dragging Emerson overseas to India, Grant suggested that the jury could send a message to the government by acquitting his client: "[I]t was open to the Jury, by their verdict, to denounce the action of Government and to send Emerson back to his home and to his wife an honourable man."[84] In his closing remarks, Judge Benson also remarked to the jury that were Emerson an innocent man, his hardship connected with the case had been burdensome.

The jury deliberated for fifteen minutes and returned a unanimous verdict of not guilty. They also asked the judge to press the government for compensation to be paid to Emerson for his troubles.[85] When he returned home, Emerson was given £30.[86] The Indian press loudly denounced the failure of the Madras High Court to deliver justice in such a clear-cut case. *Nadegannadi* went so far as to suggest that paying Emerson might "encourage crime among Europeans of low character as they might suppose it to be a new way of making money."[87]

The ambiguous promise of colonial justice and subaltern uses of law

Curzon's twin priorities in India were to make British rule both equitable and permanent. David Gilmour notes that, for Curzon, India was "'a land not only of romance but of obligation,' and, if the obligations were shirked, Britain had no right to remain."[88] To preserve the empire, Curzon was committed to fulfill a moral duty: "to fight for the right, to abhor the imperfect, the unjust and the mean, to swerve neither to the right hand nor to the left, to care nothing for flattery, applause or odium or abuse."[89]

---

[84] A verbatim account of the trial is printed in *Madras Mail*, October 5, 6, 9, and 10, 1903.
[85] *Madras Mail*, October 9, 1903.   [86] BL, IOR, L/PJ/6/652, File 2555.
[87] *Nadegannadi*, November 17, 1903, BL, IOR, L/R/5/111.   [88] Gilmour, *Curzon*, p. 166.
[89] Curzon to Hamilton, June 19, 1903, BL, IOR, Mss Eur/F111/162.

The colonial rule of law purported to treat all subjects equally, but it did not (and could not) do so given its fundamental involvement in the entrenchment and protection of British power.[90] At the end of the day, the paramount purpose of law was to maintain Britain's hold on India. But the bloodied handprints which that hold left behind revealed the unseemly fact that it was not only justice that anchored the empire, but also violence. The cases discussed in this chapter have primarily involved the military. However, British soldiers certainly did not have an exclusive preserve over the exercise of racial violence. It is likely that we know more about cases involving British soldiers both because of their large population and because the Army presented a ready framework for reporting and accountability.

It is a central argument of this book that the tension between the promise and practice of colonial law snapped around trials of violent Britons, exposing the centrality of race to the workings of colonial justice and the violence that was central to empire itself. Being British in India entitled one to a special set of legal privileges and powers, but did the celebrated right of the freeborn Englishman include the right to rape and murder with little to no culpability or consequence?

Trial outcomes at the turn of the twentieth century would seem to suggest yes. In his first year as Viceroy, Curzon not only began monitoring collisions between British soldiers and natives, he also ordered the provincial governments to report back to him about all collisions between Europeans and Indians.[91] The first available set of such reports offer a statistical account of cases that is otherwise hard to find (see Table 5.1). From 1901 to 1905, the colonial courts tried twenty-seven cases of assaults ending fatally committed by Europeans against Indians (a ludicrously small number given what we know about mortal violence in Assam at the time) and twelve assaults ending fatally committed by Indians on Europeans. In fifteen of the twenty-seven European assaults, death was determined to have resulted from an accident following a slight assault (in most cases a ruptured spleen). In two of the cases, the European defendants successfully pleaded self-defense. Only one was a clear murder case, and here the murderer was found to be insane. Of the twelve fatal assaults by Indians on Europeans, eleven resulted in murder convictions. These trial outcomes strongly, if not conclusively, point to race as the pivotal factor in legal decision-making at the turn of the century.

---

[90] For a comparative perspective, see T. Keegan, *Colonial South Africa and the Origins of the Racial Order* (Charlottesville: University of Virginia Press, 1996).

[91] Home Department Circular Letter Nos. 248–257, January 31, 1899, BL, IOR, L/PJ/6/781, File 3445.

Table 5.1 *Interracial violence*

Interracial assaults ending fatally

Year	Europeans on Indians	Indians on Europeans
1901	7	2
1902	7	1
1903	8	1
1904	3	4
1905	2	4
TOTAL	**27**	**12**

Interracial collisions generally

Year	Europeans on Indians	Indians on Europeans
1901	199	86
1902	47	32
1903	73	47
1904	45	55
1905	28	31
TOTAL	**392**	**251**

Until the very end, the non-official community remained steadfastly opposed to all efforts to subject them to laws framed for a subject population. They were indignant when their fellow Europeans were tried for violent acts committed against Indians, and, when convicted, as Henry Cotton noted, "a storm of protest was raised, the greatest anger and indignation were given vent to at every European breakfast table and tea table and no stone was left unturned to get the sentence either cancelled or modified."[92] On the other hand, when Europeans were assaulted or murdered by Indians, the pressure on the government to punish those involved was enormous. In 1907, in regard to the murder of an English indigo planter named Bloomfield who had been stoned to death by the entire village, the *Englishman* urged the government in no uncertain terms to deliver swift justice:

A crime has been committed of a kind that calls for the promptest of action on the part of the authorities. No efforts and no expense should be spared in order to bring the criminals to justice. There has been in recent affairs in which Europeans have been assaulted by mobs, a lamentable lack of police investigation, and at the

---

[92] Cotton's 1903 speech in London, quoted by Legislative Assembly Member Rangachariar in the Legislative Assembly Debates, September 15, 1921.

present moment, there are two other cases in the public eye in which nobody has been punished for the murder of the lonely planters…It is unnecessary to dwell on the dangers to which solitary Europeans in the *mofussil* are exposed at the hands of myriads of ignorant *rayats* [peasants] and others who surround them. Once the impression is allowed to get out that a European may be assaulted and even murdered without any risk there will be an end to the British prestige in India.[93]

Indian demands for justice were based both on abstract principle and on the strong and widespread conviction that the special privileges reserved to Europeans were responsible for many and grave criminal abuses. In a collection of documents sent to the British Parliament titled "Justice Murdered in India," searing questions were posed about the "catalogue" of racial cases:

Who will make a catalogue of all the cases in which natives of India have been killed by Europeans, from "mistakes" and "unfortunate circumstances" of various kinds? One has his spleen ruptured, another is mistaken for a boar, another for a pigeon, and a fourth for an elephant – as if India were a hospital of moribund patients ready to die at the slightest touch, or a jungle of beasts fit only to be killed.[94]

Colonial law not only violently touched the Indian body, it also sometimes allowed ordinary Indians to touch back at the organs of power and to demand justice. Though elite Indian demands for the British to be more fair and even-handed were sometimes self-interested (many of those who demanded legal equality were seeking administrative promotions), subaltern responses to incidents of white violence provide an opportunity to see how non-elites used and chose not to use colonial laws and law courts in ways that did not always strengthen the backbone of the empire. As Lauren Benton observes, "it is tempting but wrong to view any participation in an imposed legal system as collaboration, on the one hand, and to represent any form of rejection of the law's authority as resistance."[95]

The idea that the use of law invariably strengthened the colonial state rests on the problematic assumption that community forms of justice in India were preferable to colonial ones. For women and low-caste people especially, there is no reason to believe that a local *panchayat* (village tribunal) would be more likely than a colonial court to deliver justice. As dalit (untouchable) activists have long argued, "village India" is the original site of their oppression and not an idyllic space untouched by colonialism to which they wish to return.[96]

---

[93] *Englishman*, July 21, 1907.   [94] Ganguli, *Slavery*, pp. 64–65.

[95] Benton, *Law and Colonial Cultures*, p. 17.

[96] B. R. Ambedkar, *What Congress and Gandhi Have Done to the Untouchables* (Bombay: Thacker, 1945); and Kancha Ilaiah, *Why I am Not a Hindu: A Sudra Critique of Hindutva Philosophy, Culture and Political Economy* (Calcutta: Samya, 1996).

Two very different cases of white violence demonstrate the variety of native responses to law. The first is a case of not using law. On August 22, 1893, three soldiers of the 2nd Batallion Royal West Surrey Regiment went shooting just outside of Agra.[97] One of the soldiers, Private George Edwards, shot a breech-loading rifle at a buck that passed in front of him. After he had missed his prey, three villagers began shouting from a field 200 yards ahead directly in Edwards' line of fire. The soldiers ran over to discover that one of the villagers, Rup Ram, had been hit with buckshot in his right shoulder, causing him to fall unconscious. Begging for forgiveness, Edwards gave one of the men, Kashi Ram, 2 rupees for medical aid. Kashi Ram took the money, tied it up in his loincloth, and then, as Magistrate A. Cruickshank put it, "with Oriental duplicity, and without a word of warning, turned on Edwards and with his *lathi* [wooden club] caught him with an almost stunning blow to the head, knocking off his helmet and causing a severe bruise on the back of his head." Dazed and confused from the thrashing, Edwards handed his gun over to Kashi Ram and attempted to run away. At Kashi Ram's instructions, the three soldiers were tied to a babul tree, only to be freed two and a half hours later by a policeman who happened to pass by.

This was clearly an atypical case. Although the usual suspects played the opposite roles, the outcome was virtually the same. The government commended the soldiers for showing no resistance or retaliation, while Kashi Ram was convicted of rioting, hurt by dangerous weapon, and wrongful confinement. He was sentenced to three years of rigorous imprisonment in a case that was seen to shed "a strong light on the feeling of the ordinary villagers towards English soldiers."[98] Although Bernard Cohn has argued that culturally divergent notions about justice led Indians to have little respect for colonial courts,[99] Kashi Ram's actions suggest other possible readings. One reading is that Kashi Ram knew that justice in such a case could never be gotten in a colonial court and acted accordingly, in spite of the predictable consequences. Another is that Kashi Ram thought that justice could best be served by his own hand – by tying the soldiers to a tree. In both readings, it is clear that Kashi Ram was either unwilling or disinclined to use or rely on the colonial law and courts.

---

[97] L/PJ/6/364, File 2512.

[98] W. H. L. Impey (Allahabad) to Lyall at GOI, November 24, 1893, BL, IOR, L/PJ/6/364, File 2512.

[99] B. Cohn, *An Anthropologist among the Historians and Other Essays* (Delhi: Oxford University Press, 1988).

By contrast, a case from Madras a few years later demonstrates the deliberate use of law to obtain justice by the most oppressed subject in India, an illiterate female laborer. In August 1902, Ian Henry Baillie and Norris McGowan were tried in the Madras High Court in connection with the death of their horsekeeper, Yesu. Baillie and McGowan were partners, planters, and managers at the Cardamon Estate in the princely state of Travancore. They were charged with culpable homicide not amounting to murder, grievous hurt, and causing hurt to extort confession; they pleaded not guilty to all counts.[100]

At around 6 a.m. on the morning of March 22, 1902, Baillie and McGowan were informed by their Indian butler, Samuel, that two tin cashboxes had been found broken open and partially looted in the stables. Upon hearing the news, Baillie, McGowan, Samuel, and another servant, Sonayya Pillai, proceeded to Yesu's quarters to search for evidence of the theft. They found nothing at Yesu's home, but despite the horsekeeper's protestations of innocence they seized him and led him out to a tree in the courtyard. They stripped Yesu of his loincloth, tied him to the tree, and beat him with a *rattan*, one after the other in succession. According to the eye-witness testimony of Yesu's wife, Annapooranum, "Each gave fifteen or twenty stripes with a *rattan* (a thumb's width and 2 1/2 foot long) and hit him with their fists on the forehead and chest."[101] Another eye-witness testified that "The method of beating was that twenty or thirty stripes were given, then there would be a slight stop, and then the beating would be commenced." At 10 a.m., Yesu was locked up in the stables while Baillie and McGowan returned to their bungalow to eat their breakfast. According to Annapooranum, "After he was beaten, the skin on my husband's person peeled off."

Later that afternoon, the beatings were resumed. At one point, Yesu admitted to the theft and promised to reveal where the stolen merchandise – two watches and some petty valuables – was hidden. He was untied and taken to a spot where other workers from the estate began to dig. When nothing was found, Baillie and McGowan again began to beat and kick Yesu with their heavy leather boots, though this time witnesses stated that they saw Baillie sitting in a chair looking sickly and feverish. (Baillie later claimed that he took no active part in the beating as he was suffering from a fever. In fact, he claimed that he stuck around precisely to "see that no undue violence should be used.")[102] Yesu subsequently led the

---

[100] BL, IOR, L/PJ/6/601, File 995 and BL, IOR, L/PJ/6/634, File 877.
[101] *Madras Mail*, August 1901, BL, IOR, L/PJ/6/601, File 995.
[102] Baillie's petition to Arthur Oliver Villiers (Lord Ampthill), Governor of Madras, February 5, 1902, ibid.

planters to two more places where they dug and found nothing. For a third time, Yesu was taken back to the tree, which his wife saw shaking as her husband was mercilessly flogged.

At around 5 p.m., Sonayya Pillai and Samuel came running to Annapooranum's kitchen, grabbed a bottle of whiskey, a tumbler, and a knife and ran back to the tree, which had stopped moving. According to the testimony of another eye-witness, Baillie poured whiskey into Yesu's mouth, but "The whiskey did not go down his throat." Sonayya Pillai rubbed some whiskey on Yesu's chest and body but "There was no breath."[103] Concerned that a passer-by on the road might see the body, Baillie instructed Sonayya Pillai to move it out of sight. The next morning, Sonayya Pillai and Samuel informed Annapooranum that Yesu had died and that she should go away with her things. Along with all of the other hillmen and laborers who fled the plantation in fear, Annapooranum and her child left the estate. McGowan's cook testified that "On the following morning I went away to my village being frightened at the occurrence of the previous day."[104] Two or three days later, Baillie set fire to the rope and the *rattans* near the pear tree. The ashes were later discovered by the police.

Yesu's case would never have been tried had it not been for Annapooranum's deliberate steps to initiate a prosecution. Annapooranum traveled to a neighboring village where she elicited the help of a schoolmaster to write a petition of complaint. About one month after her husband's murder, Annapooranum's petition made it into the hands of Head Constable Lambert, who initiated an investigation.

Ironically, Baillie and McGowan had previously contacted Lambert to investigate the alleged theft. Upon receiving Annapooranum's petition, however, Lambert assigned the murder investigation to Indian Inspector Tharyan, who reached Cardamon on the evening of April 21. At 8 a.m. the next day, Tharyan requested that Baillie and McGowan provide some laborers to help him exhume Yesu's corpse, but "They said they had no coolies." They initially told Tharyan that Yesu's death was a suicide: "Yesu died by putting out his tongue and choking himself."

When Yesu's body was finally exhumed, the corpse was mostly intact, although his scalp and skin had fallen off, along with his left bicep and right calf. The hospital assistant who performed the post-mortem noted that it was difficult to detect marks of violence on his body as there was no skin. The cause of death was determined to be hemorrhage into the chest cavity: "I told the Inspector that the death must have been due to violence.

[103] *Madras Mail*, August 1901, ibid.   [104] Ibid.

A severe and continued beating by a *rattan* might be a possible cause of death. It might cause death by shock." The inquest report, written in Malayalam, was orally translated into English for Baillie and McGowan, who signed it and then went to have breakfast with a neighbor. (Baillie and McGowan later stated that the inquest report was never translated.) An Indian Medical Service officer who saw the post-mortem report confirmed that hemorrhage into the chest cavity of a healthy man "would be presumably due to severe violence." On April 24, Baillie and McGowan were arrested.

The two men were tried before a nine-person jury comprised of six Europeans and three Indians. The prosecution produced evidence from a variety of witnesses – the laborers, police, local judicial officers, medical officers, and others – all of whom corroborated in small and large detail the brutal tale of Yesu's torture. Using the £1,000 that had been raised by local planters for their defense, Baillie and McGowan's lawyers rested their case on two bare statements made by the defendants themselves. Baillie stated that he was ill with fever at the time of the alleged incident and that he did not kick, beat, or cause any violence to Yesu. McGowan asserted that he simply asked the butler to confine Yesu to the tree so he would not get away. After deliberating for thirty minutes, the jury unanimously acquitted the men of culpable homicide but convicted them of grievous hurt and causing hurt to extort confession. The Chief Justice sentenced Baillie to three years' rigorous imprisonment and McGowan (the perceived ringleader) to four years' rigorous imprisonment. Sonnaya Pillai, who was seen as having acted under the instruction of his masters, was sentenced to six months. An outraged Curzon commented: "it is one of those cases where what is called 'grievous hurt' in India bears the more uncompromising title of 'murder' at home."[105]

Baillie was sent to the Penitentiary at Madras and later transferred to Coimbatore Central Jail. Within six months, he and members of his family began petitioning the government for remission of his sentence and a transfer to England.[106] Baillie insisted that the witnesses had exaggerated and produced false evidence, and maintained that he had taken no part in the beating. He conjectured that Yesu's death was his own fault, "due primarily and mainly to the diseased condition of Yesu either to rupture of the aortic valve or of some other large artery," caused by his attempts to get free from the tree. Baillie further pleaded that the cause of death had not been definitively established by the medical evidence: "Yesu died, and he died on the day he was beaten. Ignorant, excited and superstitious

---

[105] Curzon to Hamilton, August 28, 1901, BL, IOR, MSS Eur/F111/160 (1901).
[106] BL, IOR, L/PJ/6/601, File 995.

hillmen might in their minds connect the two in the relation of cause and effect."[107]

Neither the Madras Government nor the Secretary of State accepted either Baillie's requests or the many letters of support from his previous employers and schoolteachers. In jail, Baillie's physical and mental health began to deteriorate. At first, sores and vitiligo began to spread across his hips, legs, and scalp, which the Inspector-General of Jails attributed to "much unnecessary anxiety of mind." Baillie subsequently contracted typhoid fever and quickly began to age, appearing overly suspicious, insubordinate, disrespectful, and delusional to prison authorities.[108] By August 1903, although concern about his physical health had abated, Baillie was placed on suicide watch.[109] On August 14, 1903, having served two of his three years, Baillie's sentence was remitted owing to his poor health, "his mind especially being in an unsatisfactory state."[110]

There are a number of familiar and unfamiliar elements to Baillie and McGowan's case. Familiar is the nature of the brutal beating and the efforts of the defendants to escape justice. Less familiar is the role played by a powerless Indian laborer, Annapooranum, in insisting that the colonial investigative machinery do its work and serve the ends of justice.

"The jury is not a plant of southern growth"[111]

The negative publicity surrounding "perverse verdicts" delivered by European juries in the late nineteenth century prompted official inquiries into the history and working of the jury system. Trial by jury in criminal cases was first introduced in the Mayor's Courts in 1726, where only British subjects from the Presidency towns were eligible to serve. In 1774, when the Supreme Courts supplanted the Mayor's Courts, the system of trial by jury remained unchanged. Due to prevailing notions about the dishonesty, low moral standards, ignorance, cultural backwardness, childishness, superstitiousness, and prejudicial temperament of the Indian populace, the jury system was not initially extended outside of the Presidency towns.

---

[107] Baillie's petition to the Governor-General of Madras of February 5, 1902, BL, IOR, L/PJ/6/601, File 995.

[108] Madras Government to the Secretary of State, July 15, 1903, BL, IOR, L/PJ/6/634, File 877.

[109] E. H. Gadsen, Acting Inspector-General of Prisons to the Madras Goverrnment, August 6, 1903, BL, IOR, L/PJ/6/634, File 877.

[110] Madras Government to the Secretary of State, August 26, 1903, ibid.

[111] J. L. Johnstone, Dharwar Sessions Judge to Dharwar District Magistrate, November 14, 1892, No. 142, NAI, Home/Judicial (A)/February 1893/102–150.

In 1826, the East India Jury Act provided that only Christians could serve on grand juries and that all cases involving Christians in the Supreme Courts would be tried only by Christian jurors. Indians could serve only on Petty Juries in trials of other Indians. Ram Mohun Roy was an early critic of the exclusionary nature of this system:

The consequences of this new Act is that in matters where a man's life is at stake or where banishment, imprisonment and severe punishment are awarded, we Hindoos and Mussalmans must submit to the verdict of Christians whether they be natives of Britain or the off-springs of British father by Indian mothers, whether they be the common Portuguese Armenians or the "rice Christians" of Serampore. These persons shall have the privilege of joining in cases where our lives are concerned; whereas we, although living in the same country or in the same hamlet with them and partaking in their virtues and vices, shall have no power of judging respecting them. In like manner our descendants must also submit their lives to the decisions of the sons of Christians.[112]

The official anxiety about native mendacity (discussed in Chapter 3) made colonial administrators loath to extend the jury system to ordinary Indians. In 1830, an official from Bengal noted that "the honesty and intelligence required of a juryman was unquestionably not to be found amongst the natives of India."[113] The moral and intellectual deficiencies of Indian jurors would remain a constant subject of critique.[114] As the District Magistrate of Belgaum observed in 1892, ordinary Indian jurors were no more qualified than rural schoolgirls: "if Government clerks and school masters, &c., were excluded, the whole system would be reduced to a mere burlesque, the Judge expounding legal principles to a set of men no more capable of understanding what he said than if he were to talk to an elementary class of schoolgirls in a jungle village."[115]

Efforts to extend the jury system to Indian "people of respectability" brought its own problems. In the early nineteenth century, John Shore described the difficulties of getting elite Bengalis to serve. In spite of his efforts to make being called to jury duty seem like a special distinction – Shore only called on members of the Nawab's family, respectable merchants, bankers, and *zamindars* and sat them at the same table where he sat – Indians rarely and reluctantly agreed to his personal requests,

---

[112] S. Tagore, *Rammohun Roy: His Role in Indian Renaissance* (Bengal: The Asiatic Society, 1975).

[113] Quoted from a Bengal official in Judicial Letter from Bengal, October 5, 1830, *Report from the Select Committee of the House of Lords*, 1830–32, p. 181.

[114] Belgaum District Magistrate F. L. Charles to Judicial Department, December 21, 1892, NAI, Home/Judicial (A)/February 1893/102–150.

[115] Belgaum District Magistrate F. L. Charles to the Judicial Department, December 21, 1892, NAI, Home/Judicial (A)/February 1893/148.

especially in criminal cases. As Shore noted, Indian jurors were reluctant to have blood on their hands and wanted assurances that criminal convictions would not lead to hangings. When not given such assurances, they invariably acquitted.[116]

European opposition to local criminal jurisdiction in the *mofussil* was partly based on the fact that the Company Courts did not have a jury system. As Calcutta Supreme Court Chief Justice Charles Jackson argued in 1859, "Establish good Courts and, if possible, a good Jury, in the *Mofussil*, and you would at once destroy all pretence for the exemption of British subjects from their jurisdiction."[117] Britons in India viewed their right to a jury trial as an inalienable one, although the Court of Directors noted that: "The only inalienable right of an accused Englishman is justice; and if he resides in the Interior of India, he must be content with such justice as is dispensed to the Natives."[118] Ironically, whereas non-officials clung to the jury system as their inalienable birthright, official concern with the workings of the jury system related largely to the failure of European juries to deliver justice in cases with European defendants. As Madras Governor Charles Trevelyan observed, "it is a painful but undoubted fact, that, however obvious the guilt of an Englishman may be, justice is not to be expected from any ordinary Calcutta or Madras jury composed of Europeans and East Indians."[119]

The first Code of Criminal Procedure (1861) expanded the jury system by giving local governments the discretion of where and what offenses to try by jury in the *mofussil*.[120] Without specifying which crimes could be tried by juries, it mandated only their racial composition. In criminal trials before the Sessions Courts, European British defendants were given the right to be tried by a mixed jury composed of no fewer than half European or American jurors. European (not British) and American defendants were to be tried by between five and nine jurors, more than half of whom were Europeans or Americans. Defendants who were not European or American were to be tried by juries of more than half non-Europeans and non-Americans.

In the 1860s, the Governments of Bengal, Bombay, and Madras began to experiment with the expansion of the jury system in certain districts. An early and ongoing critique of the system was that Indian jurors refused to

---

[116] Private papers of the Hon. Frederick John Shore, 1822–1858, pp. 203–218, BL, IOR, H/790.
[117] NAI, Legislative Council Proceedings, Vol. V (1859).
[118] Court of Directors to the Government of India, Home (Public) in NAI, Home (Public), Letters from Court of Directors (1834), No. 98.
[119] NAI, Home/Legislative (A)/January 1865/3.
[120] Code of Criminal Procedure (1861), section 322.

serve or convict in homicide and other capital cases no matter how obvious the guilt of the defendant because they did not approve of capital punishment. They also tended not to convict in perjury, forgery, and instituting false complaint cases because these crimes did not meet with their moral disapprobation.[121] As the Government of Burma noted, "Trial by jury in India is an exotic plant which is unsuited to the country not because people are wrongly convicted by a jury but because they are so often wrongly acquitted."[122]

Many colonial administrators, such as Judge Tweedie of the Patna Sessions Court, saw the high rate of jury acquittals as a means by which Indians resisted the statutory provisions of the colonial law. Tweedie cited three ways that Indians used their position in the jury box to protest the law:

An objection on the part of many men to much of our law – as, for example, the law of joint-liability for crime and (especially in the case of Mahomedans) to our law of evidence, which does not render "eye-witnesses" indispensable; The common feeling against convicting in any case of homicide lest the guilty person should be hanged; The further feeling that it is a good and generous action to help a guilty man to escape; Downright sympathy with some forms of crime, such as perjury and forgery.[123]

Judge Tweedie's observation offers another compelling example of how ordinary Indians engaged colonial laws and law courts on their own terms, substituting their own notions of justice in place of the crimes and punishments proscribed by the colonial state.

To secure "the ends of justice," the amended Code of Criminal Procedure (1872) gave Sessions judges the power to refer a case to the High Court when they disagreed with the jury's verdict. Law Member James Fitzjames Stephen noted that although this constituted a clear departure from English practice, it was entirely necessary as a mechanism of control.[124]

In the face of growing public concern about the perverse verdicts delivered by European juries, the Government of India was forced to review the jury system again at the end of the nineteenth century. On May 31, 1890, the government formally requested a report on the jury system from each of

---

[121] Keepwith of P. G. Meltius, August 19, 1891, NAI, Legislative/April 1896 (A)/1–408.

[122] Letter No. 1035-Q. 67, August 24, 1921, NAI *Legislative Assembly Debates*, September 15, 1921.

[123] Tweedie's fascinating note in the keepwith of P. G. Meltius, August 19, 1891, NAI, Legislative/April 1896 (A)/1–408. Also see J. P. Hewitt's keepwith of October 15, 1891, NAI, Legislative/April 1896 (A)/1–408.

[124] Stephen's note of April 16, 1872, quoted in Secretary of State to the Government of India, February 16, 1893, NAI, Home/Judicial (A)/May 1893/143–155.

the local governments.[125] Local officials were found to be more satisfied with the workings of Indian juries than they were with European juries, although the political risk of publicly admitting, much less doing anything about, this was untenable.[126] Subsequent attempts made by the Government of India to withdraw certain classes of offense from jury trials in Bengal were met with wide public condemnation.[127]

In light of the controversy concerning the failure of white juries to convict in racial cases, in 1901 the judges of the North-Western Provinces High Court proposed an amendment to the Code of Criminal Procedure that would have given High Court judges the discretion to replace a European-majority jury with a panel of three judges in cases where Europeans were accused of assaulting Indians. Still smarting from his confrontation with Cotton and the Assam tea planters, Curzon privately expressed his sympathy with the proposal but publicly capitulated to the demands of the non-official community, noting that "in spite of its occasional abuses and failures, the jury system is generally regarded in this country as a guarantee of justice and a palladium of liberty; the proposal to modify it might give rise to racial disputes or misapprehensions, which it is not desirable to awaken."[128]

The Racial Distinctions Committee and the race against empire

In July 1905, Viceroy Curzon famously (and to disastrous effect) passed a resolution approving the partition of the province of Bengal. This dramatically fueled the flames of anti-colonial nationalism and catapulted the Indian National Congress onto stronger and more stable political ground. Curzon is so closely tied to this unpopular and controversial act in historical memory that his role as an imperial watchdog and critic has been overshadowed. Following Curzon's departure from India, and in the tumultuous years between 1905 and 1911, the Government of India was largely concerned with respectively repressing and appeasing the extremist and moderate wings of the nationalist movement. Although the racialized nature of colonial justice was a long-standing historical problem that could not be totally ignored, the issue simmered slowly on the back burner.

---

[125] NAI, Home/Judicial (A)/May 1890/716–718.
[126] NAI, Home/Judicial (A)/February 1893/102–150.
[127] NAI, Home/Judicial (A)/March 1893/9–12D and NAI, Home/Judicial (A)/May 1893/143–155.
[128] Letter of December 31, 1901, NAI, Home/Judicial (A)/Dec 1901/223–225.

In March 1914, Home Member Sir Reginald Craddock introduced a Bill to amend the Code of Criminal Procedure. Five months later, Britain declared war on Germany, causing legislative action on the Bill to be postponed. After the war ended, on February 23, 1920, Bengal Advocate-General S. P. Sinha submitted what he thought was a rhetorical question to the Legislative Assembly. As Sinha had been part of a committee appointed to review Craddock's Bill, he, like others on the committee, had assumed this work would resume after the war. Thus, when he asked, "Do Government propose to assimilate and unify the procedure in trials by removing from the Code any distinctions substituting at present on the ground of race or nationality? If not, why not?," he expected a sympathetic reply.[129] Instead, Home Member William Vincent, evoking a decades-old discourse, responded that: "Government do not think that the present would be an opportune time to raise this question, which is bound to give rise to very serious controversy."[130]

The issue of legal inequality was once again poised to explode. In the post-war period, there was a massive upsurge of nationalist activity fueled by a variety of factors, including Gandhi's return to India from South Africa and the widespread disappointment across the colonial world that the Great War had not, at least for them, made the world "safe for democracy," as US President Woodrow Wilson had so hopefully promised.[131] The Government of India's pledge of "responsible government" in 1917 and the legislative reforms of 1919, which extended the role of Indians in provincial governance, seemed to be moving India towards self-rule. These reforms raised the expectations of Indian nationalists, who successfully pressured Viceroy Reading to "accept the principle that there should be equality of status for all races respecting criminal procedure."[132] On September 26, 1921, a twelve-man "Racial Distinctions Committee" was appointed to conduct public inquiries into the long-standing and still wildly controversial matter of racial distinctions in the law. Led by Law Member Dr. Tej Bahadur Sapru, the Committee accepted written and oral evidence over the next five months.

At the center of the storm was Chapter 33 of the Code of Criminal Procedure (1898), "Criminal Proceedings against Europeans and Americans." Whereas some couched their opposition to the existing statutory law in abstract terms – Sir Hari Singh Gour stated, "on first principles, on the

---

[129] NAI, Home, Judicial (B), May 1920, No. 78.   [130] Ibid.

[131] Wilson's speech to the US Congress on April 2, 1917.

[132] Judicial Resolution of December 27, 1921, NAI, Home/Judicial (A)/1922/F. 105 and the Viceroy's Telegram to the Secretary of State, January 22, 1922, NAI, *Racial Distinctions (Main Correspondence)*.

ground of international justice, on the ground of equity, no man has the right to come here to this country, suck nutrition therefrom and when he commits an offense against the laws of the country to claim immunity from the ordinary procedure which is laid down by the law of this land"[133] – most argued that the special provisions of law led to gross failures of justice in cases where European British subjects were accused of violence against Indians. As N. B. Gupta argued: "The Indian demand for the removal of all distinctions is not based on theoretical grounds but on a strong and widespread conviction that these special rules of procedure have been responsible for the many and grave miscarriages of justice."[134]

A number of prominent trials had recently re-ignited public outrage about the perverse verdicts delivered by European juries. One of the most infamous was the "Khoreal shooting case," in which the assistant manager of a tea garden in Cachar named Reid attempted to forcibly take a young female laborer as his mistress. When the girl refused Reid's overtures, he shot and killed her father. In the lower court, Reid was unanimously acquitted by a European jury.[135] When the case came before the Calcutta High Court, Reid's acquittal was confirmed by a mixed jury comprised of eight Europeans and one Indian. This time, though, the decision was not unanimous: the lone Indian juror dissented from the white majority, causing a "great commotion" in Calcutta.[136]

The Government of India was torn about how to deal with the pressure to enact a non-discriminatory law that provided a uniform mode of trial and punishment. On the one hand, failure to act offered Indian nationalists a complaint against the government around which activists of all persuasions could unify and mobilize. On the other hand, confronted by Gandhi's first non-cooperation movement, the government was desperate for allies and could not afford to start "counter agitations among Europeans."[137] The question facing the government was not just whether to remove the distinctions in criminal procedure, but how to do so. Should they "level up," so that all alike enjoyed European British privileges, or "level down", so the Briton shared in the Indian's legal disabilities?

---

[133] NAI, *Racial Distinctions (Main Correspondence)*.
[134] N. B. Gupta, Officiating Secretary to the Government of Bengal, Judicial Department, to the Government of India, Home Department, October 16, 1921, ibid.
[135] "Report on the Immigrant Labour in Assam (1919/1920)," BL, IOR, V/24/1225.
[136] K. Ahmed, NAI, Legislative Assembly Debates, January 15, 1923.
[137] "*Précis* of opinions on the reference to Local Governments, dated the 21st of July, 1921, regarding the removal of racial distinctions from the Criminal Procedure Code," NAI, *Racial Distinctions (Main Correspondence)*.

Most local officials consulted by the Government of India maintained that the time was not right to re-open this volatile issue, arguing that "racial feeling" was running especially high due to Gandhi's movement. The Madras Government observed that "owing to the present political situation, the time is not opportune for this."[138] The Bengal Government advocated a "cautious move,"[139] while the Burma Chief Court pressed the government to boldly face the inevitable:

The privileges of which it is proposed to deprive the European community are privileges which are based at bottom on a belief in racial superiority and their retention is incompatible with the proclaimed policy of the Government of India to put Europeans and Indians in India on a footing of exact equality. Their disappearance in the long run is inevitable. It is part of statesmanship to accept the inevitable, and to face the consequences now, rather than to tinker with the problem and deal with it piece-meal, and so to give handle to prolonged agitation on the part of both communities alike.[140]

Adding to the political complexity of the debate was the fact that the matter of racial distinctions was not only, as Legislative Assembly Member Sohan Lal put it, "a matter of our national self-respect,"[141] it had assumed an imperial dimension. Shortly before the Committee was appointed, an Imperial Conference met in London (June – August 1921) to determine the future constitution of the empire. One of the most contentious issues considered by the delegates was the status of Indians in the dominions.[142] At the Imperial War Conference of 1918, the self-governing dominions and India had agreed to a "Reciprocity Resolution" that recognized immigration on reciprocal terms. The 1918 Conference had also recognized the right of all colonies to "enjoy complete control of the composition of its own population by means of restriction on immigration from any of the other communities." These two policies were inherently contradictory and ignored the reality of growing anti-Indian sentiment and legislation in East and South Africa (and even in the Americas).[143]

To the dismay of many Indians, the legal disabilities placed on Indians in the colonies and the self-governing dominions stood in stark contrast to the special legal privileges afforded to subjects from the dominions and colonies in India under Chapter 33. As Sohan Lal argued: "I think the question of the condition of the Indians in the Colonies can only be solved

[138] Ibid.   [139] Ibid.   [140] Letter No. 1035-Q. 67, August 24, 1921, ibid.
[141] NAI, Legislative Assembly Debates, Vol. III, No. 40, February 19, 1923.
[142] BL, IOR, L/E/7/1188, File 148.
[143] In 1917, the US federal government established an "Asiatic Barred Zone" that banned immigration from all Asian countries except Japan. In 1924, Japanese immigration was also banned.

by our getting equal status in India. So long as we do not get equal status in India, we cannot possibly ask the Governments of Colonies to give us equal status with them in the Colonies."[144]

Not only did Indians in the colonies not have equal status, but anti-Asian sentiment across the colonial world was growing. Since the 1890s, the Natal Government had moved in an increasingly anti-Indian direction. Although Colonial Secretary Joseph Chamberlain warned the Natal Government in 1896 of "the tradition of the Empire, which makes no distinction in favour of or against race or colour," laws were passed to bar Indian representation on the Legislative Council (Franchise Act of 1896), to restrict Indian immigration (Immigration Restriction Act of 1897), and to bar Indians from owning land even indirectly. In response to the legal disabilities placed upon the 160,000 Indians domiciled in South Africa, the Indian National Congress issued a "Declaration of Indian Rights" (1918) demanding that "Indians and Europeans and the people living in the colonies must be put in the eyes of the law upon the same level."[145]

Around the same time, the Government of British Columbia barred the 4,000 or so domiciled Sikhs from bringing their wives and children over from India. In East Africa, too, anti-Indian agitation among white settlers was reaching new heights as whites tried to secure their right to settle the prized highlands in Kenya by excluding the 55,000 resident South Asians, many of whom had lived there for centuries. A report released in March 1919 by the Economic Commission in Nairobi blamed Indians for damaging Africa and Africans:

The presence of the Indians, organized as they are to keep the African out of every position which an Indian could fill, deprives the African of all incentives to ambition and opportunities of advancement...[The African] is not strong enough anywhere to stand against the competition of a more crafty race...Physically, the Indian is not a wholesome influence because of his incurable repugnance to sanitation and hygiene...The Indian is everywhere the despair of the sanitarian; here he is not only a menace to himself, but especially to the natives of the country. The moral depravity of the Indian is equally damaging to the African...The Indian is the inciter to crime as well as vice...The presence of the Indian in this country is quite obviously inimical to the moral and physical welfare and the economic advancement of the native.[146]

India's putatively equal position in the empire was at odds with both this expansion of anti-Asian legislation and with the recognized right of the

---

[144] NAI, Legislative Assembly Debates, Vol. III, No. 40, February 19, 1923.

[145] I. Narain, *The Politics of Racialism: A Study of the Indian Minority in South Africa down to the Gandhi–Smuts Agreement* (Agra: Shiva Lal Agarwala, 1962).

[146] G. H. Mungeam, *Kenya: Select Historical Documents, 1884–1923* (Nairobi: East African Publishing House, 1978), p. 548.

dominions to pass restrictive immigration laws designed to control the composition of their populations. How could India be an equal member in the empire when Indians suffered under race-based legal disabilities and discrimination at home and abroad? In June 1921, in a direct challenge to Winston Churchill, India's delegate to the Imperial Conference, Srinivasa Sastri, remarked: "In noble words you described the Empire, Sir, as a confederation of Races in which willing and free peoples had been admitted – willing and free peoples; consent is incompatible with equality of races and freedom necessarily implies admission of all peoples to the rights of citizenship without reservation."[147]

The editor of London's *Daily News* was moved by Sastri's elegant speech and his demand for a non-racial empire:

What Mr. Sastri has been sent to fight for is equal rights for Indians within the Empire…Here in reality is the supreme test of the British Empire. Is it to be a White Man's Empire or can we rise to make it something the world has never yet seen, a single and united society of peoples in which neither faith, nor colour, nor language, nor ancestry shall be a bar to full and equal citizenship? The answer to that question may decide the future of India.[148]

Richard Jebb had a more hard-line reaction. In the *Morning Post*, Jebb wrote, "there exists no such thing as a common 'citizenship' of the British Empire."[149] Jebb noted that citizenship offered political rights, whereas subjecthood entitled the people of the empire only to personal protection.[150] All of the delegates at the Imperial Conference, with the exception of South Africa, ultimately signed a resolution recognizing that "in the interests of the solidarity of the British Commonwealth, it is desirable the rights of such Indians [those legally domiciled in the Dominions] to citizenship should be recognized.[151]

During the Racial Distinctions Committee's deliberations, connections were frequently made to these anti-Indian movements elsewhere in the empire. Indian members of the Racial Distinctions Committee attempted to lower the legal status of colonials in India (as compared with the status of Britons) as an instrument of negotiation to push for full citizenship for Indians in the dominions. Why, they wondered, should white colonials get more privileges than Indians did in their own country? The pressure to "level down" colonials was one of the thorniest issues tackled by Sapru's Racial Distinctions Committee.

The Racial Distinctions Committee's work nearly collapsed under the weight of this broader imperial politics. How was a "European British

---

[147] BL, IOR, L/E/7/1227, 1425.   [148] *Daily News*, June 16, 1921.
[149] *Morning Post*, June 29, 1921.   [150] Ibid.
[151] Resolution on the Position of Indians in the Dominions, BL, IOR, L/E/7/1227, 1425.

subject" to be defined in the Indian law, if at all? J. Chaudhuri, editor of *Calcutta Weekly Notes* and representative of the Indian Association, argued that there should be no such special designation: "I think that we ought to feel that we are equal citizens of the empire. A British subject ought to be a British subject irrespective of nationality."[152] Sohan Lal similarly pressed that "There is no necessity for keeping the definition of European British subject in the Criminal Procedure Code. We have got no definition of Indian British subjects. We have got no definition of a European or of an Indian, and there is no reason why we should have the definition of a European British subject."[153] Legislative Assembly Member Munshi Iswar Saran argued that the goal was equal justice for all inhabitants of India, regardless of race:

We want justice for ourselves and we want justice for those who happen to be in this country, be they Europeans or others...[The distinction] is a constant reminder to the Indian people that there is a distinction in law between the trial of Europeans and Indians, which in other words is a hallmark of our inferiority in our own country. We claim perfect freedom and equality of treatment, and, at the same time, we are anxious that equality of treatment and of justice should not only be enjoyed by us alone but by all those Europeans who happen to be in this country. This freedom we are seeking is not for the purposes of self-aggrandizement, we desire freedom for ourselves, for the Europeans, and indeed for all the races that are to be found in this country.[154]

With the assent of all of the local governments (except Bombay), the Racial Distinctions Committee ultimately proposed a Bill that excluded people from the self-governing dominions and the colonies from the definition of a "European British subject." When Sohan Lal introduced the Bill, he noted that its object "is to uproot this tree of racial hatred and to place Indians and Europeans on the same level before the sacred altar of law and justice."[155] Emphasizing the essential solidarity of the empire as a whole, the Secretary of State refused to pass the Bill unless colonials were included in the definition of "European British subject."[156] To murmurs in the crowd that the changes to the Committee's report "are the instructions of a reactionary Secretary of State, no friend of India," the Legislative Assembly presented a revised Bill that defined "European British subjects" as "any subject of His Majesty of European descent in the male line born, naturalized or domiciled in the British Islands or any

[152] Evidence before Racial Distinctions Committee, NAI, Home/Judicial/1924/File 638.
[153] NAI, Legislative Assembly Debates, Vol. III, No. 40, February 19, 1923.
[154] NAI, Legislative Assembly Debates, September 15, 1921.
[155] NAI, Home/Judicial (A)/1922/F. 105, Part I, Nos. 1–4.
[156] Viceroy to the Secretary of State, December 20, 1922, NAI, Home/Judicial/1922/Files 105–111.

Colony or any subject of His Majesty who is the child or grandchild of any such person by legitimate descent."

The Criminal Law Amendment Act (XII of 1923) represented yet another "compromise" solution worked out with representatives of the non-official community in Calcutta. The law maintained racial distinctions for European British subjects, including the right to request a panel with a majority of European and American jurors. In an effort to "level up" natives, Indians could request a panel with a majority of Indian jurors. To the horror of many, the amended Code also contained a special provision for British soldiers that allowed them to be tried, at the government's discretion, by a High Court in any of the five major offenses for which they could not by law be tried by court-martial (murder, manslaughter, rape, treason, and treason-felony).

This came as a disappointment, but not a surprise, to the many Indians who had fought so long and hard on this issue, including Hafiz Muhammad Abdul Rahim, who had the prescience to observe in 1922 that "unless there is *Swaraj* [self-rule] there will be no real reform."[157] Indeed, it was not until after independence, with the passage of the Criminal Law (Removal of Racial Distinctions) Act of 1949, that the last vestiges of racial discrimination in criminal procedure were finally abolished from the Code of Criminal Procedure.

---

[157] Written evidence of Hafiz Muhammad Abdul Rahim, January 3, 1922, NAI *Racial Distinctions (Main Correspondence)*.

(challenging empire → nation-state process)

Conclusion

On the eve of the Great War, the British empire consisted of eighty territorial units ranging from self-governing dominions to informal and formal colonies, 11 million square miles of territory, and 400 million subjects in Africa, Asia, Australia, and the Americas who recognized Britain as their sovereign power. When the war ended, the empire swelled further still as Britain took control of certain German and Ottoman territories in Africa and the Middle East. Contrary to J. R. Seeley's famous quip over a century ago that British imperial expansion occurred in "a fit of absence of mind," it stands to reason that the growth and consolidation of this global powerhouse required considerable focus and attention. Although the British colonizers may not have been all-knowing, ill-intentioned, or unambiguous, they could not afford to be absent-minded if they wished to retain control of their massive empire.

This book argues that an important challenge to British imperial power and stability in India came from within. By foregrounding the menace of white violence and the uneven efforts of the colonial state to control it, this study demonstrates that violence was central to the empire in India in ways that simultaneously subverted and sustained British dominance. While some Company men may have "responded to India by slowly shedding their Britishness like an unwanted skin and adopting Indian dress and taking on the ways of the Mughal governing class they came to replace,"[1] other Britons, like William Orby Hunter, were gruesomely shedding the skin of others and (for the most part) getting away with it.

The eighteenth-century world of British India was populated not only by "White Mughals" but also by white marauders. As important as it is that we remember the unforgettable love story between Khair-un-Nissa and James Achilles Kirkpatrick, so too we must be careful to recall what William Orby Hunter and his Bibi did to their three female servants.[2]

---

[1] W. Dalrymple, "Plain Tales of British India," *The New York Review of Books*, 54, 7 (April 26, 2007).
[2] Dalrymple, *White Mughals*.

Through their murderous and criminal conduct, this unruly third group of whites in British India caused widespread anxiety about what could happen when the wrong sorts took part in the right to rule. They threatened the early Company state by besmirching the English character, disturbing the peace, and presenting a serious law-and-order crisis. The official response to this problem of European lawlessness was to codify the law, which ultimately expanded the legal authority of the colonial state, even if it did little to quell the violence or ensure justice.

In the nineteenth century, as the ranks of non-officials in India grew, so too did their rogue behavior and their influence over the formal organs of governance. Despite a rhetorical stance of legal equality, successive colonial administrations conferred special legal privileges upon European British subjects in criminal trials, thereby making law complicit in acts of white violence rather than a protection against them. This, combined with the prejudicial practices of British judges, juries, and police, guaranteed that Britons accused of assaulting and murdering Indians were booked on lesser (if any) criminal charges, which resulted in little to no punishment. In 1844, Bombay Supreme Court Puisne Judge Erskine Perry proudly observed that "one of the most valuable boons, which it lies within the competence of Government to confer upon this vast country, consists in the establishment of a rational and intelligible system of Law."[3] Only fifty years later, a series of "perverse verdicts" delivered in well-publicized trials of violent Europeans led the Bombay newspaper *Pratod* to conclude that "the law appears to sanction whatever is done by a European."[4]

This study of white violence in colonial India expands our knowledge of the "tensions of empire." British colonial society in India was not monolithic. In relation to each other, Britons were deeply divided, particularly along the lines of class. Law, however, conferred a certain stability and cohesion to their identity. In the Code of Criminal Procedure, *all* European British subjects could lay claim to the same privileges and protections regardless of their occupation or class background. In this way, law defined and defended what in social reality were unstable and porous boundaries, thereby making fuzzy distinctions between the colonized and the colonizer into something that was (literally and figuratively) more black and white.[5]

law defined social reality

[3] Bombay Supreme Court Puisne Judge Erskine Perry to the Governor-General in Council, May 22, 1844, *Report on the Civil Judicature in the Presidency Towns* (1844).
[4] *Pratod*, February 27, 1893, NAI, *Report on Native Newspapers from Bombay*.
[5] A. L. Stoler brilliantly demonstrates the instability of colonial categories in "Rethinking Colonial Categories: European Communities and the Boundaries of Rule," *Comparative Studies in Society and History*, 13, 1 (1989),134–161.

For some, what it meant to be a Briton in India was not an official appointment in the Indian Civil Service, or a summer stay in a hill station, or entry into an all-white social club. What set them apart from the ruled, and what provided a sense of solidarity with the rulers, was a colonial system of law that allowed Britons to behave violently towards Indians with impunity. Although law was not the originator of racial attitudes or the direct cause of violent actions, by denying the imperial promise of impartiality and equal protection, law normalized the violence that sustained British dominance.

In conducting the research for this book, among the many shocking stories and cases I came across, probably the most astounding thing I discovered is the abundance of available written evidence about colonial violence. That is, I did not have to read against the grain of the official archive to tell this dark and lesser-told tale about the empire in India. (Finding images, I will admit, was a lot more challenging.)

The shortage of secondary literature as compared with the abundance of archival evidence – which is to make no mention of other types of source material not consulted in the preparation of this manuscript, including Indian-language literature, fiction, and drama – raises a curious question: why are there so few written histories about white violence in colonial India? To answer this question, we might begin by considering the tradition of imperial history, which was born in and of the empire itself. The work of nineteenth-century imperial historians, such as James Mill and J. R. Seeley, in many ways reflected imperial self-representations and promoted imperial policy. It certainly comes as no surprise that men who tied the march of historical progress to the expansion of England did not stop to consider some of the more sinister ways in which colonialism functioned. But why have successive generations of historians turned a blind eye to this open secret?

In recent years, there has been a resurgence of scholarly and public interest in the history of empires and empire-building. Historians representing the "new imperial history" have restored the history of Britain's empire to the history of the British nation by placing metropole and colony in a unitary field of analysis.[6] This body of exciting work has placed questions about culture, race, identity, and "theorizing

---

[6] See, for example, C. Hall and S. O. Rose (eds.), *At Home with the Empire: Metropolitan Culture and the Imperial World* (Cambridge: Cambridge University Press, 2006); J. MacKenzie, *Propaganda and Empire: The Manipulation of British Public Opinion, 1880–1960* (Manchester: Manchester University Press, 1984); S. Stockwell (ed.), *The British Empire: Themes and Perspectives* (London: Blackwell, 2008); Walvin, *Fruits of Empire*; and K. Wilson (ed.), *A New Imperial History: Culture, Identity and Modernity in Britain and the Empire, 1660–1840* (Cambridge: Cambridge University Press, 2004).

difference"[7] at center stage and has demonstrated that the empire existed at home as much as it did in the world. The question of culture has also been of central importance to historians of the colony interested in exploring the complex nature of colonial power and its impact on colonized people.[8]

This book shifts attention away from questions of culture and takes up the history of physical violence as a site for reframing our view of the British empire in India. Violence was not an exceptional but an ordinary part of British rule in the subcontinent, even if the word "ordinary" may seem incongruous with the extraordinary brutality found in many of the cases presented in this study. Although it is difficult to definitively explain why everyday white violence, and its handling in the criminal courts of British India, has remained largely hidden from view, there can be no doubt that it is of central importance to the understanding of British colonialism and, perhaps, colonialism in general.

In India, the rule of law was a tool of empire that served both practical and ideological functions. Practically, law provided the colonial stage with a mechanism of regulation, extraction, and control. Ideologically, law legitimized the exercise of British power by promising India's colonized subjects a fair and impartial system of justice, thereby advancing Britain's civilizing mission. Emphasis in this study is placed on colonial law as it evolved in response to an unusual problem: the menace of white violence. The enduring crisis of European misconduct reveals not only the intrinsic violence associated with the exercise of colonial authority but also the messy work of running the empire.

Although the Indian subcontinent occupies the primary focus of this book, I would suggest that the everyday acts of racial violence committed by individuals in local Indian settings did not have exclusively Indian origins. It is clear that colonial law enabled and protected certain kinds of violence in India, largely by placing European British subjects above the law. Racial violence was not just practiced but also condoned by a colonial system of law that institutionalized legal inequality. I have sought to provide a comparative dimension to this study by suggesting that white violence in India is best understood within the global framework of

[7] C. Hall, *Cultures of Empire: Colonizers in Britain and the Empire in the Nineteenth and Twentieth Centuries: A Reader* (Manchester: Manchester University Press, 2000), p. 16.

[8] The literature on culture and colonialism is vast. For India, see Cohn, *Colonialism and Its Forms of Knowledge*; and Dirks, *Castes of Mind*. A different perspective on colonial power and cultural interventions is offered by C. A. Bayly, *Empire and Information: Intelligence Gathering and Social Communication in India, 1780–1870* (Cambridge: Cambridge University Press, 2000); and E. Irschick, *Dialogue and History: Constructing South India, 1795–1895* (Berkeley: University of California Press, 1994).

empire. The explicitly racial discourse espoused by critics and perpetrators of white violence in India about how "blacks" and "niggers" should
be treated reveals continuities in racial attitudes and actions across the
British empire, from the eighteenth-century slave plantations on Britain's
Caribbean colonies to the nineteenth-century British Raj.

The echoes of chattel slavery that resonated in the brutal acts of violence
and the scandalous acquittals of Britons accused of murdering Indians
also provided opponents of colonialism with a powerful platform and
potent language of critique. The notion that Britons looked at Indians as
less than human was not only shocking to Indians but also to many British
missionaries, reformers, and administrators including Viceroy Curzon,
who struggled to align his moral conscience with the imperial imperative.
Whether the promise of colonial justice ultimately softened or hardened
the practice of colonial power, I leave it to the reader to determine.

Select bibliography

Archives and libraries consulted

All India Institute of Medical Science, New Delhi, India
Arthur W. Diamond Law Library, Columbia University, NY, NY
Biddle Law Library, University of Pennsylvania, Philadelphia, PA
British Library, India Office Records, London, UK (BL, IOR)
Falvey Memorial Library, Villanova University, Villanova, PA
Indian Law Institute, New Delhi, India
Lahore High Court Library, Lahore, Pakistan
Library of Congress, Washington, DC
National Archives of India, New Delhi, India (NAI)
Nehru Memorial Museum and Library, New Delhi, India
New York University Law Library, NY, NY
Wellcome Library, Wellcome Trust, London, UK

Case law reports

Arbuthnot, A. J., *Select Reports of Criminal Cases Determined in the Court of Foujdaree Udalut of Madras, 1826 to 1850* (Madras, 1851)
Bengal Law Reports of Decisions of the High Court at Fort William (Calcutta, 1868–1875)
Bombay High Court Reports: Reports of Cases Decided in the High Court of Bombay (Bombay, 1866–1879)
Criminal Law Journal of India (Lahore: Law Printing Works, 1904–1946)
Indian Law Reports (various series; see http://pegasus.law.columbia.edu)
Madras High Court Reporter (Madras, 1861)
Madras Weekly Notes (Madras, 1910–)
Morley, William H., *An Analytical Digest of All the Reported Cases Decided in the Supreme Courts of Judicature in India* (Calcutta, 1850)
Punjab Record (Lahore, 1866–)
Reports of Cases Determined in the Court of Nizamut Adawlut (Calcutta, 1805–1850 [old series, vols. I–VI], 1851–1859 [new series, vols. I–IX])
Sutherland's Weekly Reporter (Calcutta, 1864–1877)

Statutory law, legal digests, and legal commentaries

Arbuthnot, A. J., *Select Reports of Criminal Cases Determined in the Court of Foujdaree Udalut of Madras, 1826 to 1850* (Madras, 1851)

Atkyns, J. T., *Reports of Cases Argued and Determined in the High Court of Chancery During the Time of Lord Hardwicke*, 3 vols. (London, 1765–1768)

Auber, Peter, *Supplement to an Analysis of the Constitution of the East India Company* (London, 1828)

Banerjee, A. C. (ed.), *Indian Constitutional Documents, 1757–1947*, vol. I (Calcutta: A. Mukherjee & Co., 3rd edn., 1961)

Baynes, Charles R., *The Criminal Law of the Madras Presidency, As Contained in the Existing Regulations and Acts with Statement of Crimes and Punishments and also Circular Orders of the Foujdaree Udalut 1805–1848* (Madras, 1848)

Beaufort, F. L., *A Digest of the Criminal Law of the Presidency of Fort William and a Guide to All Criminal Authorities Therein* (Calcutta, 1849)

Bellasis, A. F., *Reports of Criminal Cases Determined in the Sudder Foujdaree Adawlut of Bombay* (Bombay, 1850)

Carrau, J., *The Circular Orders of the Court of the Nizamut Adawlut Communicated to the Criminal Authorities from 1796 to 1853* (Calcutta, 1855)

Cases Disposed of by the Sudder Foujdaree Adaulut of Bombay, 1854–1857 (Bombay, 1857)

Colebrooke, Sir Henry Thomas, *Regulations and Laws Enacted by the Governor-General in Council for the Civil Government of the Whole of Territories under the Presidency of Fort William in Bengal* (Calcutta, 1793–1834)

Harrington, E., *Index to and Digest of Morris' Reports of the Sudder Foujdaree Adawlut, 1854–1858* (Bombay, 1860)

Marshman, J. C. *The Darogah's Manual* (Serampore, 1850)

Norton, John Bruce, *The Law of Evidence Applicable to the Courts of the East India Company* (Madras, 1858)

Stokes, Whitley, *The Anglo-Indian Codes: Adjective Law* (Oxford, 1888)

The Anglo-Indian Codes: Substantive Law (Oxford, 1887)

Thayer, J. B. *A Preliminary Treatise on Evidence at the Common Law* (Boston, 1898)

The Circular Orders Issued by Government in the Police Branch of the Judicial Department (1852–53) (Bombay, 1853)

The Circular Orders of the Court of Foujdaree Udalut, from 1805 up to the end of 1841 (Madras, 1842)

The Indian Evidence Act, with James Fitzjames Stephen's Speech Delivered on the Occasion of Presenting to the Supreme Council of India the Report of the Select Committee on the Bill to Define and Amend the Law of Evidence (Madras, 1873)

The Statutes of the United Kingdom of Great Britain and Ireland (London, 1807–1869)

Woodroffe, John and Ameer Ali, *Law of Evidence Applicable to British India* (Calcutta, 1898)

Printed sources (pre-1947)

Acharyya, Bijay Kisor, *Codification in British India* (Calcutta: S. K. Banerji & Sons, 1914)

Ambedkar, B. R., *What Congress and Gandhi Have Done to the Untouchables* (Bombay: Thacker, 1945)

Barker, George, *A Tea Planter's Life in Assam* (Calcutta: Thacker and Spink, 1884)

Bentham, Jeremy *"Swear Not At All": Containing an Exposure of the Needlessness and Mischievousness as well as Antichristianity of the Ceremony of an Oath* (London, 1817)

Bolts, William, *Considerations on Indian Affairs Respecting the Present State of Bengal* (London, 1772)

Buckingham, J., *Tea-Garden Coolies in Assam: Replying to a Communication on the Subject which appeared in the "Indian Churchman"; Reprinted with an Introduction and an Answer by the Rev. Charles Dowding* (London, 1894)

C. S., *Hindu Witnesses and the Judicial Oath* (Madras, 1882)

Chevers, Norman, *A Manual of Medical Jurisprudence for Bengal and the North-Western Provinces* (Calcutta, 1856)

   A Manual of Medical Jurisprudence for India, Including an Outline of a History of Crime against the Person in India (Calcutta, 1870)

   "Report in Medical Jurisprudence in the Bengal Presidency," *Indian Annals of Medical Science*, 3 (October 1854), 243–426

Cotton, Henry, *Indian and Home Memories* (London: T. Fisher Unwin, 1911)

Crawford, Arthur T., *Reminiscences of an Indian Police Official* (London, 1894)

Crawford, D. G., *A History of the Indian Medical Service 1600–1913* (London: W. Thacker, 1914)

Crawfurd, John, *Letters from British Settlers in the Interior of India Descriptive of Their Own Condition, and that of the Native Inhabitants under the Government of the East India Company* (London, 1831)

   Notes on the Settlement of British Subjects in India (London, 1833)

Das, Rajani Kanta, *Plantation Labor in India* (Calcutta: R. Chatterjee, 1931)

Dharker, C. D., *Lord Macaulay's Legislative Minutes* (New York: Oxford University Press, 1946)

Dowding, Charles, *Coolie Notes* (Dibrugarh, 1895), in BL, IOR, L/PJ/6/832, File 3639

Earl of Ellenborough, *Tyranny in India! Englishmen Robbed of the Blessings of Trial by Jury and English Criminal Law. Christianity Insulted!* (London, 1850)

Field, C. D., *Some Observations on Codification in India* (Calcutta, 1880)

   The Law of Evidence in British India (1st edn. Calcutta, 1867); (2nd edn. Calcutta, 1873)

Ganguli, Dwarkanath, *Slavery in British Dominion* (Calcutta, 1872)

Ghose, Ram Gopal, "Remarks on the 'Black Acts,'" reprinted in *Nineteenth-Century Studies* (Calcutta), 12 (1975), 412–432

Gilmore, J. R., "The 'Poor Whites' of the South," *Harper's New Monthly Magazine*, vol. 29 (1864), 115–124

Gribble, J. D. B., *Outlines of Medical Jurisprudence for Indian Criminal Courts* (Madras, 1885)

Hansard's Parliamentary Debates

Hansard, T. C., *The Parliamentary History of England, from the Earliest Period to the Year 1803*, vol. xxx (London, 1817)

Harvey, Robert, *Report on the Medico-Legal Returns, Received from the Civil Surgeons in the Bengal Presidency during the Years 1870, 1871, and 1872* (Calcutta, 1876)

Hope, A., *The "Black Acts": A Dialogue between a Free-Born-Briton-Indigo-Planter and an Impartial Man* (Calcutta, 1850)

Hough, William, *A Case Book of European and Native General Courts-Martial Held from the Years 1801 to 1821* (Calcutta, 1821)

The Practice of Courts-Martial (London, 1825)

Hunter, William, "On the Uncertainty of the Signs of Murder in the Case of Bastard Children," *Medical Observations and Enquiries*, 6 (1784), 266–290

Ilbert, Courtenay, "Codification," *The Law Quarterly Review*, 5, 20 (1889), 347–369

Kaye, J., *The Administration of the East India Company* (London, 1853)

Johnston, Charles, "Helping to Govern India," *The Atlantic Monthly*, November 1911, 643–653

Lambert, Donald, *The Medico-Legal Post-Mortem in India* (London: J. & A. Churchill, 1937)

Locke, John, *Second Treatise of Government* (1690)

Long, James, *Strike but Hear! Evidence Explanatory of the Indigo System in Lower Bengal* (Calcutta, 1861)

Lyon, Isidore B., *Lyon's Medical Jurisprudence for India with Illustrative Cases* (reprint Calcutta: Thacker, Spink, 1953)

Macaulay, Thomas Babington, *Critical and Historical Essays Contributed to the Edinburgh Review* (London, 1883)

Speeches and Poems with the Report and Notes on the Indian Penal Code (New York, 1867)

The Miscellaneous Writings and Speeches of Lord Macaulay (London, 1880)

Mittra, Kissory Chand, "Great Non-Exemption Meeting," reprinted in *Nineteenth-Century Studies*, 12 (1975), 433–448

Mookherji, Hurrish Chunder, *Selections from the Writings of Hurrish Chunder Mookherji* (Calcutta: Cherry Press, 1910)

Moore, A. T., *Notes for Officers Proceeding to India* (Chatham: Royal Engineers Institute, 1912)

Morley, William H., *An Analytical Digest of All the Reported Cases Decided in the Supreme Courts of Judicature in India* (Calcutta, 1850)

Pal, Bipin Chandra, *Memories of My Life and Times* (reprint Calcutta: Bipin Chandra Pal Institute, 1973)

Parliamentary Papers

Peet, L. M., *Courts-Martial in India* (Calcutta: Thacker and Spink, 1923)

Richards, Frank, *Old Soldier Sahib* (London: Faber and Faber, 1936)

Russell, William Howard, *My Indian Mutiny Diary* [reprint of *My Diary in India, in the Year 1858–59*, 1860] (London: Cassell, 1957)

Sanyal, Ram Gopal, *History of Celebrated Criminal Cases and Resolutions* (Calcutta, 1888)

Record of Criminal Cases as Between Europeans and Natives for the Last Hundred Years (Calcutta, 1896)

Record of Criminal Cases as Between Europeans and Natives for the Last Sixty Years (Calcutta, 1893)

Stephen, Leslie, *The Life of Sir James Fitzjames Stephen* (London, 1895)

Sunderland, J. T., *India in Bondage: Her Right to Freedom* (New York: L. Copeland, 1929)

Taylor, Alfred Swaine, *Elements of Medical Jurisprudence with a Copious Selection of Curious and Instructive Cases and Analyses of Opinions Delivered at Coroners' Inquests* (London, 1836)

The Principles and Practice of Medical Jurisprudence (London, 1865)

Trevelyan, George O., *The Competition Wallah* (reprint Delhi: HarperCollins, 1992)

The Life and Letters of Lord Macaulay (reprint London: Lowe and Brydone, 1959)

Wallace, R. G., *Fifteen Years in India; or, Sketches of a Soldier's Life* (London, 1822)

Wigmore, John Henry, *Wigmore on Evidence: A Treatise on the Anglo-American System of Evidence in Trials at Common Law* (Boston: Little, Brown, 1904)

Yule, Henry (ed.), *The Diary of W. Hedges*, vol. III (London, 1887)

Printed sources (post-1947)

Adas, Michael, "From Avoidance to Confrontation: Peasant Protest in Precolonial and Colonial Southeast Asia," *Comparative Studies in Society and History*, 23, 2 (1981), 217–247

Machines as the Measure of Men: Science, Technology, and Ideologies of Western Dominance (Ithaca: Cornell University Press, 1989)

Agamben, Giorgio, *The State of Exception* (Chicago: University of Chicago Press, 2005)

Anderson, Clare, *Legible Bodies: Race, Criminality and Colonialism in South Asia* (Oxford, New York: Berg, 2004)

"Multiple Border Crossings: Convicts and Other Persons Escaped from Botany Bay and Residing in Calcutta," *Journal of Australian Colonial History*, 3, 2 (2001), 1–22

Anglesey, Marquess of, *A History of the British Cavalry, 1816–1919* (London: Secker and Warburg, 1986)

Antrobus, H., *A History of the Assam Company, 1839–1953* (Edinburgh: T. and A. Constable, 1957)

Arnold, David, "European Orphans and Vagrants in India in the Nineteenth Century," *Journal of Imperial and Commonwealth History*, 7, 2 (1979), 104–127

(ed.), *Imperial Medicine and Indigenous Societies* (Manchester: Manchester University Press, 1989)

"White Colonization and Labor in 19th Century India," *Journal of Imperial and Commonwealth History*, 11 (1983), 133–158

Bagal, J. C., *History of the Indian Association, 1876–1951* (Calcutta: Indian Association, 1953)

Bailkin, Jordanna, "The Boot and the Spleen: When Was Murder Possible in British India?" *Comparative Studies of Society and History*, 48 (2006), 462–493

Ballantyne, Tony, "Race and the Webs of Empire Aryanism from India to the Pacific," *Journal of Colonialism and Colonial History*, e-journal, 2, 3 (2001)

Ballhatchet, Kenneth, *Race, Sex and Class under the Raj: Imperial Attitudes and Policies and Their Critics* (London: Weidenfeld and Nicolson, 1980)

Banerjee, Anil Chandra, *Indian Constitutional Documents, 1757–1947* (Calcutta: A. Mukherjee, 1961)

Baruah, Sanjib, *India against Itself: Assam and the Politics of Nationality* (Delhi: Oxford University Press, 1999)

Basu, B. D., *The Colonization of India by Europeans* (Calcutta: R. Chatterjee, 1925)

Bayly, C. A., *Empire and Information: Intelligence Gathering and Social Communication in India, 1780–1870* (Cambridge: Cambridge University Press, 2000)

Behal, Rana P., "Forms of Labour Protest in Assam Valley Tea Plantations, 1900–1930," *Economic and Political Weekly*, 20, 4 (January 26, 1985), PE19–PE26

   Wage Structure and Labor: Assam Valley Tea Plantations, 1900–1947 (Noida: V. V. Giri Labour Institute, 2003)

   and Mohapatra, Prabhu P., "'Tea and Money versus Human Life': The Rise and Fall of the Indenture System in the Assam Tea Plantations, 1840–1908," *Journal of Peasant Studies*, 19, 3/4 (1992), 142–172

Benton, Lauren, *Law and Colonial Cultures: Legal Regimes in World History, 1400–1900* (Cambridge: Cambridge University Press, 2001)

Bolt, Christine, *Victorian Attitudes to Race* (London: Routledge and Kegan Paul, 1971)

Bose, Ambica Charan, *A Handbook of Criminology* (Calcutta: Sri Gouranga Press, 1960)

Bose, Nemai Sadhan, *Racism, Struggle for Equality and Indian Nationalism* (Calcutta: Firma KLM Limited, 1981)

Brown, Christopher Leslie, *Moral Capital: Foundations of British Abolitionism* (Chapel Hill, NC: University of North Carolina Press, 2006)

Buettner, Elizabeth, *Empire Families: Britons and Late Imperial India* (Oxford: Oxford University Press, 2004)

Burney, Ian, *Bodies of Evidence: Medicine and the Politics of the English Inquest, 1826–1930* (Baltimore: Johns Hopkins University Press, 2000)

   Poison, Detection and the Victorian Imagination (Manchester: Manchester University Press, 2007)

Cannadine, David, *Ornamentalism: How the British Saw Their Empire* (Oxford: Oxford University Press, 2002)

Canny, Nicholas, "The Ideology of English Colonization: From Ireland to America," *The William & Mary Quarterly*, 30 (1973), 575–598

Cesaire, Aimé, *Discourse on Colonialism* (reprint New York: Monthly Review Press, 2000)

Chandra, Bipin, *The Rise and Growth of Economic Nationalism in India, 1880–1905* (New Delhi: Anamika, 1966)

Chanock, Martin, *Law, Custom and Social Order: The Colonial Experience in Malawi* (Cambridge: Cambridge University Press, 1985)

The Making of South African Legal Culture, 1902–1936: Fear, Favour and Prejudice (Cambridge: Cambridge University Press, 2001)

Chatterjee, Partha, *The Nation and Its Fragments: Colonial and Postcolonial Histories* (Princeton: Princeton University Press, 1993)

Churchill, Ward, *Perversions of Justice: Indigenous Peoples and Angloamerican Law* (San Francisco: City Lights Books, 2003)

Coetzee, J. M., *Waiting for the Barbarians* (London: Penguin, 1980)

Cohn, Bernard, *An Anthropologist among the Historians and Other Essays* (Delhi: Oxford University Press, 1988)

Colonialism and Its Forms of Knowledge: The British in India (Princeton: Princeton University Press, 1996)

Colley, Linda, *Captives: Britain, Empire and the World, 1600–1850* (London: Jonathan Cape, 2002)

Collingham, Elizabeth M., *Imperial Bodies: The Physical Experience of the Raj, c. 1800–1947* (Cambridge: Polity Press, 2001)

Comaroff, John L., "Symposium Introduction: Colonialism, Culture, and the Law: A Foreword," *Law and Social Inquiry*, 26, 2 (2001), 305–314

Cooper, Frederick and Stoler, Ann Laura (eds.), *Tensions of Empire: Colonial Cultures in a Bourgeois World* (Berkeley: University of California Press, 1997)

Crawford, Catherine, "The Emergence of English Forensic Medicine Medical Evidence in Common-Law Courts, 1730–1830," unpublished D.Phil. thesis, University of Oxford (1987)

"Legalizing Medicine: Early Modern Legal Systems and the Growth of Medico-Legal Knowledge," in Michael Clark and Catherine Crawford (eds.), *Legal Medicine in History* (Cambridge: Cambridge University Press, 1994)

Curtin, Philip D., *The Image of Africa: British Ideas and Action, 1780–1850* (Madison: University of Wisconsin Press, 1964)

Dalrymple, William, "Plain Tales of British India," *The New York Review of Books*, e-journal, 54, 7 (April 26, 2007)

White Mughals: Love and Betrayal in Eighteenth-Century India (London: Viking, 2002)

Dirks, Nicholas B., *Castes of Mind: Colonialism and the Making of Modern India* (Princeton: Princeton University Press, 2001)

The Scandal of Empire: India and the Creation of Imperial Britain (Cambridge, MA: Harvard University Press, 2006)

Drescher, Seymour, "The Ending of the Slave Trade and the Evolution of European Scientific Racism," *Social Science History*, 14, 3 (1990), 415–450

Dubber, Markus Dirk, "The Historical Analysis of Criminal Codes," *Law and History Review*, 18, 2 (2000), 433–440

Edwardes, Michael, *Bound to Exile: The Victorians in India* (London: Sidgwick and Jackson, 1969)

Elkins, Caroline, *Imperial Reckoning: The Untold Story of Britain's Gulag in Kenya* (New York: Henry Holt, 2004)

Evans, Julie, "Colonialism and the Rule of Law: The Case of South Australia," in Barry Godfrey and Graeme Dunstall (eds.), *Crime and Empire 1840–1940: Criminal Justice in Local and Global Context* (Portland, OR: Willan Publishing, 2005)

Evans, Julie, Grimshaw, Patricia, Philips, David, and Swain, Shurlee, *Equal Subjects, Unequal Rights: Indigenous Peoples in British Settler Colonies, 1830–1910* (Manchester: Manchester University Press, 2003)

Fanon, Frantz, *The Wretched of the Earth* (reprint Manchester: Grove, 2005)

Farmer, Lindsay, "Reconstructing the English Codification Debate: the Criminal Law Commissioners," *Law and History Review*, 18, 2 (2000), 397–425

Fede, Andrew, "Legitimized Violent Slave Abuse in the American South, 1619–1865: A Case Study of Law and Social Change in Six Southern States," *American Journal of Legal History*, 29, 2 (1985), 93–150

Fisch, Jorg, *Cheap Lives and Dear Limbs: The British Transformation of the Bengal Criminal Law 1769–1817* (Wiesbaden: Franz Steiner Verlag, 1983)

Fischer-Tiné, Harald, "Flotsam and Jetsam of the Empire? European Seamen and Spaces of Disease and Disorder in Mid-Nineteenth-Century Calcutta," in Ashwini Tambe and Harald Fischer-Tiné (eds.), *The Limits of British Colonial Control in South Asia: Spaces of Disorder in the Indian Ocean Region* (New York: Routledge, 2009), pp. 121–154

  Low and Licentious Europeans: Race, Class and White Subalternity in Colonial India (Delhi: Orient BlackSwan, 2009)

  and Gehrmann, Susanne (eds.), *Empires and Boundaries: Rethinking Race, Class and Gender in Colonial Settings* (London: Routledge, 2008)

Forbes, Thomas Rogers, *Surgeons at the Bailey: English Forensic Medicine to 1878* (New Haven, CT: Yale University Press, 1985)

Gallanis, Thomas P., "The Rise of Modern Evidence Law," *Iowa Law Review*, 84, 3 (March 1999), 499–560

Ganachari, Aravind, "'White Man's Embarrassment': European Vagrancy in 19th Century Bombay," *Economic and Political Weekly*, (June 22, 2002), 2477–2486

Genovese, Eugene, *Roll, Jordan, Roll: The World the Slaves Made* (New York: Pantheon, 1974)

Ghosh, Durba, "Household Crimes and Domestic Order: Keeping the Peace in Colonial Calcutta, c. 1770–1840," *Modern Asian Studies*, 38, 3 (2004), 598–624

  Sex and the Family in Colonial India: The Making of Empire (Cambridge: Cambridge University Press, 2006)

Ghosh, Suresh Chandra, *The Social Condition of the British Community in Bengal, 1757–1800* (Leiden: E. J. Brill, 1970)

Gilmour, David, *Curzon: Imperial Statesman* (London: John Murray, 1994)

Golan, Tal, "The History of Scientific Expert Testimony in the English Courtroom," *Science in Context*, 12, 1 (1999), 7–32

Guha, Amalendu, *Planter-Raj to Swaraj: Freedom Struggle and Electoral Politics in Assam, 1826–1947* (New Delhi: Indian Council of Historical Research, 1977)

Guha, Ranajit, "The Prose of Counter-Insurgency," in R. Guha and G. C. Spivak (eds.), *Selected Subaltern Studies* (New York: Columbia University Press, 1988), pp. 45–88

  A Subaltern Studies Reader, 1986–1995 (Minneapolis: University of Minnesota Press, 1997)

Gupta, Bishnupriya, "The History of the International Tea Market, 1850–1945," http://eh.net/encyclopedia/article/gupta.tea

Hall, Catherine, *Civilising Subjects: Metropole and Colony in the English Imagination, 1830–1867* (Chicago: University of Chicago Press, 2002)
  Cultures of Empire: Colonizers in Britain and the Empire in the Nineteenth and Twentieth Centuries: A Reader (Manchester: Manchester University Press, 2000)
  and Rose, Sonya O. (eds.), *At Home with the Empire: Metropolitan Culture and the Imperial World* (Cambridge: Cambridge University Press, 2006)
Hall, Stuart, "Conclusion: The Multi-Cultural Question," in B. Hesse (ed.), *Un/settled Multiculturalisms: Diasporas, Entanglements, Transruptions* (London: Zed Books, 2000), pp. 209–241
Hallward, N. L., *William Bolts: A Dutch Adventurer under John Company* (Cambridge: Cambridge University Press, 1920)
Harris, Cheryl, "Whiteness as Property," *Harvard Law Review*, 106, 8 (1993), 1709–1791
Havard, J. D. J., *The Detection of Secret Homicide: A Study of the Medico-legal System of Investigation of Sudden and Unexplained Deaths* (London: Macmillan, 1960)
Hawes, C. J., *Poor Relations: The Making of a Eurasian Community in British India 1773–1833* (London: Curzon, 1996)
Hay, Douglas and Craven, Paul (eds.), *Masters, Servants, and Magistrates in Britain and the Empire, 1562–1955* (Chapel Hill, NC: University of North Carolina Press, 2004)
Herbert, Christopher, *War of No Pity: The Indian Mutiny and Victorian Trauma* (Princeton: Princeton University Press, 2008)
Hirschmann, Edwin, *"White Mutiny": The Ilbert Bill Crisis in India and Genesis of the Indian National Congress* (Delhi: Heritage, 1980)
Holmes, Richard, *Sahib: The British Soldier in India, 1750–1914* (London: HarperCollins, 2005)
Hula, Richard C., "Calcutta: The Politics of Crime and Conflict, 1800 to the 1970s," in Ted Robert Gurr, Peter N. Grabosky, and Richard C. Hula (eds.), *The Politics of Crime and Conflict: A Comparative History of Four Cities* (London: Sage Publications, 1977), pt. V
Hussain, Nasser, *The Jurisprudence of Emergency: Colonialism and the Rule of Law* (Ann Arbor: University of Michigan Press, 2003)
Hyams, Paul R., "Trial by Ordeal: The Key to Proof in the Early Common Law," in Morris S. Arnold, Thomas A. Green, Sally A. Scully, and Stephen D. White (eds.), *On the Laws and Customs of England* (Chapel Hill, NC: University of North Carolina Press, 1981)
Ilaiah, Kancha, *Why I am Not a Hindu: A Sudra Critique of Hindutva Philosophy, Culture and Political Economy* (Calcutta: Samya, 1996)
Irschick, Eugene, *Dialogue and History: Constructing South India, 1795–1895* (Berkeley: University of California Press, 1994)
Jasanoff, Maya, *Edge of Empire: Lives, Culture and Conquest in the East* (New York: Vintage, 2006)
Jha, Jagdish Chandra, *Aspects of Indentured Inland Emigration to North-East India, 1859–1918* (New Delhi: Indus Publishing, 1996)
Keay, John, *The Honourable Company: A History of the English East India Company* (London: HarperCollins, 1991)

Keegan, Timothy, *Colonial South Africa and the Origins of the Racial Order* (Charlottesville: University of Virginia Press, 1996)

Kennedy, Dane, *The Magic Mountains: Hill Stations and the British Raj* (Berkeley: University of California Press, 1996)

Kenny, A., "The Expert in Court," *Law Quarterly Review*, 99 (1983), 197–216

Kiernan, Victor, *The Lords of Human Kind: European Attitudes Towards the Outside World in the Imperial Age* (London: Weidenfeld and Nicholson, 1969)

Kincaid, Dennis, *British Social Life in India, 1608–1937* (London: George Routledge and Sons, 1938)

Kling, Blair B., *The Blue Mutiny: The Indigo Disturbances in Bengal, 1859–1862* (Philadelphia: University of Pennsylvania Press, 1966)

Kolsky, Elizabeth, "Rape on Trial in Early Colonial India, 1805–1857," *The Journal of Asian Studies*, 69, 4 (November 2010)

"'The Body Evidencing the Crime': Rape on Trial in Colonial India, 1861–1947," *Gender and History*, 22, 1 (March 2010)

Kuiters, Willem G. J., *The British in Bengal, 1756–1773: A Society in Transition Seen through the Biography of a Rebel: William Bolts (1739–1808)* (Paris: Indes Savantes, 2002)

Kumar, Dharma, Raychaudhuri, Tapan, and Desai, Meghnad (eds.), *The Cambridge Economic History of India*, vol. II (Cambridge: Cambridge University Press, 1983)

Landsman, Stephan, "From Gilbert to Bentham: The Reconceptualization of Evidence Theory," *The Wayne Law Review*, 36, 3 (1990), 1149–1186

"Of Witches, Madmen, and Products Liability: An Historical Survey of the Use of Expert Testimony," *Behavioral Science and the Law*, 13, 2 (1995), 131–157

"The Rise of the Contentious Spirit: Adversary Procedure in Eighteenth-Century England," *Cornell Law Review*, 75, 3 (1990), 497–609

Langbein, John H., "The Criminal Trial before the Lawyers," *University of Chicago Law Review*, 45, 2 (1978), 263–316

Linebaugh, Peter and Rediker, Marcus Buford, *The Many-Headed Hydra: Sailors, Slaves, Commoners, and the Hidden History of the Revolutionary Atlantic* (Boston: Beacon Press, 2001)

Lobban, Michael, "How Benthamic was the Criminal Law Commission?," *Law and History Review*, 18, 2 (2000), 427–432

López, Ian Haney, *White by Law: The Legal Construction of Race* (New York: New York University Press, 2006)

MacKenzie, John, *Propaganda and Empire: The Manipulation of British Public Opinion, 1880–1960* (Manchester: Manchester University Press, 1984)

Marshall, P. J., "British Immigration into India in the Nineteenth Century," *Itinerario*, 14, 1 (1990), 25–41

"British Society in India under the East India Company," *Modern Asian Studies*, 31, 1 (1997), 89–108

East Indian Fortunes: The British in Bengal in the Eighteenth Century (Oxford: Clarendon Press, 1976)

"The White Town of Calcutta under the Rule of the East India Company," *Modern Asian Studies*, 34, 2 (2000), 307–331

McCulloch, Jock, *Black Peril, White Virtue: Sexual Crime in Southern Rhodesia, 1902–1935* (Bloomington: Indiana University Press, 2000)

"Empire and Violence, 1900–1930," in Philippa Levine (ed.), *Gender and Empire* (Oxford: Oxford University Press, 2004), pp. 220–239

Mehrotra, S. R., *The Emergence of the Indian National Congress* (Delhi: Vikas Publications, 1971)

Merry, Sally Engle, *Colonizing Hawai'i: The Cultural Power of Law* (Princeton: Princeton University Press, 2000)

"Law and Colonialism," *Law and Society Review*, 25, 4 (1991), 889–922

"Resistance and the Cultural Power of Law," *Law and Society Review*, 29, 1 (1995), 11–27

Metcalf, Thomas, *Ideologies of the Raj* (Cambridge: Cambridge University Press, 1994)

Mitter, Partha, "Cartoons of the Raj," *History Today*, 47, 9 (1997), 16–21

Mizutani, Satoshi, "A 'Scandal to the English Name and English Government': European Pauperism in Colonial Calcutta, 1858–the 1920s," unpublished paper presented at the European Association for South Asian Studies (2004)

"Historicizing Whiteness: From the Case of Late Colonial India," *Australian Critical Race and Whiteness Studies Association*, 2, 1 (2006), 1–15

"Rethinking Inclusion and Exclusion: The Question of Mixed-Race Presence in Late Colonial India," *University of Sussex Journal of Contemporary History*, 5 (2002), 1–22

Morris, Thomas D., *Southern Slavery and the Law, 1619–1860* (Chapel Hill, NC: University of North Carolina Press, 1996)

Mukherjee, Rudrangshu, *Awadh in Revolt 1857–1858: A Study of Popular Resistance* (Delhi: Oxford University Press, 1984)

Mungeam, G. H., *Kenya: Select Historical Documents, 1884–1923* (Nairobi: East African Publishing House, 1978)

Narain, Iqbal, *The Politics of Racialism: A Study of the Indian Minority in South Africa down to the Gandhi–Smuts Agreement* (Agra: Shiva Lal Agarwala, 1962)

Nemec, Jaroslav, *Highlights in Medicolegal Relations* (Washington, DC: US Government Printing Office, 1976)

O'Brien, Gail Williams, *The Color of the Law: Race, Violence, and Justice in the Post-World War II South* (Chapel Hill, NC: University of North Carolina Press, 1999)

Oldham, James, "Truth-Telling in the Eighteenth-Century English Courtroom," *Law and History Review*, 12, 1 (1994), 95–121

Orwell, George, *Shooting an Elephant and Other Essays* (New York: Harcourt, Brace and World, 1966)

Pagden, Anthony, *Lords of All the World: Imperial Ideologies in Spain, Britain and France, c. 1500–1800* (New Haven, CT: Yale University Press, 1995)

Paton, Diana, *No Bond but the Law: Punishment, Race, Gender and Jamaican State Formation, 1780–1870* (Durham, NC: Duke University Press, 2004)

Patterson, Orlando, *Slavery and Social Death: A Comparative Study* (Cambridge, MA: Harvard University Press, 1982)

Peers, Douglas M., *Between Mars and Mammon: Colonial Armies and the Garrison State in India, 1819–1835* (London: Tauris, 1995)

"Privates off Parade: Regimenting Sexuality in the Nineteenth-Century Indian Empire," *International History Review*, 20, 4 (1998), 844–853

Pierce, Steven and Rao, Anupama (eds.), *Discipline and the Other Body: Correction, Corporeality, Colonialism* (Durham, NC: Duke University Press, 2006)

Pinney, Chris, *Camera Indica: The Social Life of Indian Photographs* (Chicago: University of Chicago Press, 1997)

Pitts, Jennifer, *A Turn to Empire: The Rise of Imperial Liberalism in Britain and France* (Princeton: Princeton University Press, 2005)

Pouchepadass, Jacques, *Champaran and Gandhi: Planters, Peasants and Gandhian Politics* (New York: Oxford University Press, 1999)

Reddy, V. S., "Side Lights on the Medicolegal Problems of the Mouryan Era," *Indian Medical Record*, 64 (1944), 97–101

Renford, R. K., *The Non-Official British in India to 1920* (Delhi: Oxford University Press, 1987)

Said, Edward, *Culture and Imperialism* (New York: Vintage Books, 1994)

Schneider, Wendie, "'Enfeebling the Arm of Justice': Perjury and Colonial Administration under the East India Company," in Markus Dirk Dubber and Lindsay Farmer (eds.), *Modern Histories of Crime and Punishment* (Stanford: Stanford University Press, 2007), pp. 299–327

Schofield, Philip, "Jeremy Bentham and Nineteenth-Century English Jurisprudence," *Journal of Legal History*, 12, 1 (1991), 58–88

Scott, James C., *Weapons of the Weak: Everyday Forms of Peasant Protest* (New Haven, CT: Yale University Press, 1987)

Sen, Sudipta, *Distant Sovereignty: National Imperialism and the Origins of British India* (New York: Routledge, 2002)

Sharma, Jayeeta, "An European Tea 'Garden' and an Indian 'Frontier': The Discovery of Assam," *Centre of South Asian Studies Occasional Paper*, e-journal, 6 (2002)

Sharpe, James A., *Crime in Early Modern England, 1550–1750* (London: Addison Wesley Longman, 1999)

Singha, Radhika, *A Despotism of Law: Crime and Justice in Early Colonial India* (Delhi: Oxford University Press, 1998)

"The Privilege of Taking Life: Some 'Anomalies' in the Law of Homicide in the Bengal Presidency," *Indian Economic and Social History Review*, 30 (1993), 181–215

"Providential Circumstances: The Thuggee Campaign of the 1830s and Legal Innovation," *Modern Asian Studies*, 27, 1 (1993), 83–146

Sinha, Mrinalini, "Britishness, Clubbability, and the Colonial Public Sphere: The Genealogy of an Imperial Institution in Colonial India," *Journal of British Studies*, 40, 4 (2001), 489–521

Colonial Masculinity: The "Manly" Englishman and the "Effeminate Bengali" in the Late Nineteenth Century (Manchester: Manchester University Press, 1995)

Smith, Roger and Wynne, Brian (eds.), *Expert Evidence: Interpreting Science in the Law* (London: Routledge, 1989)

Spear, Percival, *Nabobs: A Study of the Social Life of the English in 18th Century India* (London: Oxford University Press, 1963)

Stepan, Nancy Leys, *The Idea of Race in Science: Great Britain, 1800–1960* (London: Macmillan, 1982)

Stern, Philip Jared, "The Fringes of History: The Seventeenth-Century Origins of the East India Company-State," in Sameetah Agha and Elizabeth Kolsky (eds.), *Fringes of Empire: People, Power and Places on the Margins of Colonial India* (Delhi: Oxford University Press, 2009)

Stockwell, S. (ed.), *The British Empire: Themes and Perspectives* (London: Blackwell, 2008).

Stokes, Eric, *The English Utilitarians and India* (Oxford: Clarendon Press, 1959)

Stoler, Ann Laura, *Capitalism and Confrontation in Sumatra's Plantation Belt, 1879–1979* (New Haven, CT: Yale University Press, 1985)

"Making Empire Respectable: The Politics of Race and Sexual Morality in 20th-Century Colonial Cultures," *American Ethnologist*, 16, 4 (1989), 634–660

"Rethinking Colonial Categories: European Communities and the Boundaries of Rule," *Comparative Studies in Society and History*, 13, 1 (1989), 134–161

Tabili, Laura, "The Construction of Racial Difference in Twentieth-Century Britain: The Special Restriction (Coloured Alien Seamen) Order, 1925," *Journal of British Studies*, 33, 1 (1994), 54–98

Tagore, Soumendranath, *Rammohun Roy: His Role in Indian Renaissance* (Bengal: The Asiatic Society, 1975)

Thirsk, J. and Cooper, J. P. (eds.), *Seventeenth-Century Economic Documents* (Oxford: Clarendon Press, 1972)

Thompson, E. P., *Whigs and Hunters: The Origin of the Black Act* (New York: Pantheon, 1975)

Tinker, Hugh, *A New System of Slavery: The Export of Indian Labour Overseas, 1830–1920* (London: Oxford University Press, 1974)

Travers, Robert, *Ideology and Empire in Eighteenth-Century India* (Cambridge: Cambridge University Press, 2007)

Twining, William (ed.), *Bentham: Selected Writings of John Dinwiddy* (Stanford: Stanford University Press, 2003)

Varma, Nitin, "Coolie Strikes Back: Collective Protest and Action in the Colonial British Indian Tea Plantations of Assam, 1880–1920," *Indian Historical Review*, 33 (2006), 259–287

Walvin, James, *Fruits of Empire: Exotic Produce and British Taste 1660–1800* (London: Macmillan, 1997)

Washbrook, David, "India, 1818–1860: The Two Faces of Colonialism," in Andrew Porter (ed.), *Oxford History of the British Empire*, vol. III (Oxford: Oxford University Press, 1999)

Weiss, Gunther A., "The Enchantment of Codification in the Common-Law World," *The Yale Journal of International Law*, 25, 2 (2000), 435–532

Wiener, Martin, *An Empire on Trial: Race, Murder, and Justice under British Rule, 1870–1935* (Cambridge: Cambridge University Press, 2009)

Wilson, K. (ed.), *A New Imperial History: Culture, Identity and Modernity in Britain and the Empire, 1660–1840* (Cambridge: Cambridge University Press, 2004)

Windschuttle, Keith, *The Fabrication of Aboriginal History* (Paddington: Macleay Press, 2002)

Yang, Anand (ed.), *Crime and Criminality in British India* (Tucson: University of Arizona Press, 1985)

Young, Robert E., *Postcolonialism: An Historical Introduction* (Oxford: Blackwell, 2001)

Index

248

Cambridge Studies in Indian History and Society

Other titles in the series